Twayne's United States Authors Series

Sylvia E. Bowman, *Editor*

INDIANA UNIVERSITY

Francis Parkman

FRANCIS PARKMAN

By ROBERT L. GALE

University of Pittsburgh

 220

Twayne Publishers, Inc.   ::   New York

74-173

To my Brother
EUGENE C. GALE
Affectionately and in
Gratitude for a Half-
Century of No Conflict

Preface

Francis Parkman deserves to be more thoroughly known than he is. He writes so much better than the average professional, academic historian that critics from the ranks of history teachers tend to dismiss him as outmoded. Not one history teacher in a hundred would trouble to read his journals and letters, attempt to integrate his personal character and his writings, take the belletristic elements in his production as a challenge to improve their own style, or praise him for what he is—the finest historian America has yet produced. By comparison, William Hickling Prescott, who was personally as heroic as Parkman but who insisted upon a repellent Johnsonian style, and John Lothrop Motley, who had a lesser vision than Parkman and dealt with subjects remote from our experience, are decidedly lower in any scale of values. And Jared Sparks, George Bancroft, Richard Hildreth, John Bach McMaster, and John Fiske are still more dated. Only Henry Adams, who was a personal friend of Parkman, can match him as a historian of long ago whose works are alive today. This fact is true because both men were more than historians: they were vital personalities with fascinating lives, and they wrote works that were more than simply historical ones.

Parkman, born into a rich Boston Brahmin family, went to Harvard; he took a grand European tour; he went to Harvard Law School, for no particularly impressive reason; and then he traveled west briefly and returned to write *The Oregon Trail,* a book which ironically made him famous but which was tangential to the main purpose of his life—to write the history of the clash of England and France for dominance in North America. He fought bad health and family tragedies, but he lived to complete his massive history. His life, as well as his work, should be an inspiration to anyone who feels cursed by his fate.

Curiously, Parkman combined a reactionary personal philosophy with a writing style which is modern in subtle ways and which should make him attractive to modern literary, if not historical, critics. I have been obliged by my background and cast of mind to see Parkman's life and his extensive writings— totaling about seven thousand pages (histories, travel book, journals, letters, novel, and handbook on roses)—from the point of view of a literary critic. I make no apology for this fact because, after all, Parkman is a literary historian in the sense that his histories have literary merit.

If I were to suggest a course of reading in Parkman for the young scholar, I would recommend *The Oregon Trail* first, with the warning that the reader should not take the apparent superciliousness of its young author as an indication of his real personality, which was warm, humor loving, and ultimately mellow. Then I would prescribe *Montcalm and Wolfe*, both because of its historical interest and because of its almost musical suspense. Next would be *La Salle and the Discovery of the Great West*, the hero of which had a life of incredible adventure and was revealingly dear to Parkman. The *Journals* and the *Letters* might come after that, for the light they shed on Parkman's own adventures, personality, and professional activities. If the young scholar still has the stamina, let him then turn to *The Conspiracy of Pontiac, Pioneers of France in the New World*, and *Count Frontenac and New France under Louis XIV*, after which he would be a Parkman buff and could stand to read *The Jesuits in North America in the Seventeenth Century, The Old Régime in Canada*, and even *A Half-Century of Conflict*. He might then wish to complete his reading of Parkman's entire canon by turning to his pleasant little *Book of Roses*, his wretched novel *Vassall Morton*, and his minor, short pieces. Reading these twenty-six or so volumes would be taxing but also informative and rarely dull because they light up corners of our national past which are growing obscure and also teach much about a writer of extraordinary charm, humor, wisdom, and stoicism.

The most efficient way to understand Parkman, however, is first of all to read the following pages. In them I begin by narrating the main events of his life, with its solid academic and cultural preparation, its manifold uncertainties, and finally its triumphs. Then I consider in chronological order his major works, telling what they are about, how they succeed in moving dramat-

Preface

ically and pictorially, what their stylistic virtues and weaknesses are, and how they reveal their author's human qualities. Works especially stressed are *The Oregon Trail, The Conspiracy of Pontiac,* and *Montcalm and Wolfe.*

Every scholar incurs certain specific debts, which it is a pleasure for him to acknowledge. Five earlier specialists on Parkman have been especially helpful: Wilbur L. Schramm, whose pioneering Parkman reader is full and is also graced by a solid introduction and by other critical apparatus; Mason Wade, who wrote the first modern biography of the historian and also edited his *Journals;* Otis A. Pease, whose monograph on Parkman's literary skill has incalculable value; Wilbur R. Jacobs, the highly professional editor of Parkman's *Letters;* and Howard Doughty, whose long critical biography of Parkman vibrates with brilliant insights. Others by whose wisdom I have been taught are listed in my footnotes and bibliography.

In addition, I gratefully acknowledge receipt of permission to quote from the following: *The Journals of Francis Parkman,* published in 1947 by Harper and Brothers (now Harper and Row), and copyrighted by the Massachusetts Historical Society; *Letters of Francis Parkman,* Vols. I and II, published in 1960 by the University of Oklahoma Press in cooperation with the Massachusetts Historical Society; and the edition of *The Oregon Trail* prepared by E. N. Feltskog and published in 1969 (Madison: The University of Wisconsin Press, © 1969 by the Regents of the University of Wisconsin). I am also grateful for sabbatical time and grant-in-aid funds from the Faculty of Arts and Sciences and the English Department of the University of Pittsburgh; expert advice and courteous assistance from personnel at the Massachusetts Historical Society in Boston, the Houghton Manuscript Library at Harvard University, the Hillman Library of the University of Pittsburgh, and the Hunt Library of Carnegie-Mellon University in Pittsburgh; and, finally, encouragement and invaluable editorial advice from Dr. Sylvia E. Bowman.

ROBERT L. GALE

University of Pittsburgh

Acknowledgments

Selections from THE JOURNALS OF FRANCIS PARKMAN, VOLS. I & II, edited by Mason Wade. Copyright 1947 by the Massachusetts Historical Society. Reprinted by permission of Harper & Row, Publishers.

Selections from LETTERS OF FRANCIS PARKMAN, VOLS. I & II, edited and with an Introduction by Wilbur R. Jacobs. Copyright 1960 by the University of Oklahoma Press.

Selections from Francis Parkman, THE OREGON TRAIL, edited by E. N. Feltskog. Madison: The University of Wisconsin Press; © 1969 by the Regents of the University of Wisconsin.

Contents

Contents

Chronology

1823   Francis Parkman, Jr., born September 16 in Boston. Older son of the Reverend Mr. Francis Parkman (1788–1852) and his second wife, Caroline Hall Parkman (1794–1871); other children were Sarah (by father's first marriage), Caroline, Mary, Eliza, and John Eliot.

1829   Moved with family from Beacon Hill to 1 Green Street, Boston.

1831   Began to live on farm of maternal grandfather at Medford, Massachusetts, to improve health (until 1835); began to attend private schools (until 1840).

1838   Moved with family to home of paternal grandfather at 5 Bowdoin Square, Boston.

1840   Began to attend Harvard.

1841   July-August, explored White Mountains and wilds of Maine.

1842   July-August, took second forest trip; also visited Albany and southern Canada; during Christmas vacation, visited friends in Keene, New Hampshire.

1843   November, sailed from Boston for Europe. Went to Italy, Switzerland, France, England, and Scotland; returned to Boston in June, 1844.

1844   August, graduated from Harvard, vacationed in New England (including Berkshires) before and after; entered Harvard Law School in fall.

1845   Published five pieces in *Knickerbocker Magazine*. July, went to New York, Harrisburg, Detroit, Niagara, and elsewhere on research concerning Pontiac.

1846   January, received law degree from Harvard. January–February, went to New York and Baltimore on historical research. March, left Boston to start exploring along California and Oregon Trail: April 28–October 7, went on trail, leaving from St. Louis and going by steamer up Mississippi and Missouri rivers to Independence, then on horseback to Platte River and along it to Fort Laramie, then after camping with Sioux Indians going east of Rockies to Pueblo and Bent's Fort, then back again to St. Louis. Returned to Boston later in October. November, to New York to study in law office and undergo treatment for weakened eyes. Terrible misery and nervousness began.

1847 February, first installment of *California and Oregon Trail* (published serially) in *Knickerbocker*.

1849 Published revised edition of *California and Oregon Trail* (called *Prairie and Rocky Mountain Life; or, California Trail*, in 1852 edition, and *Oregon Trail* in 1872 edition).

1850 May, married Catherine Scollay Bigelow (three children: Grace Parkman Coffin, 1851–1928; Francis Parkman III, 1854–57; and Katharine Parkman Coolidge, 1858–1900).

1851 *History of Conspiracy of Pontiac.*

1856 October–November, traveled to Montreal, Ottawa, and Quebec. *Vassall Morton.*

1858 September, death of wife. December, to Paris to consult physician about nervous and mental disorders.

1859 Returned to Boston; began to cultivate extensive rose garden.

1865 June, visited Washington, D.C., and Richmond. *Pioneers of France in New World.*

1866 March, began correspondence with Abbé Henri-Raymond Casgrain (lasting until Parkman's death). August, visited Canada. *Book of Roses.*

1867 July–August, visited Iowa, Illinois, Missouri, and Minnesota. *Jesuits in North America in Seventeenth Century.*

1868 November, to Paris to rest and visit archives; returned to Boston, March, 1869.

1869 *Discovery of Great West.*

1870 Revised and enlarged *Pontiac* (as *Conspiracy of Pontiac and Indian War after Conquest of Canada*).

1871 May, welcomed Casgrain to Boston for their first meeting. July–August, visited Nova Scotia and New Brunswick.

1872 July–October, to Europe; met Pierre Margry in Paris. Extensively revised *Oregon Trail.*

1873 August, visited Canada.

1874 July, visited Quebec. *Old Régime in Canada.*
1876 August–September, visited Lake Champlain and Ottawa. November, sold his *lilium Parkmanni.*
1877 *Count Frontenac and New France under Louis XIV.*
1878 August, began to publish articles on democracy and suffrage (to 1880). November, visited Lake George, Fort Ticonderoga, and Quebec; became center of partisan controversy over Canadian honorary degree (until March, 1879). Revised *Discovery of Great West* (calling it *La Salle and Discovery of Great West*).
1879 August, visited Quebec and inspected Louisbourg fortress.
1880 January, helped to found St. Botolph Club in Boston; served as first president (until 1886). July–September, to Paris and London.
1881 May–August, to Paris and London.
1884 *Montcalm and Wolfe.*
1885 May, traveled to South Carolina and Florida. Enlarged and revised *Pioneers.*
1887 April, visited Spain briefly, returned via Paris and London.
1889 LL.D., Harvard.
1892 *Half-Century of Conflict.* Slightly revised *Oregon Trail.*
1893 Revised *La Salle* and *Old Régime.* November 8, died at Jamaica Pond, in Boston.
1947 *Journals of Francis Parkman.*
1960 *Letters of Francis Parkman.*

CHAPTER *1*

Preparatory Years, 1823-1844

IT WAS NOVEMBER, 1893. Only a few days earlier, Francis Parkman, the heroic old historian, had taken advantage of the mild autumn weather to row his boat around Jamaica Pond on his estate at Brookline, just south of Boston. But now, suddenly stricken with peritonitis, he lay dying. He reread an old favorite of his, Lord Byron's *Childe Harold*, in the intervals between assaults of pain. He lay back, slept fitfully, and dreamed. Once he sat up suddenly. His white hair crowned a poetic brow. His little eyes showed pain, but merriment was etched about them by wrinkles deepened from much smiling. His nose was fine enough for sculpture. His jutting jaw and chin indicated determination. Suddenly he began to describe a dream he had just had. He was in the vast American forest. Before him was a huge bear. He shot the shaggy beast. His friends listened attentively and then watched him sink back to rest.[1]

If the literary works of his life passed in review before his inner vision at that time, Francis Parkman must have been pleased: eight big historical works comprised his study of France and England in North America; in addition, there were his valuable *Oregon Trail*, a charming book about roses, a novel of no great worth except as disguised partial autobiography, a set of careful journals, and many letters. Perhaps, as he lay dying, he smiled in recollection of the heroic struggle his life had been against adverse forces which not merely would have crippled but surely would have completely stopped a man of lesser will. Perhaps his dream of conflict with the bear, symbol of an elemental enemy, summarized his life. The unceasing struggle—the courage not to give in until he had accomplished what he had determined early in life to do—was Parkman's goal and glory.

[19]

I *Historian's Tree*

Like many other nineteenth-century men of letters born in Boston, Francis Parkman could point with pride to an illustrious family tree. His father's line went back to Devonshire, England, which sent forth Elias Parkman to Massachusetts Bay in 1633. One of Elias' grandsons, Ebenezer Parkman, was graduated from Harvard College in 1721, served as a tough-fibered minister at Westborough for more than half a century, and died toward the close of the American Revolution. Among Ebenezer's sixteen children by two wives was Samuel Parkman, the future historian's grandfather, who by dint of hard and honest work made himself one of the wealthiest merchants in Boston. One of his sons, Francis Parkman, Sr., who was born in 1788, was graduated from Harvard at the age of nineteen; and, after study under William Ellery Channing and in Edinburgh, became a Boston Unitarian minister. In addition to ministers and merchants, the Parkman family could boast of brave Indian fighters and a host of philanthropic citizens.[2]

Parkman's mother, who came from an equally renowned family, could proudly name John Cotton of Boston, grandfather of the incredible Cotton Mather, as one forebear; and another was John Cotton the second, a Plymouth divine who preached to the Indians—as did his son Rowland—in their own language. Rowland married a Saltonstall, and their daughter's daughter married a brilliant, liberal minister named Edward Brooks, who was a Revolutionary War chaplain and then a prisoner of the British at Halifax. His daughter Joanna married Nathaniel Hall, a Medford distiller; and their daughter Caroline became Parkman's mother.[3]

Parkman's Unitarian father preached at the New North Church in Boston, published ethical and religious essays of note, and was also remembered for his phenomenal fluency and his kindly humor. His son Francis, Jr., enjoyed a full measure of both these traits himself but is said by those who knew him intimately to have more closely resembled his mother. So thought Parkman's sister Eliza, who was later his devoted companion and assistant, and who once wrote that "Whatever characteristics Frank inherited from his parents came from her [their mother]. He was like her in many ways, and the expression of his face grew more and more like hers. She had, I think, a peculiar tenderness toward him, her oldest child." [4]

Parkman's father had been married before and brought a daughter, Sarah Cabot, to his second marriage, a union which resulted in Francis, Jr., three daughters—Caroline, Mary, and Eliza—and a second son, John Eliot. Caroline later married John Cordner, an Ulster-born Unitarian minister in Montreal, whose delightful household Parkman greatly relished and who in turn valued Parkman's companionship so much that, upon his retirement from the ministry, he moved to Boston to share the aging historian's final decade of life. [5] Earlier, both Caroline and Mary acted as Parkman's secretaries during his trying bouts with near-blindness. After Mary's premature death in 1866, his youngest sister Eliza dedicated her life to his Chestnut Street home, since somewhat before this time the unfortunate man's wife had died. It seems that Lizzie, as his favorite sister Eliza was called, idolized her dashing brother. Now she managed his affairs, cared for his two daughters—Grace and Katharine (his son too had died)—read to him, took dictation from him, and made him the central subject of a now evidently lost diary. [6] Parkman's one and only brother, John Eliot Parkman—"Elly," as he was nicknamed—joined the United States Navy early in the Civil War, was taken prisoner and later released, and was killed in a fall while serving with the Pacific Fleet. [7]

So it appears that Francis Parkman, Jr., was favored by the gods when they placed him in a remarkable family. Because of the commercial acumen of Grandfather Samuel, there would always be money. The warmth and brilliance of Parkman's father, together with the devotion of his mother and sisters, guaranteed that the household would be a vibrant, stimulating one. But the gods devised sinister trials for the young man, who later posited in an autobiographical letter a theory of hereditary mental aberration: his father suffered a nervous breakdown, and his sister Caroline and his brother John were mildly unstable. [8] Parkman's own physical maladies were enough to render a normal person insanely frantic: for much of his adult life the historian suffered from weak eyes, blinding headaches, arthritis in his knees, indigestion, and insomnia. But he converted these afflictions into spurs to goad himself into keener compensatory activity.

II *Boyhood*

Parkman, who was born on September 16, 1823, in Somerset Place (now Alston Street), Boston, divided his childhood between Boston and its vernal suburbs. Everyone who has read *The Education of Henry Adams* remembers that young Adams did the same: he was a schoolboy in winter in Boston, but he summered in Quincy.[9] With Parkman, Beacon Hill contrasted with the rustic wildness of Medford, where he lived with his maternal grandfather on his farm outside the village. Medford was then a few miles north of Boston but is now part of the city, which violently expanded during Parkman's lifetime, to his regret. In his youth, however, the Hall farm was adjacent to a four-thousand-acre area of rocks and wild forest then called the Five Mile Woods but later the Middlesex Fells.[10] Young Frank proving sickly, his parents decided when he was only eight years old to rusticate him out there.

The experiment, which lasted for about five years, seems to have been a good one; for the boy made the rugged Fells his particular domain. He collected rocks, eggs, bugs, and snakes; trapped small animals; and shot arrows at birds with more persistence than success. He always felt that this outdoor school taught him more than the indoor one run by John Angier in Medford a mile away, to which the boy trudged twice daily to learn little or nothing, as he later recorded. He added that Angier's school had a "high but undeserved reputation." [11] An indoor seat of learning somewhat more to Parkman's liking was located behind his father's house, in a shed which contained an amateur laboratory. Here Frank conducted experiments of various sorts. Writing of himself in the third person, as Henry Adams regularly did, Parkman dourly described this phase as follows: "Chemical experiment was his favorite hobby, and he pursued it with a tenacious eagerness which, well guided, would have led to some acquaintance with the rudiments of the science, but which in fact served little other purpose than injuring him by confinement, poisoning him with noxious gases, and occasionally scorching him with some ill-starred explosion." [12]

When he was thirteen, Parkman returned home to his parents in Boston and began to attend Gideon Thayer's famous private school at Chauncey Place, in order to prepare for Harvard Col-

lege, the only proper institution of higher learning for a proper
Bostonian. A little later, the Parkman family moved from its home
at 1 Green Street, where it had lived since Frank was about six,
into his paternal grandfather's sumptuous town house at 5 Bowdoin Square. Frank must have been uncommonly comfortable
within this three-story, colonial brick mansion, which was pilas-
tered, had a Doric-pillared porch, and was surrounded by chestnut trees for shade; but he was assuredly happier in the sloping,
terraced gardens, the pride of which was his now dead grandfather's luscious pears.[13]

The tug of academe, however, was now strong; and Parkman
began to spend more time indoors. At Thayer's busy Chauncey
Hall School, he studied Latin, Greek, English, French, and science. Turning from his chemical experiments, his former fondness
for which he later attributed more to "bodily defect than a mental
superiority," [14] he began to toy with home-made electrical equipment, which he even employed to give shocks to rows of little
girls who stoically assembled themselves before him for that purpose. Fortunately for American history, Parkman preferred English composition to the study of either Greek or Latin. One of
his teachers at Chauncey Hall recalled later that his essays were
fine and that he volunteered to versify descriptions of adventurous
action, for example, the tournament in *Ivanhoe* by Sir Walter
Scott.[15] Parkman himself preferred to recall that while he was in
Thayer's school he chanced to fall under the direction of William Russel, whom he called "a teacher of excellent literary tastes
and acquirements." As Parkman observed when praising Russel,

> It was his constant care to teach the boys of his class to write
> good and easy English. One of his methods was to give us lists
> of words to which we were required to furnish as many synonyms
> as possible, distinguishing their various shades of meaning. He
> also encouraged us to write translations, in prose and verse, from
> Virgil and Homer, insisting on idiomatic English, and criticising
> in his gentle way anything flowery or bombastic. At this time I
> read a good deal of poetry, and much of it remains *verbatim* in
> my memory. As it included Milton and other classics, I am con-
> fident that it has been of service to me in the matter of style.[16]

Here we have the foundation of Parkman's sinewy, masculine
prose style, which is a splendid combination of the bracingly
Romantic and the Realistically idiomatic.

During his pre-college years, Parkman also participated in amateur theatricals and scientific entertainments. For a couple of seasons he was a leading managerial hand and actor in an amateur group, the Star Theater, which offered a variety of bills in a local barn. Other participants included several of Parkman's cousins, one of whom was Quincy Adams Shaw, later his companion on the Oregon Trail. Parkman's lifelong flare for the histrionic, which he displayed with such brilliance in all of his historical writing, must have been developed profoundly, if indirectly, by these juvenile shows. Finally, it should also be mentioned that, rigorous though his school reading may have been at Chauncey Hall, Parkman found time to start what became a lifelong habit of devotion to the works of Scott, Lord Byron, and James Fenimore Cooper.

III *Harvard College*

Parkman's next four years, like much of his boyhood, were divided between town and country, between making himself both an intelligent Boston Brahmin and a full-hearted lover of the American woods.[17] Parkman entered Harvard in August, 1840, just before he turned seventeen; and he would have been admitted even if his father had not that year donated five thousand dollars to the institution, then just entering upon a period of expansion under the leadership of President Josiah Quincy, who did much to make Harvard University the admiration of the academic world.[18] Parkman did well at Harvard, especially after his freshman year. But he always insisted while there, in an early display of his celebrated independence of mind and will, upon studying conscientiously—as Ralph Waldo Emerson had done earlier—only what suited his already forming purpose in life. Part of his program was to toughen himself physically and therefore to take every opportunity, like Henry David Thoreau, to get back to nature. Therefore, unlike his friend Richard Dana, Jr., he cared little about achieving a distinguished academic record but treasured most his invigorating and informative summer vacations, spent hiking through various New England locales hallowed by the French and Indian War.

Parkman could do little map-reading, however, in the fall of 1840; for he was deep in a required reading of Xenophon, Herodotus, and Livy and in the study of French, geometry, and algebra. In January, 1841, his curriculum included Thucydides, Cicero, trigonometry, and Greek and Roman history. During his sophomore year, he continued to study the classics, the *Iliad* and several Greek plays, Juvenal, and more Cicero; and he worked through more history, turning now with relish to Sismondi and Guizot. In addition, he had the distinct pleasure of coming under the influence of an excellent professor of rhetoric, Edward Tyrrel Channing, also known as "Potty," whose sensible instruction improved the prose styles of Emerson, Oliver Wendell Holmes, Dana, Thoreau, and Motley, among many others. What Russel had started to do for Parkman's prose, Channing was able to continue.[19] Another notable Harvard professor at this time was the chemist and mineralogist John White Webster, who in 1850 was hanged for murdering Parkman's uncle, Dr. George Parkman, in the laboratory of Harvard Medical College.

At the start of his sophomore year, Parkman discontinued rooming at Holworthy Hall with Benjamin Apthorp Gould, son of the Boston Latin School headmaster and later a distinguished astronomer. Thereafter, Parkman roomed alone, first at the corner of Appian Way and Garden Street and then, during his junior and senior years, in different rooms in Massachusetts Hall. He was not a recluse, like Nathaniel Hawthorne both before and after his Bowdoin College years. At the noisy boardinghouse where Parkman had his meals, he earned the ironic sobriquet "The Loquacious" by virtue of his habit of listening when several people were present. But he was sufficiently convivial and extremely popular, as may be proved by citing his membership in several undergraduate clubs: the literary and forensic Institute of 1770, the Hasty Pudding (of which he was once president), the I.O.H. (whatever that was), and the C.C. [Chit-Chat] Club (which he helped to found).[20]

In at least two respects, Parkman was an unusual Harvard undergraduate. In debate, he was unconventionally savage. When he was once assigned the affirmative of the topic "Does attendance on theatrical exhibitions have a bad effect on the mind and morals?" he started well but then, perhaps recalling his Star Theater smash hits, startled his audience at Harvard by switching sides and blasting the hidebound.[21] With other topics as well, he showed vehemence and sarcasm. "His manner in debate, always forcible and trenchant, is said also to have been sometimes downright belligerent"—reports his most recent biographer, Howard Doughty, who then suggests a penetrating explanation—"as if, perhaps, he were bringing to these verbal clashes the same spirit of combat that would later have found its outlet in competitive sports." [22]

A second unconventional trait in Parkman also appeared during his Harvard years. In his free time, which he insisted should be ample and which he had intelligence and money enough to make so, he grabbed his rifle and took to the wilds near Cambridge and north to his beloved Five Mile Woods. Few classmates had stamina enough to maintain his gait on these furious hikes, and still fewer had the inclination. One of his bewildered cronies noted that Parkman "even then showed symptoms of 'Injuns on the brain'" and added that "His tales of border life, his wampum, scalps, and birch-bark were unsurpassed by anything in Cooper." [23] In addition, Parkman took boxing lessons from a former professional, addressed himself to gymnasium dumbbells as unremittingly as if they were authorities he might never consult again, practiced horsemanship until he was as adept as a circus equestrian, vigorously rowed boats, and generally drove himself to the edge of a breakdown. [24]

By this time, Francis Parkman knew what he wanted to do with his life. So his eclectic reading program, his indifference to college subjects which did not concern him, and his arduous regimen of hiking, studying the woods, and ferocious physical exercise should not be considered eccentric or willful but Spartan and farsighted. A third-person, autobiographical letter of his, written in 1868, reads in part as follows: "After the usual boyish phases of ambitious self-ignorance, he resolved to confine his homage to the Muse of History, as being less apt than her wayward sisters to requite his devotion with a mortifying rebuff." [25] In a second autobiographical letter composed in 1886, Parkman in an often-quoted passage explained what was to become the intellectual business of his life:

> My favorite backwoods were always in my thoughts. At first I tried to persuade myself that I could woo this new mistress in verse; then I came down to fiction, and at last reached the sage though not flattering conclusion that if I wanted to build in

her honor any monument that would stand, I must found on
solid fact. Before the end of the sophomore year my various
schemes had crystallized into a plan of writing the story of what
was thus known as the "Old French War;" that is, the war that
ended in the conquest of Canada; for here, as it seemed to me,
the forest drama was more stirring and the forest stage more
thronged with appropriate actors than in any other passage of
our history. It was not till some years later that I enlarged the
plan to include the whole course of the American conflict between France and England; or, in other words, the history of the
American forest; for this was the light in which I regarded it. My
theme fascinated me, and I was haunted with wilderness images
day and night.[26]

Thus, when he was only eighteen, this assiduous reader, woodsman, and lover of his young country's past projected the grand
scheme for what would be the work of almost his entire mature
life. The hero of his autobiographical novel *Vassall Morton* similarly plans early in his career his life's work—to be an ethnologist,
thus combining scholarship and adventurous exploration.[27]

Parkman's junior year at Harvard was not materially different
from the first two. The young man continued to study hard,
especially in those subjects which he felt would most immediately
help him to realize his dream of writing the history of the American forest. He had plenty of spare time to continue his teen-age
pursuits of drinking, stag dinners, Boston play-going, dancing,
and the like. And, thinking it essential, he continued to prepare
his physique to withstand the rigors of future New England,
Canadian, and Ohio and Mississippi valley explorations. As
Samuel Eliot Morison sagely observes, "His symptoms form a
now recognizable pattern of neurosis. Consciously or unconsciously, he created a 'struggle situation.' Given his worship of
manliness and contempt for weakness, he could be content with
no less than mastery of 'the enemy,' as he personified the terrible
headaches, the insomnia and the semiblindness"[28] which later
shook him almost nightly.

His senior year at Harvard was easy in those day of sometimes
relaxed academic standards. The term had hardly well begun, in
August, 1843, when Parkman showed signs of nervous exhaustion
and near-collapse, induced by a combination of too much physical
exercise and mental activity. And so, evidently with the blessing

of his Harvard supervisors and with plenty of money from his
generous father, Parkman set sail early in November for a grand
tour of Europe which lasted until the following June, at which
time he simply rejoined his tolerant Class of 1844. The most energetic studying he accomplished after his return was to explore
the shoreline around Nahant and then the Berkshire Hills of
western Massachusetts in July and August, toward the end of the
latter month returning to Harvard to pick up the diploma attest-
ing that he was now a bachelor of arts. His senior year had undoubtedly been the most valuable of his four in college, but many
undergraduates today would envy Parkman the fact that he spent
his last year of study off campus except for about three months.

IV *Forest Research*

During his tenure at Harvard as an undergraduate scholar,
Parkman enjoyed several splendid vacation trips in addition to
other extracurricular activity closer to Cambridge such as the
already mentioned clubbing, tavern-visiting, and theater-going.
As soon as his freshman year was over, Parkman set his keen
woodsman's eyes on the lovely White Mountains. On July 19,
1841, as his earliest extant journal records, he and a companion
named Daniel Denison Slade caught a train from Boston through
Portsmouth to Dover, then took a crowded stage bound for Alton
but impatiently got out twelve miles short of that New Hampshire
town and walked the rest of the way, and soon sighted Lake
Winnipesaukee. Discovering the next day that there was no steamboat, they trudged, carrying full packs, toward Center Harbor.
The heat and dust discouraged them; so they stopped short at
Meredith Bridge, which Parkman described as "a disgusting little
manufacturing village, with no single point of attraction, either
as concerns scenery or anything else" (*Journals*, 9).*

* The following short titles of Parkman's works will be used par-
enthetically in the text and also in the footnotes: *Conflict* (for *A
Half-Century of Conflict*), *Frontenac* (*Count Frontenac and New
France under Louis XIV*), *Jesuits* (*The Jesuits in North America in
the Seventeenth Century*), *Journals* (*The Journals of Francis Parkman*), *La Salle* (*La Salle and the Discovery of the Great West*), *Letters* (*Letters of Francis Parkman*), *Montcalm* (*Montcalm and Wolfe*),
Morton (*Vassall Morton: A Novel*), *Pioneers* (*Pioneers of France in*

Though they had resolved to make it on foot to Center Harbor next morning, they changed their strategy and hired a wagon. Slade soon collapsed into a deep sleep on his hotel bed in Center Harbor, while the hardier Parkman forgot the heat in reading Washington Irving's *Alhambra*. The following morning their hiking began in earnest in an assault on Red Hill. Parkman reveled in both the climb and the view from the two-thousand-foot peak; but he reviled the natives for desecrating nature by burning the timber in a stupid "Yankee spirit of improvement" (10). By this time Slade was complaining so much about the heat and his sore feet that Parkman privately wished he might go on alone. When afternoon came, however, they were happy companions aboard the stage bound for Conway and were passing through wildly beautiful scenery.

The following day they started by stage, had breakfast at Bartlett, and pressed on through a rugged mountainous area rendered more Byronic by mists and oceans of rain. Parkman was sitting on the driver's seat and therefore put up an umbrella, until he noted that it was conducting "a small torrent of dirty water directly into the laps of the ladies behind" (12). When the party arrived at Notch House, it was soaked to the skin and anxious to try the warming effects of brandy and conviviality.

Parkman knew all about the dreadful avalanche of August 28, 1826, which had swept nine people to death in this very region; [29] and he was therefore impatient to explore its ruinous path, a deep ravine cut in the already steep mountainside. Soon he was clawing his way alone up sheer precipices of rotting granite, drenched by the spray of a nearby stream and threatened by an approaching rain cloud. When he decided to return to the Notch House, he found that he could not safely retrace his steps and should therefore climb on and around. At one point he nearly fell when his fingers dislodged a projecting stone, and he had to cut a foot support with his jackknife and then stab his way forward along the crumbling rock face. Safely down again, he heaved a sigh of relief, cut a fishing pole, and tried a trout stream for an hour to calm his nerves. The entire account of this rather foolhardy

the New World), *Pontiac* (*The Conspiracy of Pontiac and the Indian War after the Conquest of Canada*), *Old Régime* (*The Old Régime*), *Roses* (*The Book of Roses*), and *Trail* (*The Oregon Trail*). For bibliographical details, see pp. 183–85 below.

escapade, which he carefully penned into his journal, makes thrilling reading and reveals that Parkman was master of a captivating prose style before he had turned eighteen, and that he also early in life quietly set for himself tough physical challenges.[30]

On July 25 ten men and women, including Parkman, enjoyed climbing to Mount Clinton, went on to Mount Pleasant, then up to the summit of Mount Franklin, and finally stopped before the summit of 6,288-foot Mount Washington, the highest point in New Hampshire. Parkman was thrilled almost beyond words, and his entire account is absorbing. The setting was perfect: at a ridge Parkman alone on horseback, with thunder, a rainbow, and boiling mists about and beneath him: "No scene among the Andes could have been wilder or more picturesque. . . . The mountains were like a sea of lashing waves" (15, 16). The party penetrated through the mist to Mount Monroe, passed the Lake of the Clouds, and camped for almost an hour on the summit of Mount Washington, sipping brandy and waiting vainly for a clearing in the windy, sleety storm to permit a view of the panorama beneath. The descent fatigued all the party but the sinewy Parkman, who was unsympathetic, and a young lady named Miss Pamela Prentiss of Keene, New Hampshire, whom Parkman so admired that she provides some of the traits of Fanny Euston, a charming secondary character in *Vassall Morton*. Of Miss Prentiss he wrote that her "strength and spirit and good humor would have invigorated at least a dozen feeble damsels" (17).[31]

The next day was so filled with a dull rain that only Parkman ventured forth to climb another mountain. His gloomy temper worsened when, upon his return to the Notch House, he found that Miss Prentiss and most of the others had decamped for Franconia, which he and Slade aimed at on foot the next morning. This day was the finest one yet, and the two young men enjoyed their twenty-two-mile hike and also a partridge and a pigeon which Parkman brought down with his rifle. On the following day they trudged south to see the Great Stone Face, immortalized by Hawthorne, and on down across the Appalachian Trail to Lincoln and a vile little tavern there, complete with drunken host but no water. Next day they set forth to explore the famous Flume before breakfast but soon became lost and had to return for a guide. When he got to the Flume, Parkman was thrilled by its combination of rocky cliffs, rotten tree trunks, dripping moss, and riotous waters.

July 30 found Parkman in Lancaster, north of the Connecticut River. He had just heard of a mountain pass near Dixville, still farther north. Disappointed in his efforts to hire as a guide a famous Dartmouth College Indian named James Annance from Quebec, Parkman was lucky enough to fall in with Dr. Charles T. Jackson, a versatile Harvard man who at this time was beginning a New Hampshire geological survey.[32] "The country about . . . is a wilderness where moose and other wild game are still common," Parkman jotted in his journal (21); and he was as excited by the place as was Thoreau when he visited it a few years later.[33] Parkman's enthusiasm, however, was not contagious; and the future historian was obliged to argue convincingly to induce Slade to press on with him to Colebrook, seven hours north by wagon. By now they were only ten miles from the Canadian border. The day after their arrival was Sunday, August 1. The Reverend Dr. Parkman's son implied his partial independence of the family's Unitarianism in the following journal entry: "Sunday in the country is a day of most unmitigated and abominable dulness. . . . I went to church in the morning, but the minister being unfortunately an Unitarian, the dulness of his discourse and the squall of his choir were not varied and relieved by any novel fanaticism or methodistical blunders" (23).

When Monday came, Parkman and Slade pushed east through forests and over streams which no one but Indians and intrepid white hunters had ever before seen. Parkman was ecstatic. They found their sought-for opening in the blocky green range. Evening found them at the lumber settlement of rugged Captain James Bragg, on the banks of the Androscoggin River, where they "slept to the roar of the rapids" (24). As Mason Wade, the first modern biographer of Parkman, concludes at this point, "At last, when only seventeen, he had reached the real wilderness he had often dreamed of in his childhood." [34] He hastened to preserve his impressions in his journal by the light of his forest camp fire.

Bragg advised the young men to follow animal tracks and thus avoid quagmires on their way to Lake Umbagog and the Magalloway River.[35] They did so and then turned north and headed for a settlement which ultimately was called Wilson Mills, Maine, near Aziscoos Mountain. On August 4, the pair, in a borrowed skiff above some rapids, prepared to rendezvous with Jerome, the nephew of Annance the Indian, thirty miles up the Magalloway. The treacherous waters which were too fast to paddle and pole against, flies which bit more than did the fish they hoped to catch, and the rocky shallows—all failed to depress Parkman, whose journal pictures the shaggy forests about them more poetically and a good deal more honestly than any lines in Henry Wadsworth Longfellow's *Evangeline*. For example, one reads with pleasure that "From the high banks huge old pines stooped forward over the water, the moss hanging from their aged branches, and behind rose a wall of foliage, green and thick . . ." (29).

When Jerome paddled on schedule into camp the following morning, he found his tired employers under a cloud of carnivorous mosquitoes. Since their provisions were nearly exhausted, and since Slade was disconsolate, they decided for the present to turn their backs on Canada and to head south. As Parkman explains to himself, "My chief object in coming so far was merely to have a taste of the half-savage kind of life necessary to be led, and to see the wilderness where it was as yet uninvaded by the hand of man" (31). So, with Jerome leading the way in his bark canoe, the two Americans drifted back south again. Parkman had reason to feel that his magnificent first lesson in the woodsman's life was thorough enough when he sighted a huge female moose and broke her spine with a single quick shot. They flayed and cut her up, found the still-smouldering fire at their first night's camp site, and soon enjoyed a juicy meal of moose steaks.

August 7 found them on the fringes of civilization again. As though to test their endurance to the utmost, they covered the forty miles back to Colebrook that day. They quickly paddled ten miles in their skiff down to Bragg's, where they devoured a huge nine-cent breakfast and then hiked west so fast that Slade, who, like Parkman, was now unused to civilized food, became thoroughly sick. Parkman stoically prescribed a freezing bath in a nearby stream, took one himself, and on they went.

On August 8, another Sabbath, Parkman slept and caught up with his journal. Next day they went by foot and wagon to Lancaster, and on the way Parkman chanced to meet again the surveyor Dr. Jackson. This learned man offered to lend him his notebooks, crammed with Indian legends; and Parkman gratefully accepted, knowing that they would help him in his future writing. Soon the young man went to Littleton and then Hanover, then crossed the Connecticut River to Windsor, Vermont, and traveled by train to Boston. One of the last entries in his 1841 journal is revealing: "My pilgrimage . . . must come to an end, and next Saturday will find me at home. I regard this journey but 'as the beginning of greater things' and as merely prefatory to longer wanderings" (35).

His first extant journal, covering his trek through the White Mountains and eastern Maine, is hypnotic. The reader admires the maturity of his already well-formed prose style. One follows the resolute young man breathlessly as he picks up the gauntlet flung down by nature and history. And one nods his head in agreement as he reads between the lines the implicit avowal of Parkman's certainty that this rugged life suits him perfectly, both because of its physical good and because it trains him to follow the track of the past through forest and archives.

Two signs, however, are less auspicious. In the first place, Parkman was developing an antisocial attitude so far as travelers less Spartan than himself were concerned. Forced to join "softies" at the Notch House, he skewers a pair of them with his sharp pen: "a couple of the most consummate fools I ever saw. They set out for the mountain this morning, though the lady uttered the most piercing shrieks her limited power of lungs could compass the instant she was seated in the saddle" (17). Even Slade's complaints are mercilessly preserved—for example, his perfectly understandable "Devil take the Flume—I wish we had never come, or else had brought a guide" (20).[36] And, in the second place, Parkman regularly made things more difficult for himself than he needed to do, or should have done. For example, one reads this account of his trek to the High Rock in the Notch: "The way was through a tangled wood, rocky, bushy, and strewed in all directions with rotten trunks, many of which, when stepped upon, straightway burst to pieces, and, unless I was extremely careful, seated me among their rot. There was a path, but I did not avail myself of it" (17). Morison is surely right when he notes that Parkman created a "struggle situation" for himself; and it is tempting to wish that he had decided to take the easier path to acceptance of less rugged social types and also to less ruinous physical activity.[37]

V *More Extracurricular Education*

Never one to let college interfere with his real education, young Francis Parkman took another trip, even more extensive, in the summer of 1842, this time to Lake George and its environs. Then, during a brief respite from his Harvard assignments in the winter of 1842–43, he headed for Keene, New Hampshire, the home of Pamela Prentiss, whom he had not forgotten. Next, in the summer of 1843 he made a long but easier and more scholarly foray into Canada, with Lake Champlain figuring on the way to Montreal and Quebec, and the White Mountains, again, on his return. Finally, as though to complete the broadening of his undergraduate perspective, he set his sights on Europe that fall. Since these three New England-Canadian trips following his first venture into the White Mountains and the Magalloway area were not materially different, though they were somewhat more rewarding intellectually, there is no need to describe them thoroughly. Always, however, one should remember that Parkman was dedicated by this time to making himself the rugged historian of the English and French in the New World.

Before following Parkman on his tour of the Lake George region, one should glance at a significant little letter he wrote in April, 1842, to Jared Sparks, who at Harvard was the first history professor in America, was later Harvard's president, and still later wrote an important biography of George Washington. In his letter the young sophomore explained that he desired to study the history of the Seven Years' War, that he found the usual authorities insufficiently detailed, and that he wanted material on the "military operations around Lake George—the characters of the officers—the relations of the Indian tribes—the history, the more minute the better, of partisan exploits—in short, all relating to the incidents of the war in that neighborhood" (*Letters*, I, 9). Sparks, a kind man and a friend of Parkman's father, sent the neophyte historian a sizable bibliography and an invitation to converse on the subject of his intense interest.

In order to explore Fort Ticonderoga, Parkman traveled by train on July 15, 1842, to Albany. This time his companion was Henry Orne White, who, because of his sniveling ways and his propensity to sleep, was a poor substitute for Dan Slade. In due time, the travelers passed through Albany and went on to Schenectady, which the young journal-writer called a tissue of canal docks, rotting boats, dirty children, and dung-caked pigs. The next stop was Saratoga. By stage they traveled through scenes hallowed by the French and Indian War to Caldwell (now the town of Lake George) and to the beginning of Parkman's wilderness challenge.

For more than a week Parkman inspected the southern half of Lake George, happy until White, unable to endure the mosquitoes so well as his stoical leader could, threatened to quit. "His scruples I trust to overcome in time," noted Parkman (*Journals,* 57), who sweetened the sour young man with a view of Fort Ticonderoga and with a luxurious steamboat ride on to Burlington, Vermont, where they arrived July 27. Soon they were tramping northeast toward Mount Mansfield, Vermont's highest peak. At Cambridge that night, Parkman was delighted to be taken for an Indian by a garrulous old farmer. Next, a stage carried the two young men from Johnson to Stanstead, east of Lake Memphremagog in Canada, where Parkman happily shared a draft of mead with a garrison of British troops quartered there.

On the first of August, Parkman began to aim for his old haunt, the Magalloway, since his whining companion could not have made it to their original target, the recently discovered Mount Katahdin in Maine, immortalized later in Thoreau's essay on it. To get to the Magalloway, Parkman and White took a wagon to Barnston, Quebec, then walked back into New England at Canaan, Vermont, a trek of twenty miles southeast, punctuated by rain and stops at log cabins along the way. Instead of heading south down the nearby Connecticut River, Parkman began next day to push east to the two Connecticut Lakes and to lure White along with stories of the trout he might catch when they reached the Magalloway. At the First Lake Connecticut they hired a farmer named James Abbot to guide them south to familiar terrain. "Abbot was a rough-hewn piece of lumber enough, but his wife was a perfect barbarian, as far as the entire absence of all manners can make one," Parkman recorded with relish (68).

From August 4 until August 9, Parkman, with Abbot for help and White for an anchor, traversed the watery, mountainous region from the northernmost tip of Vermont past Rosebuck Mountain, bushwhacking, floating through rapids in improvised canoes and rafts, and finally wallowing down to Bragg's old settlement.

Here Parkman renewed acquaintances with several white men whom he had met the summer before, and he even terrified poor White by introducing him to ugly Jerome, his old Indian guide. Next Parkman walked to Colebrook, waiting there for the stage which finally came and took him on to Lancaster, Littleton, and Plymouth. All along the way, far from being happy at the thought of returning home, he reveled in seeing old familiar notches, gorges, and rocky profiles, which, he wrote, "seemed to press me to stay in a manner that nothing but necessity enabled me to resist" (83). Necessity was college again. Parkman's second grand forest exploit ended August 10, at Plymouth.[38]

Of Parkman's two Magalloway trips, Doughty concludes aptly: "They were, so to speak, his Oregon Trail of the East. . . . These few days . . . yielded an extraordinary harvest of impressions that was the life in epitome of his whole history: the great series of explorers' voyages from Champlain to La Salle that fills its first half; the innumerable wood marches of scouts, partisan bands, and armies that fill its second. The eastern forest, not the plains of the West, was his scene, and he here came closest to its heart." [39]

Information is scarce concerning Parkman's brief visit to his classmates George Silsbee Hale and Horatio Justice Perry, at Keene, during their 1842 Christmas vacation from Harvard. Parkman probably had the usual holiday fun. He was handsome, virile, and popular. In addition, he probably looked up Pamela Prentiss, whose high spirits he had admired in the White Mountains two summers before.[40]

Considerable material is available about Parkman's third major foray into rural New England, which occurred in the summer following his junior year. Since this trip was undertaken not primarily for muscle-building—indeed, evidently in spite of slightly worsening health—but to gather historical data, it is less exciting to follow but more significant. The 1843 entries in the journal are, as its editor Mason Wade notes, incomplete, terse, and bad tempered, in contrast to the buoyancy of the earlier notebooks.[41] But Parkman did his outdoor homework thoroughly, for he scoured the Hudson and Mohawk valleys for still-available oral traditions. He also gathered priceless information about Sir William Johnson, the British leader of the Iroquois; about early Dutch inhabitants of Albany and Schenectady; about Joseph

Brant, the formidable Mohawk chief educated by Dartmouth's Eleazar Wheelock in Lebanon, Connecticut, and commissioned a colonel by the British for services rendered during the American Revolution; about Brant's sister Molly, who was one of Sir William's ruddy mistresses; and about much else. Parkman went on to Lake George to revisit battlegrounds thereabouts. And this time he satisfied his desire to see Montreal and Quebec, where he inspected cathedrals, nunneries, forts, barracks, and military monuments. Soon he was on his way home by way of his beloved White Mountains, this time for the purpose of hearing and recording yarns from the oldest inhabitants who would talk to him. He also evidently asked everyone to recommend reliable books about the past of the area, for his sparse notebook includes several titles of such items.

Parkman had hardly rested in Boston from this informative tour than he set out again, this time with his sister Caroline, for Gardiner, Maine, where she stayed with friends while he went to Bangor to interview Penobscot Indians on their reservation north of town.[42]

VI *See Naples, etc.*

Home again and reconciled to the prospect of re-entering Harvard, Parkman soon found that his regimen of camping in the rain and of trying later to recover from its lingering ill-effects by swinging on the gymnasium trapeze was taking a dreadful toll. He was as incapable of continuing his college studies as Dana had been a decade earlier because of his measles and consequent eye weakness. Dana had refused to take a gentlemanly grand tour to Europe or anywhere else; instead, as everyone knows, he shipped as a common seaman for two years before the mast. The Parkmans had more money than the Danas, but Frank also disdained an easy voyage. He chose to sail in mid-November, 1843, as the only passenger aboard the *Nautilus*, a Boston fruit barque bound for Gibraltar. He followed pretty much the route Emerson had taken in 1833. Parkman went to Gibraltar ("Here, in this old world, I seem, thank heaven, to be carried about half a century backwards in time" [*Journals*, 125]); Malta, Sicily ("The country inns of Sicily are notorious" [148]); Naples ("I would go farther for one look into the crater of Vesuvius than to see all the ruined temples in Italy" [165]); Rome and its environs, Florence

("... everything speaks of the middle ages and of the Medici" [199]); Bologna, Milan, the Lake of Como ("Give me Lake George, and the smell of the pine and fir!" [209]); the Splügen, Zurich, Basel, Strasbourg, Paris (" 'Let envious Englishmen sneer as they will,' I thought, 'this *is* the Athens of Modern Europe!" [219]); London, Abbotsford ("I ... consider the day better spent than the whole four months I was in Sicily and Italy" [226], Edinburgh, Liverpool, and home again—arriving late in June, 1844.

The journal of fifty thousand words which Parkman kept during his active seven months in Europe is a remarkable document; bursting with facts and impressions, it is informed throughout by the joyful traveler's engaging personality. The writer is obviously an intelligent young American Protestant, willing to be shown anything of interest but refusing to call something an eloquent message from the past if it does not seem so to his candid vision. His European journal reveals Parkman to be a combination of Mark Twain's innocent abroad and Henry James's passionate pilgrim, of Twain's raucous American shrewdness and James's aristocratic culture. When Parkman sees filth and superstition, he says so as frankly—and as unsympathetically—as the author of *The Innocents Abroad;* yet he responds intelligently when a Sicilian recites part of Virgil's *Eclogues* to him. Parkman plays hookey from conventional groups of tourists with the relish of Tom Sawyer and Huckleberry Finn; yet he takes to Abbotsford as thorough a memory of Sir Walter Scott's novels as James's Isabel Archer or Lambert Strether ever could.

The voyage from Boston to Gibraltar took thirty-two days but, once Parkman got over a bout of seasickness, was filled with variety. His journal contains a predictable number of adverse comments about the members of the *Nautilus* crew, especially the first mate Jonathan Snow. But Parkman liked Hansen, the tough, experienced second mate, and plied him with brandy to learn details of his Indian-fighting days in Oregon. When they had been five days at sea, Snow called Parkman from his reading of *Don Quixote* to rush on deck to see a rousing gale. It lasted four days, until they were close to the Azores: "The wind was yelling and howling in the rigging in a fashion that reminded me of a storm in a Canada forest" (112). This storm, other circumstances of his voyage—including a tedious calm off the Azores—and even the name Hansen, Parkman used in his novel *Vassall Morton*.[43]

While the *Nautilus* was off Gibraltar, Parkman lost no time in getting ashore to inspect this locale of many historic battles. He admired the noble-looking Moors, obtained permission to visit excavations and fortifications, but by Christmas was happy to board the *Polyphemus*, a British troop steamer bound for Malta, where he landed in five days. Transportation problems permitted him to devote only a single crowded day to seeing the sights of colorful Valetta. Then he caught a Neapolitan steamer bound for Messina; stopped on the way at storied Syracuse; and arriving at Messina on New Year's Eve, disembarked and toured Eastern Sicily for several arduous days and then took a little steamer which plied between Sylla and Charybdis, "the scene of Ulysses' submarine adventures" (139), to Palermo. Parkman had a glorious week there enjoying Mount Pellegrino, the Capuchin Convent, Monreale, and donkey rides through sections of the vivid city.

On January 17, 1844, he engaged Luigi, a professional guide, for four dollars a day to "pilot" him for a couple of weeks around the entire Western part of Sicily—Marineo, Castel Termini, Caltanizetta, Agrigentum, Sciacca, Castelvetrano, Mazzara, Marsala, Trapani, Segesta, and back to Palermo. This jaunt through flea-riddled *alberghi* and over grim terrain on donkeys suited Parkman but was not good for a young man with a supposedly weakened heart. Luigi, who took his role seriously and seems to have been an unusually honest *vetturino*, pointed out spots of geographical and historical interest, introduced his employer to antiquarians and patrons of art and the homes of friends, found him samples of ancient coins, led him to temples and ruins and churches, and saw to it that the best of food and accommodations were made available to his *signore americano*. "In short the fellow is a jewel, and shall be my particular friend henceforward," Parkman noted (151). As usual, he made the most of his opportunity: he saw an incredible variety of Sicilian objects—geographical, architectural, religious, commercial, and domestic. He did not spare himself physically, and in his limited moments of rest he took the trouble to record his impressions in lavish detail.

Parkman arrived in the matchless Bay of Naples during a miserable storm, but the Mediterranean sun soon appeared. Making the most of his week or ten days there, he visited the Royal

Museum (now the Nazionale), Pozzuoli and its caves, Lake
Avernus and the nearby Cumaean Sybil, Baiae Bay, the flat volcanic field of Solfatara, and Virgil's tomb at Posillipo. Here his
mountain-scaling zeal prompted him to try to climb out on a rock
for a Virgilian memento, but a crowd of solicitous Neapolitans
mistook him for a madman, seized him for a while, and thus
deterred him.[44] At his hotel in Naples, Parkman chanced to meet
Theodore Parker, the Unitarian minister, controversial Transcen-
dentalist, and splendid linguist who was vacationing in Europe.
They climbed Vesuvius together at a time when both the approach and the hellish view into its vivid crater were more dangerous than they are now. The two Bostonians were tolerant
enough to sample some famed Lagrima Cristi wine on their way
down the dry volcanic slope. Returning to Naples, they were
caught in the carnival crowds swirling about the masked figure
of King Ferdinand, who was firing sugarplums at his subjects
and was being pelted in return as he passed along the Toledo
(now Via Roma), the most colorful street in Naples. Parkman
next examined the San Carlo opera house but recorded his amateurish preference for the Punch and Judy street shows with their
lively indecencies. Best of all, according to this scion of New
England divines, were the dark-skinned beauties whose presence
made the street audiences even more enticing than puppets:
"There is something particularly attractive about these women
[Parkman allowed], who are seldom, however, handsome, properly speaking—but there is the devil in their bright faces and full
rounded forms" (171–72). Pompeii and Herculaneum also beck-
oned, and then Parkman accompanied the Parkers on a wild
diligence ride to Rome.

As the three New Englanders were spinning through the streets
of the Eternal City, Mrs. Parker's inquiry as to the identity of the
nearby Coliseum occasioned "an untheological interjection" (175)
from her ministerial spouse. The carnival was in its hectic closing
days here too. After three or four weeks in Rome, beginning late
in February, Parkman was weary and needed a change. As he
recorded it, "I . . . have been presented to his Holiness the Pope
—have visited churches, convents, cemeteries, catacombs, common
sewers including the Cloaca Maxima, and ten thousand works
of art. This will I say of Rome—that a place on every account
more interesting—and which has a more vivifying and quickening

influence on the faculties—could not be found on the face of the earth—or at least I should not wish to go to it, if it could" (179–80). The change for Parkman took the form of a jackass tour with the expatriate painter William Morris Hunt around Tivoli, Subiaco, Palestrina, and Velletri.

What occurred next Howard Doughty calls the climax of Parkman's Roman days.[45] The young man decided to spend a week or so in a convent. Denied admittance by the Passionists at Albano and then by the Capuchins in Rome, Parkman was finally allowed to join a group of Italian Easter retreatists in the Passionist convent in Rome. Soon he was happily writing as follows: "The Coliseum is close to the window of my room, with Rome behind it—gardens in front, and endless ruins—arches—columns—walls—and fountains—around. Now—about sunset—a hundred different church bells are ringing in the city, and the dome of St. Peter's is red in the light of the setting sun. It is a sight that would intoxicate an antiquary, and is pleasant enough to anybody" (193). Of more value to a historian than the picturesque view was Parkman's being permitted to share simple repasts with the monks, hear their vesper chants, talk gaily and frankly with them, and begin to admire their Spartan regimen.

Parkman retained some vivid images of these men: "A thin, hollow-eyed father tried to start my heresy this morning, but was horrified at the enormity of my disbelief; and when I told him that I belonged to a Unitarian family, he rolled up his bloodshot eyes in their black sockets, and stretched his skinny neck out of his cowl, like a turtle basking on a stone in summer" (194). But Parkman was glad to leave and witness the Holy Week in Rome, during which he insinuated himself into throngs to come as close as possible to the Pope. In his journal, Parkman traces the successive stages of his mounting interest in Catholic pageantry with a kind of unsuccessful sarcasm, until the climax, which was Easter Sunday, April 7, when the Pope blessed an army before St. Peter's during the day and that edifice was flooded by candlelight after dark. "It was a sight well worth all the rest of Holy Week," Parkman tersely noted (198), then departed for Florence the next day.

Thus began another period of wearying travel. After a few days in Florence, during which he inspected the Duomo, the picture galleries, the American sculptor Hiram Powers' popular studio, and the Arno shops, Parkman galloped on, unhappy that his

"cursed injury" (201)—that is, his strained heart and hypertension
—was causing him to forego Granada. He had to content himself
with Bologna, Modena—where he bought an Italian translation of
Cooper's *Last of the Mohicans*—and then Parma. In that city he
was directed to a filthy restaurant, which prompted the following
proud comment: "On occasions of necessity, I can eat anything
that a dog can, but I had no mind to banquet gratuitously on dirt;
so, telling the *padrone* that his establishment was not to my taste,
I went off leaving him growling in the rear" (203). After Pia-
cenza, where he recorded his impression of the differences between Northern and Southern Italians, he crossed the Po River
into territory dominated by Austria, and proceeded to Milan on
April 21. Though the cathedral there engaged him, he was more
pleased to see the Alps shimmering in the distance and challenging the mountain man in him.

Parkman was soon cursing Napoleon for building roads in the
mountains instead of leaving the Alps alone. The highest, wildest
Alpine pass he could find, the Splügen, disappointed him, and he
compared it unfavorably with his beloved Notch in the White
Mountains; but the village in the valley just beyond reminded
him happily of New England, for it was surrounded by mountain
scenery of proper savageness. Of one wild stream he wrote, "Last
night I followed it for a mile or two, back into the mountains—
not Cooper himself could do it justice" (212).[46] Parkman, en-
thralled by this entire Grisons region, left it with regret after days
of happy hiking. Zurich and Basel called, and Parkman sampled
a sermon emanating from a Calvinist parson equipped with "all
the dignity of Geneva bands and gown," and "a scowling countenance" besides (218). Leaving Strasbourg by train, Parkman
soon arrived in Paris, where he was conducted about the glittering city for two weeks by his knowledgeable uncle, Dr. Samuel
Parkman (the man later murdered by J. W. Webster). Parkman
so completely neglected his journal that only the hiatus proves
that he was delighted there.

By May 17, Parkman was in London and the "mother country,"
as he called England (220). It immediately seemed familiar to
him, because of his introduction to a host of British types by
Charles Dickens. Parkman tried the theaters and restaurants. St.
Paul's he found dirty and gloomy, but the view from the cupola

was wonderful. He liked the scenery about Richmond tolerably well but was ecstatic in Westminster Abbey.

One last spot remained for Parkman to visit before he left for Liverpool and a westbound ship. Giving the Lake District short shrift, he sped to Scott country and Abbotsford: "We were in the region where one thinks of nothing but of Scott, and of the themes which he has rendered so familiar to the world. . . . Three days was all the time I had to spare for these places; but rising at six and going to bed at ten, and being on my legs during the whole interval, I managed to see almost every spot of note for eight or ten miles around" (225, 226). Taking a coach to Edinburgh, he enjoyed the architecture of that superb city, and heard stories of Scott and Bobby Burns everywhere. Finally he tore himself away, went to Glasgow to catch a boat to Liverpool, and soon was steaming west with a motley assortment of fellow passengers. It seems that half of them were insular British and the other half Anglophobic Americans, Scotsmen, and Irishmen. Parkman had a grand time superciliously observing them. He landed at Boston late in June, 1844, ready to tackle new problems—academic, physical, and professional.

Although he did not quite know it, his apprenticeship was over. Parkman, not yet twenty-one years of age, was now ready to embark upon his life's work. He was well schooled: he was a master woodsman, he had begun his study of the British and French in the American forest, and his grand tour of Europe had widened his somewhat provincial intellectual perspective. His trip abroad, to the fountains of Classicism and the heart of Catholicism, had converted a Romantic young Puritan into a self-reliant, stoical American scholar.

CHAPTER 2

Uncertain Years, 1845-1865

FOR THE NEXT two decades, Parkman was alternately active in the pursuit of his main goal in life, writing the history of the American forest, and diverted from it, if not positively laid low—by circumstances beyond even his will to control. When he had his way and his health permitted, he listened to the muse of history. At other times, he was forced to sit in a darkened room, with such incredible pain in his head and eyes that he could not look anywhere except within. What he saw there was an image of a man resolved never to give up.

I *Law School and Little Trips*

Immediately before and just after his graduation from Harvard in August, 1844, Parkman took brief research and pleasure trips through New England. He celebrated the Fourth of July at Concord, admiring the orderly rowdiness of his fellow Americans and discussing "the she-philosophers of W[est] Roxbury [at Brook Farm]," all of which he found "striking and amusing after seeing the manners of Paris and London" (*Journals*, 256). His notebooks also contain historical and topographical comments, summaries of information offered by hardy old survivors of the French and Indian War, and descriptions of scenes of old battles and mouldering forts. There is also one refreshing little personal note which shows that Parkman was more than a mere antiquarian: "*Lee* [Massachusetts] is full of factory girls. The very devil beset me there. I never suffered so much from certain longings which I resolved not to gratify, and which got me into such a nervous state that I scarcely slept all night" (259-260).

A little later Parkman visited Stephentown, New York, for the express purpose of observing the anti-renters, whose cause he deplored while conceding its inevitable success: "I have never seen a viler concourse in America," he undemocratically allowed; but he also opined that "feudal tenure, so strangely out of place in America, has probably lived its time" (268). He returned to Boston from such trips laden with information but often nervous. His mind was teeming with visions of Rogers' Rangers, Bish-Bash Falls, frontier women who spoke about nights of terror in log huts, and accounts of nocturnal scalping parties and ambushes in sun-drenched corn fields.

He was already formulating a theory as to the tragedy of his forest: "For a thousand ages her trees rose, flourished, and fell. In the autumn the vast continent glared at once with yellow and red and green; and when winter came, the ice of her waters groaned and cracked to the solitudes; and in the spring her savage streams burst their fetters, and bore down the refuse of the wilderness. It was half a world consecrated to the operations of Nature!" (258). The forest was thus heroic. And the villain? Curious, almost shorthand notes at the end of this 1844 Berkshire journal imply the answer: "Every possible thing done to ruin the face of nature—but unsuccessful." To him, "America's remaining beauty" was "Her wildness" (277).[1]

A historian-to-be, with historical and wilderness associations crowding his brain, should never have entered law school. Parkman did so, however, in the fall of 1844. Yet, judging at least from a charming letter in October to George Hale, his friend from Keene, he did not let his juridical studies siphon much energy from his dearer intellectual pursuits: "I am down at Divinity [Hall], devoting one hour *per diem* to law—the rest to my own notions. It is a little dismal here with the *fellers* . . . We have in the Law-School a sprinkling of fine fellows from north, south, east, and west—some in the quiet studying line, some in the *all-Hell* style, and some a judicious combination of both" (*Letters*, I, 18). Many of his journal comments about his fellow law students are viciously sarcastic. He usually avoided their company and continued to address himself to his historical "notions."

Doughty concludes rather too easily that, since Parkman was faced with the traditionally acceptable careers of law, medicine, and the ministry, and found that law "ran least against the grain of his inclinations," he entered law school in "good faith."[2] Such an opinion seems too charitable. When Parkman let his father talk him into going to law school, he was taking a short path of no resistance to a dead end for him. Once in Divinity Hall, he kept busy, not at studying the law but in reading European and American history; and he also wrote a few semi-fictional sketches based on his New England camping trips. In 1845 he published anonymously and pseudonymously in the *Knickerbocker Magazine* "The Ranger's Adventures" (about a ranger and some Indians), "The Scalp Hunter" (about a murderous white bounty hunter), "A Fragment of Family History" (apocryphal but vividly scenic), "The New Hampshire Ranger, by Captain Jonathan Carver, Jr." (a historical narrative poem cast near Lake George), and "Satan and Dr. Carver, by Captain Jonathan Carver, Jr." (a slight, humorous sketch against a real backdrop). No matter how fast Parkman might have written, these five pieces would have interfered with any conscientious study of Blackstone. Parkman's early biographer Henry Dwight Sedgwick is correct in labeling his subject "a make-believe law student." [3]

The semi-autobiographical sketches were enough to tell Parkman that his muse was historical rather than narrowly literary. By now he had determined to begin work on the history of the uprising of Pontiac, the last great Indian leader who had even a chance to stem the English tide after Quebec fell. To this end, Parkman spent the summer of 1845 on a research trip to New York, Philadelphia, Lancaster, Harrisburg, Buffalo, Detroit, Mackinaw, Sault Ste. Marie, Niagara, Oswego, Syracuse, and Oneida, and home again by Albany and New York.

Although Parkman relished everything he saw, the goal of his summer was Detroit and its environs. Therefore he spent a minimum of journal-words on Mennonites at Lancaster, the beauties of the Susquehanna River, Locofocoism in Harrisburg, Senecas at Buffalo, and Norwegian emigrants on the Detroit steamer. Once stimulated by the former habitat of fierce Pontiac, his mind and sensibilities expanded gratefully. He observed skinny, pockmarked, rum-drinking descendants of Pontiac's lieutenants, then went up the Eastern coastline of Michigan to Thunder Bay, and journeyed north to Mackinaw. "The place is a picture of an ancient Canadian settlement—the little houses in Canadian style—some of them log, with roofs thatched with bark—the picket fences, of rough sharpened stakes, that surround them all—the canoes and Ind[ian]. huts on the shore give them a wild and picturesque air. Wild-looking half-breeds in abundance" (*Jour-*

nals, 303). Parkman struck up an immediate friendship with Lieutenant Henry Whiting, an intelligent army officer stationed at the Mackinaw post who showed him around. When he went on to Sault Ste. Marie, he took along letters of introduction from Whiting to Henry Rose Schoolcraft and Robert Stuart. Schoolcraft was a Lake Superior Indian agent with pretensions to anthropological acumen, and Stuart was a knowledgeable retired Astor Fur Company trader.[4] Parkman made abundant use of these fortunate contacts.

Next he headed west for Palmer, Michigan, because he had heard that out there were some papers of a soldier named Lieutenant M'Dougal, who had been captured by Indians while on a mission to Pontiac in 1763. His day in Palmer being Sunday, poor Parkman first had to go to a frontier church service conducted by a clergyman described as "a vile-looking fellow, tall and sallow, with a loud voice and a bad obtrusive face." Parkman also noticed, however, "A very pretty face in the choir" (308). Then he got down to research "in overhauling *six trunks* of old McDougall's [*sic*] papers" (309). Unwilling to leave any stone unturned, Parkman returned home by way of Windsor, Ontario, to consult François Baby, the grandson of a French trader who had known Pontiac.

By August 17, Parkman was at Niagara, exhausted by his researches and explorations but prepared to admire the stupendous cataract, though never the little tourists who made it their summer Mecca. "What a pack of damned fools," the Brahmin recorded even as he gawked. He was always better at appreciating nature than man, as is shown in the following entry, which is reminiscent of Emerson's "Hamatreya" and "Seashore":

Old Niagara pours bellowing on forever, as it has poured since the beginning of time, and generation after generation of poor little devils of human beings play their little pranks and think their little thoughts around him. He roars on undisturbed, while age after age of the manikins look at him, patronize him with their praises, and go to the devil before his eyes. What does he care for their pranks, their praises, or their fault-finding? His tremendous face never changes; his tremendous voice never wavers; one century finds him as the last did, in his unchanging power and majesty. (312) [5]

Still heading home, Parkman paused at Syracuse long enough to go by horse to Onondaga Castle to check topography and to search for Indians who might tell him about the Iroquois confederation of the Five Nations (Mohawks, Oneidas, Onondagas, Cayugas, and Senecas) which had held councils there. Although he plied every available redskin with cigars, he was compelled to record his failure: "They are the worst people in the world to extract information from: the eternal grunted 'yas' of acquiescence follows every question you may ask, without distinction" (315).[6]

II Go West, Young Historian

The greatest emotional experience of Parkman's life was soon to begin. Dane Law School meant little to the restless young man in the fall of 1845; though he continued to do his modicum of work there (being read to from Blackstone by his sisters when his eyes became worse), the several letters he wrote at this time to professional historians and possessors of historical information show where his mind and heart lay. After he took his Harvard law degree in January, 1846, he repaired almost instantly to New York and Baltimore for a month of research. The pressure of conforming to the rigors of law school while conducting historical investigations now afflicted him: his eyesight began to fail alarmingly. So he and his adventure-loving cousin, "Quin" Shaw, decided to go west, really west, to the Oregon Trail,[7] for information, fun, and physical challenges which might prove tonic. Parkman went west primarily to study the Indians in their still pristine vigor. Only secondarily did he go west to improve his eyes, which in fact were almost fatally weakened by the burning glare of the plains and by the alkali dust.

At the end of March, 1846, Parkman left New York for the West. Simply getting to Pittsburgh was no easy task. A freshet swept away a bridge near Harrisburg. Phlegmatic, stolid Dutchmen had to be endured around Carlisle. Then Parkman had to take a coach leaving Chambersburg at midnight; as dawn came, he saw the ranges of the Allegheny Mountains and was delighted. Once in Pittsburgh, he paused to visit the ruins of Fort Pitt and the scene of General Edward Braddock's disastrous defeat. Then Parkman boarded an Ohio River steamboat in April, accompanied by a generally unacceptable variety of fellow passengers. He was honest enough to rebuke himself in his journal for his offishness, a trait which is especially notable in the first few chapters of *The Oregon Trail.*

The first thing he observed when he arrived in St. Louis in mid-April was Henry Clay, who was campaigning among his unwashed constituents. "So much for the arts by which politicians —even the best of them—thrive," Parkman noted (410). He preferred talking with Pascal Louis Cerré, octogenerian veteran of the fabulous fur trade, and with Pierre Chouteau, another trader; visiting Cahokia, the locale in Illinois across from St. Louis which was rumored to have been the scene of Pontiac's assassination; digesting everything he could get hold of concerning the Indians of the region; and inspecting Jefferson Barracks, the army post outside St. Louis.

The real trip started on April 28 from St. Louis. Parkman and Quin Shaw boarded a steamer for Independence, Missouri, along with some beggarly Kaw Indians, a party of flashy Baltimorians headed for California, and Henry Chatillon, Parkman's incomparable hunter and guide. Parkman was delighted by the muddy Mississippi River and then the lighter Missouri. Ominously, as soon as they got to Independence, he recorded a feeling of depression, partly, it may be supposed, because he was embarking on yet another unearned youthful lark and partly because he sensed the passing of time. "I felt as I had felt many years before, but I was no longer the same man, either in knowledge or in character" (417).

On May 5 they went on to Westport (now part of Kansas City, Missouri), and they soon gazed upon "the great green ocean of the prairies" (417), an alluring cure for lingering melancholy. Parkman was intrigued by galloping bands of Shawnees and tales of the Delawares and Wyandots, all on nearby reservations. He observed the efforts of the emigrants to choose leaders and prepare to roll west. For sixty dollars he bought a fine horse which he promptly named Pontiac (usually spelled "Pondiac" in the journal). Then he and Shaw purchased a pair of mules and rode back to camp just as a violent thunderstorm bombarded the vast prairie (*Trail*, Ch. I).

After a few delays, Parkman, Shaw, Chatillon, and their French-Canadian muleteer Deslauriers (spelled "Delorier" in the journal) from Kansas Landing headed out from Westport toward Fort

Leavenworth. Next day they ferried the Kansas River, then moved through Delaware territory until they saw "the white walls of Leavenworth . . . in the distance" (*Journals*, 421; *Trail*, Ch. II). On the following day Parkman rode into the fort to meet its commanding officer, Colonel Steven Watts Kearny (later of Santa Fe and California fame), and then went over to a semi-civilized Kickapoo Indian village (*Trail*, Ch. III). "Some of the scenery— the rich, sunlit, swelling prairies with bordering hills and groves— was very beautiful" (*Journals*, 422).[8]

On May 13 they joined a wagon train of Britishers who were aided by a pair of French-Canadian hunters and a muleteer from St. Louis. This party included Captain Bill Chandler, his happy-go-lucky brother Jack, their British friend Romaine, their hunters Sorel and Boisvert (spelled "Boisverd" in *The Oregon Trail*), and their muleteer—named Wright (*Trail*, Chs. I, II). The whole group headed out from Leavenworth, only to take a wrong turn and get lost until they wandered into a fresh dragoon trail in time for an evening thunderstorm. The next day the horse Pontiac showed his native wisdom by disappearing until Parkman chased him and brought him back roped. Soon the party struck the St. Joseph's Trail (Ch. IV) and began following what they judged to be Mormon camp sites. One day after they had covered twenty dusty miles, "nooned," and then traversed more of the endless prairie, "We struggled through bushes, reeds, and mud till we came to a nasty pool, rich in mud, insects and reptiles, where we washed as we could. Dor-bugs swarmed in the prairie and camp" (*Journals*, 424). Within a few days they were having trouble with the British party, which had its own reasons for wanting to hurry,[9] whereas the two Brahmins and their cohorts preferred to saunter along through the brooding land. One rainy day they came upon a stray Mormon cow, which they promptly shot and devoured (*Trail*, Ch. V).

Parkman amused himself on the trail by observing the personnel of the British party and by pumping Chatillon for Indian lore. Chatillon knew plenty, since he was married to Bear Robe, an Oglala chief's daughter (Ch. X). But Mason Wade says that Parkman displays "anthropological naivete" in being unduly impressed by some of the things Chatillon reported—for example, a commonly known primitive taboo concerning mothers-in-law.[10]

On May 24 the group struck the Oregon Trail, seven days from the Platte River (in what is now Nebraska). Then they spotted a twenty-wagon emigrant party and its herd of cattle. Parkman and his friends passed them while they were breakfasting. Soon, according to Romaine, who stayed behind to get his horse shod, the emigrants had a little insurrection and broke up into smaller units, one of which—a party of four wagons—joined Parkman's group, much to his annoyance in spite of the fact that their cows gave milk regularly and their oxen once pulled his wagon out of a gully.

Two days later Parkman began to feel the first adverse effects of his reckless adventure: "Afternoon, not well—sat slouching on horse, indulging an epicurian [*sic*] reverie—intensely hot—dreamed of a cool mountain spring, in a *forest* country—two bottles of Champagne cooling in it, and cut-glass tumblers, full of the sparkling liquor" (*Journals,* 429). Wade explains that the altitude of the subhumid region and the alkali water often caused tenderfoot travelers to suffer from vomiting, depression, and dysentery.[11] Toward the end of May, Parkman and the others suspected that they were lost. Their bacon was running low, and they could not bring down any antelopes with their rifles. As they drifted on and on, "Immense masses of blue, lurid clouds in the west shadowed the green prairie, and the sun glared through purple and crimson" (430). They made contact with a pair of Indians out hunting. Finally they reached the Platte on May 30 (*Trail,* Ch. VI).

Early in June, still moving westward and now encountering sleety winds, they noted traces of buffalo moving ahead of them. Tempers were getting raw. Shaw was for breaking away from the Englishmen and going alone to Laramie, but they all remained together. One afternoon Parkman and Chatillon galloped after some elusive buffalo, shot two, skinned and cut them up, and returned to camp well provisioned but chilled by a freezing rain and envious of the prairie dogs in their snug burrows. The next morning, June 4, Chatillon returned from reconnoitering to report that a fleet of eleven boats was wallowing down the shallow Platte a month out of Laramie. Parkman eagerly visited the boatman and their rough-looking boss, Pierre Papin, and gave him some letters to mail (Ch. VII). The hills around their afternoon camp reminded Parkman of Sicily; and, a day later, while lying on the ridge of a barren hill and glowering about for antelope, he "contrasted my present situation with my situation in the convent at Rome" (*Journals*, 434).

Becoming restive and worried, Parkman and Shaw now decided to part company with "old-womanish" Bill Chandler (434), his party, and the emigrant train as soon as they crossed the Side Fork (now known as the South Platte, near the northeastern tip of what is now Colorado). A report from some emigrants up ahead that Indians had stolen ten of their horses and had driven off more than a hundred head of cattle enlivened one "nooning" but distressed Chandler. They forded Side Fork at a picturesque spot—"river half a mile wide and no where more than three feet deep—swift and sandy . . ." (435)—whereupon Parkman's group bid farewell on June 10 to the British party, and pushed on alone through monotonous scenery rife with sand flies, invisible Sioux, and buffalo dung—variously called *bois de vache* and prairie chips.[12]

On June 12 Parkman sighted Chimney Rock, the famous natural landmark (in Western Nebraska), and a day later pressed on to join an emigrant party led by one of the famous Robidoux brothers (Parkman spells the name "Roubideau" in both his journal and his *Oregon Trail*). They went on together and camped at Scott's Bluff near what is now the Wyoming border. After a night of rain, Parkman and his friends rendezvoused with Old Smoke, a canny old Oglala chief known to Chatillon (Parkman spells the tribe "Ogillallah"). Parkman rushed to record his impressions in his journal of Old Smoke's twenty lodges. "The camp was a picturesque scene. The squaws put up temporary sun shades, and scattered their packs and utensils about—the boys splashed in the river—the horses were picketed around. The shield and three poles hung up for each lodge—medicine—Smoke's was pure white" (439). The immediacy of such vivid jottings makes some critics think that the journal is superior to *The Oregon Trail* in several ways.

At last, on June 13, they rode into sight of Fort Laramie (*Trail*, Ch. VIII). The area was alive with intense activity and variety, and Parkman was jubilant now that a long-held curiosity was satisfied. Here he was thrilled to meet such genuine Western stalwarts as James Bordeaux (boss of the fort since Pierre Papin was boating on the Platte), Pierre Louis Vasquez (who was a partner of legendary Jim Bridger and whose name is spelled "Vaskiss" in

The Oregon Trail), and Simoneau (a French-Canadian hunter whose prowess rivaled that of Chatillon himself).

For nearly a week Parkman and his group remained at Fort Laramie. He stoically downed boiled puppy with Old Smoke, welcomed tardy Captain Chandler and his cohorts, ecstatically observed the local Indians, recorded much information, and declined an Indian mistress to be paid for by his horse Pontiac (Ch. IX), which he instead traded for a little mare promptly christened Pauline after its former owner Paul Dorion (Ch. XIII). Next, for almost two weeks he camped at Chugwater, ten miles southwest of Laramie. At this time he hired as *engagés* two pleasant young fellows named Raymond and Reynal. Raymond remained with Parkman in the Sioux camp and on down to Bent's Fort. Reynal was related by marriage to Indians in the Oglala village in Laramie Basin, where Parkman also stayed; in addition, Reynal replaced Chatillon later as Parkman's interpreter. One night Parkman galloped from Chugwater back to Laramie and learned that Chatillon and Shaw had left on a sad mission—to attend the funeral of Bear Robe, Chatillon's squaw. Parkman later learned from Shaw various details of Indian mourning and burial practices (Ch. X).

For a while Parkman vibrated to the rumor that the great Sioux chief Tunica (also called Whirlwind) was moving about nearby and was planning to make war on the Snake Indians; but, because of an inadequate supply of horses, he was dissuaded, much to the curious diarist's disappointment. "So much for Indian constancy—in fact they are the most uncertain people living—their resolutions no more to be trusted than those of children" (*Journals*, 449). Obviously, the historian wanted a war staged for his particular elucidation (*Trail*, Chs. X, XI, XV).

Shortly after Tunica's portable Sioux village appeared on July 3, Parkman moved camp to Laramie Creek, then Bitter Cottonwood Creek, and then Horseshoe Creek, where he hoped to wait until the trader Bissonnette ("Bisonette" in *The Oregon Trail*) arrived. But the elusive man was not to be seen (Ch. XII), even though Shaw rode out and lost his horse trying to find a trace of him. Parkman and his guides Raymond and Reynal rode lazily about; then a few days later they all began to follow the trail of a nomadic Indian village. They saw Laramie Peak and the Medicine Bow Mountains in the distance. They were in some trepidation because of rumors that fierce Snakes, Gros Ventres, and Arapahoes might be in the vicinity (Ch. XIII). On July 15 they came upon a small circle of friendly Oglala lodges, to their immense relief (Chs. XI, XII). Although their supplies were low, the white men feasted the Indians, and smoked and conversed with them pleasantly in their lodges before moving west after the vacillating Oglalas, whose uncertain aim was to find buffalo and execute a surround—much to Parkman's joy.

Shaw decided to return to Laramie, but Parkman and Raymond sought, and finally found, the elusive Oglala village (Ch. XIII). Then, during more than two weeks of milling about with the Oglalas —"a wild, helter-skelter, hurrying group" (*Journals*, 460) —moving generally westward, Parkman, together with Raymond and Reynal, saw a great deal of lodge leveling and recorded bits of new information (*Trail*, Chs. XIV, XV). He hunted happily through hills that reminded him of New England (Chs. XVII, XVIII) and finally rejoined Shaw at Fort Laramie on August 3 (Ch. XIX). Parkman's depiction of lodge life is perhaps the high point of his *Oregon Trail*.

On the next day, Parkman, Shaw, Chatillon, and their guides Deslauriers and Raymond, together with a trapper named Rouville and his squaw, left Laramie headed in the direction of Bent's Fort in Southeastern Colorado. Three noons later, when they met the slippery trader Bissonnette at Little Horse Creek, he was safe and sound in the midst of Tunica's forty-lodge entourage. Stories of Pawnee and Arapahoe outrages just over the horizon spiced their time for a while. After a few days, Bissonnette's group, including the mass of Indians, split off; and Parkman and his four companions continued along Crow Creek, across the South Fork of the Platte, then beside Cherry Creek northeast of stormy Pikes Peak toward Bent's Fort. They saw evidence of an Arapahoe party which was keeping ahead of them. They had to dig for water. They ate wild cherries and currants. By now, mid-August, they were hoping soon to strike the Arkansas River and turn east. On August 20 they "saw the valley of the Arkansas and, soon after, the cornfields and the low mud wall of the Lower Pueblo" (*Journals*, 473, *Trail*, Ch. XX).

At this point, Parkman sank into dangerously poor health, and his journal entries become for a time staccato rather than literary and informative. For several days he quietly explored the Arkansas from Pueblo to Bent's Fort, observed Mormons in the area with great disapproval, visited the fort and interviewed the invalids there, digested rumors about the Mexican War to the south, and talked with a few persons disillusioned with the Far West and on their way overland home. Four of these individuals joined Parkman's group as it prepared to move along the Arkansas River toward Independence, more than five hundred miles east. The four were an ex-soldier named Hodgman (called "Tête Rouge" in *The Oregon Trail* [Ch. XXII] because of his red hair), Munro (returning from California), a sailor called both Ben and Jim (named "Jim Gurney" in *The Oregon Trail* [Ch. XXI]), and a homesick emigrant (called "Ellis" in *The Oregon Trail* [Ch. XXI]).

On August 27, Parkman and his party began their return trek. They talked with Santa Fe wagoners, who dispensed rumors of murderous Pawnees. They saw a roving band of Arapahoes and were bold enough to visit their slovenly village, which reeked of newly butchered meat (Ch. XXIII). August gave way to September, and on they loped, until suddenly they spied a herd of game:

> . . . the prairie in front was literally black with buffalo. Q[uin]. and I put after them, driving them up the hills on the right. The mare [Pauline] brought me upon the rear of a large herd. In the clouds of dust I could scarcely see a yard, and dashed on almost blind, amidst the trampling of the fugitives. Their rumps became gradually visible, as they shouldered along, but I could not urge the mare amongst them. Suddenly down went buffalo after buffalo, in dust and confusion, into an invisible ravine some dozen feet deep, and down in the midst of them plunged the mare. I was almost thrown, but she scrambled up the opposite side. As the dust cleared, I fired—the wounded beast soon dropped behind—I plied him with shot after shot, and killed—not a cow—but a yearling bull! (*Journals*, 476-77)

When Chatillon alone had killed four cows (*Trail*, Ch. XXIV), they camped in this area for four days to dry some meat for the remaining part of their trip back to Independence. They experienced heat, clouds, rain at night, buzzards and wolves, and then sunshine (Ch. XXV). Soon they crossed what became the Colorado-Kansas border. When they encountered little bands of Missouri volunteers bound for the Mexican War, the soldiers seemed to Parkman "a set of undisciplined ragamuffins" (*Journals*, 478). They even had to buy a few horses from the Easterners since some of their own mounts had strayed. A little farther east, Parkman and Shaw caught the strays, complete with their saddles (*Trail*, Ch. XXVI).

On September 9, they left the Arkansas River and angled slightly north onto what was called the Ridge Road (Ch. XXVII), which was near the famous Cimarron Crossing Route. The next day they covered without water twenty-five scorching miles. That evening they found not only a sizable stream but more Missouri volunteers and a battalion of Mormons bound for Santa Fe. At this point, Parkman and his cronies had to give up the stray army mounts they had been gathering.

Across Pawnee Creek more signs of civilization came into view: more people, fruit trees, camps of wagons, grape vines, and even walnut trees. They crossed Cow Creek in mid-Kansas and were obliged to drink from mud puddles. Cottonwood Creek, Diamond Spring, then Council Grove—only now did they stop posting a nightly guard. Soon their casual traveling companions, the men who had become disillusioned with the West, went on ahead. Parkman, who evidently felt superior to all such persons, once wrote of two of the men traveling with him: "Hodgman afflicted with a variety of complaints. Ellis impudent to S[haw]. and effectually silenced" (*Journals*, 480).

On September 21, only five days west of Westport, where they had started, Parkman and Shaw met some wagons, whose curious drivers hammered at them with questions: " 'Whar are ye from? Californy?' 'No.' 'Santy Fee?' 'No, the Mountains.' 'What yer been doing thar? Tradin'?', 'No.' 'Trappin'?' 'No.' 'Huntin'?' 'No.' 'Emigratin'?' No.' 'What *have* ye been doing then, God damn ye?' " (481). The final question was a good one. Parkman had been on the California and Oregon Trail but had seen neither California nor Oregon. He had gone west to fraternize with mountain men, hunters, trappers, traders, soldiers, and Indians; yet he had remained aloof.

One of his original purposes had been to improve his eyesight and general constitution, but his eyes were worse than ever and his system had been enervated by dysentery. He had collected much information but with it much misinformation as well. Parkman would probably not have put into these words what he had been doing—having the last lark of his youth, undergoing the Western initiation of the Eastern tenderfoot, and starring in the title role of an ageless drama—the trial of the young man in an unknown land, complete with archetypal dangers, temptations, helper figure, mysterious malady, and return to the first threshold. Parkman and Shaw, back in civilization at Westport, sold the remnants of their equipment. Then they rode to Kansas Landing and slept under a roof again for the first time since their challenging trek had begun five months before at this same spot (*Trail*, Ch. XXVII). On October 1, Parkman ended the journal of his Western adventures with the terse note that he was in a riverboat on his way home.

II *Historian, Friend, and Husband*

Parkman took back to Boston not only an image in his mind of the young man surviving trials in the West but also many impressions: arrow-straight Indians reminiscent of Pontiac, the wailing of grief-stricken squaws in hellishly stinking lodges, rough-shouldered buffalo, stretches of waterless wastelands, French-Canadian fur traders, and American soldiers and settlers pushing west. As Sedgwick says of Parkman at this point, "On his return he felt that he had qualified himself by practical experience to write the history of the Indian and French wars. . . ." [13]

But an extensive period of restlessness and suffering began, one which tried Parkman's mettle more severely than the Magalloway, Sicily, or the Oregon Trail ever could have. As soon as the ambitious young historian returned home, the consequences of his overexertions for the past several years concentrated in his eyes, which quickly became almost useless. Within a month he agreed to study law in a New York office and to put himself under the care of Dr. Samuel Mackenzie Elliott, a famous Scotch oculist then practicing on Staten Island.

Parkman could hardly have been of use in a law office, and the physician did not effect the quick cure promised. (Later, Parkman wrote that Dr. Elliott "nearly blinded me, and for this and other reasons hated me to the extent of his capacity" [*Letters*, II, 6].) The uneasy patient turned back to his only real occupation, writing, for he had already started *The Oregon Trail*. Shaw and a few others read him sections from his journal; then he composed sentences and paragraphs in his head, and finally dictated them. The work appeared in the *Knickerbocker Magazine*, starting in February, 1847, and running for two years. Parkman rewrote the serial installments for book publication in 1849; and Wade insists that "the book lost much of its vitality in the triple distillation," and that *The Oregon Trail Journal* has more appeal and verisimilitude.[14] In addition to this literary project, Parkman began to compose his first book of history, one about the Indian chief Pontiac. In his 1864 autobiographical letter, Parkman describes his physical plight and his method of circumventing it:

> The difficulties were threefold: an extreme weakness of sight, disabling him even from writing his name except with eyes closed; a condition of the brain prohibiting fixed attention except at occasional and brief intervals; and an exhaustion and total derangement of the nervous system, producing of necessity a mood of mind most unfavorable to effort. . . .
>
> He caused a wooden frame to be constructed of the size and shape of a sheet of letter-paper. Stout wires were fixed horizontally across it, half an inch apart, and a movable back of thick pasteboard fitted behind them. The paper for writing was placed between the pasteboard and the wires, guided by which, and using a blacklead crayon, he could write not unlegibly with closed eyes. He was at the time absent from home, on Staten Island, where, and in the neighboring city of New York, he had friends who willingly offered their aid. . . . He chose for a beginning that part of the work which offered fewest difficulties and with the subject of which he was most familiar, namely, the Siege of Detroit. The books and documents, already partially arranged, were procured . . . and read to him at such times as he could listen to them, the length of each reading never, without injury, much exceeding half an hour, and periods of several days frequently occurring during which he could not listen at all. Notes were made by him with closed eyes, and afterwards deciphered and read to him till he had mastered them. For the first half year, the rate of composition averaged about six lines a day. The portion of the book thus composed was afterwards partially rewritten.
>
> His health improved under the process, and the remainder of the volume . . . was composed in Boston, while pacing in the twilight of a large garret . . . It was afterwards written down from dictation by relatives under the same roof . . . His progress

was much less tedious than at the outset, and the history was completed in about two years and a half.[15]

The drama of the resolute historian at this time was intense but is easily summarized. Until the publication of *The History of the Conspiracy of Pontiac* (1851), Parkman walked in a curtained world, his brain reeling with images of Pontiac, the aboriginal genius whose bravery, cunning, and leadership momentarily made America's destiny anything but manifest. Parkman was encouraged to complete his *Pontiac* by the favorable reception of his *Oregon Trail* and by his being made an honorary member of the New-York Historical Society in 1847. Of great help also were two friendships formed at this time with Charles Eliot Norton and Ephraim George Squier. Gentle, effeminate Norton, who acted as a kind of literary mentor to Parkman, merited his confidence, encouraged him, and read proof for the coming book edition of *The Oregon Trail*, an activity Parkman appreciated although the result was a slight dilution of the text.[16]

Squier, on the other hand, was an energetic anthropologist, archaeologist, and diplomat whose resolution Parkman admired and whose works on Indians he studied. Early in 1849, Parkman wrote Squier to introduce Norton: "He takes an interest in ethnology, and though I do not think your ideas and his are in all respects congenial—as his [Harvard] education has been rather of the strict and precise sort—yet you will find him a most capital fellow and well able to appreciate all that you have done" (*Letters*, I, 58). In himself Parkman combined the grace of Norton and the rough-and-readiness of Squier, to whom he wrote later in 1849 of his determination to push *Pontiac* through to the end: ". . . I can bear witness that no amount of physical pain is so intolerable as the position of being stranded and doomed to be rotting for year after year. However, I have not abandoned any plan, which I have ever formed and I have no intention of abandoning any until I am made cold meat of" (I, 64).

Though Norton and Squier provided different kinds of masculine friendship and stimulation, Parkman, as has already been observed, needed the companionship of women. He had already been attracted to tomboyish Pamela Prentiss of Keene; and, later in the 1840's, he seems to have been in love with Ellen Dwight, the sister of one of his classmates. She was beautiful and in-

telligent; but when he met her he was profoundly sick and
nervous, and nothing came of their relationship.[17] In May, 1850,
he married Catherine Scollay Bigelow, the daughter of Jacob
Bigelow, a leading Boston physician, a member of the Harvard
Medical College faculty, and an amateur botanist. Curiously,
Parkman in 1844 had visited Miss Prentiss at the doctor's home—
"merely out of politeness," his journal insists, since he was "quite
indifferent to her charms." But the doctor, who thought otherwise,
whisperingly urged him to outstay another young gentleman
caller so as to have the field to himself. Parkman chose to become
annoyed at Dr. Bigelow's "contemptible suspicion" and, labeling
himself as "a man of sense," recorded in his journal his thoughts
on the "blockhead's folly" (285, 286). The suspicious blockhead
was destined to become the sensible man's father-in-law, after
which the two got along splendidly.

Parkman was happily married for eight years, during which
time Kate bore him three children: Grace, born in 1851; Francis,
1854; and Katharine, 1858. Most people might think that Parkman was brave to undertake marriage, given his afflictions; but
his wife deserves at least as much credit for agreeing to marry
a man who seemed to be an almost hopeless invalid and who was
without much money until after his father's death. Kate, who was
calm, practical, and understanding, read to Parkman from many
books and manuscripts which probably bored her. When he wrote
Vassall Morton, his 1856 autobiographical novel, and put a former
girl friend into it, his wife was uncommonly tolerant. As Morison
has neatly stated, "An awful novel it was, and difficult for the
young wife to take; since the hero was obviously her husband,
and the heroine the high-spirited Amazon from Keene who had
been his first love. Mrs. Parkman must have been blessed with a
sense of humor, and an unusually strong conviction of marital
security." [18]

A year after the novel appeared, domestic tragedy smote the
Parkmans. Their little son Francis was not yet three when in
February, 1857, he contracted scarlet fever and died. Of the in-
consolable mother, Sedgwick writes as follows: "The death of her
little son, Francis, broke her heart, and it never healed; after that
she went about like one who belonged in another world." [19]
Her hubsand's intermittently alarming health had been growing
worse, and this misery also weakened her. The following summer

she gave birth to their second daughter, but within a week, in September, 1858, she herself died.[20] After this calamity, friends of Parkman feared for his sanity and were relieved when he set sail for Paris to consult the same eminent brain specialist who had seemingly relieved Charles Sumner after the Free Soil congressman had been caned almost to death in the United States Senate a couple of years earlier.

IV *The Education of a Stoic*

During the eight years of his married life, Parkman was domestically happy but was in physical and professional anguish much of the time. Since he was of a stoical temperament, he evidently concealed his pain from Kate, his wife. On one occasion, in April, 1853, he wrote an amazing letter to Mary Dwight Parkman, his cousin-in-law and the sister of Ellen Dwight, his former girl friend. In it he deplores the fact that he is in pain: ". . . I cannot look unmoved at the future which now opens before me—a weary death in life, with the remembrance of worthy purposes unfulfilled, the consciousness of strong energies paralyzed, high hopes crushed to the dust—a blank of passive endurance, where courage and determination avail nothing." After realizing that the recipient of his letter may wonder why he is disburdening himself to her rather than to his wife, he admits that "It is simply that I am oppressed with reiterated and protracted disaster—that expression is a relief—and that I . . . indulge myself with this relief. . . . I know but one other person [his wife] to whom I would use this kind of language, and she has too much sorrow of her own, for me to increase it by my complaints. Before her, I am bound to assume what pretence of cheerfulness I can." Since pain was battering down his habitual reserve, Parkman uniquely discusses his emotional state before his marriage; and he makes this tribute: "The change from then to now is a change from tempest to calm. Out of that tempest, I saw a harbor of refuge; and looking for peace and rest, I found happiness. I owe unbounded gratitude to the source of that happiness, and feel far more than gratitude" (*Letters*, I, 103, 104).

His wife and her sister, Mary Bigelow, helped Parkman put the finishing touches on *Pontiac*, which after many delays was published late in 1851 by Little and Brown.[21] The next year his father died, leaving Parkman a great deal of money which enabled the Parkmans to move from rather restricted quarters—first they had lived in a cottage at Milton and then in a house in Brookline, both now part of greater Boston—to three acres which they purchased south of Boston on Jamaica Pond. Here Parkman had a cottage for more than two decades (in 1874, he renovated it); and here he lived for most of his remaining years, especially during the milder seasons.[22]

With tranquillity, money, and strong-willed intelligence, Parkman hoped to press on with his literary endeavors. But then he began to suffer additional blinding headaches combined now with water on the left knee, which made it almost impossible for him to indulge in the long walks that he had always found salutory for his overexcited mind: ". . . I was attacked with an effusion of water on the knee, which subsided in two or three months, then returned, kept me a prisoner for two years. . . . The consequence was that the devil which had been partially exorcised returned triumphant. The evil now centred in the head, producing cerebral symptoms of such a nature that, in 1853, the physician who attended me . . . said in a low and solemn voice that his duty required him to warn me that death would probably follow within six months. . . ."[23] Elsewhere Parkman describes his headaches thus:

> The most definite of the effects produced was one closely resembling the tension of an iron band, secured round the head and contracting with an extreme force, with the attempt to concentrate the thoughts, listen to reading, or at times engage in conversation. . . . The brain was stimulated to a restless activity impelling through it a headlong current of thought which, however, must be arrested and the irritated organ held in quiescence on a penalty to avert which no degree of exertion was too costly. The whirl, the confusion, and strange undefined torture attending this condition are only to be conceived by one who has felt them. . . . Sleep, of course, was banished during the periods of attack, and in its place was demanded, for the exclusion of thought, an effort more severe than the writer has ever put forth in any other cause. (*Letters*, I, 181–82)

Naturally, under such circumstances, Parkman had to write slowly, if at all. Since his eyes were still so dangerously weak that he had to be read to, and since he could travel only with great difficulty, he was compelled to conduct much of his research by means of voluminous correspondence, some by dictation, some in his grid-guided hand. There were times when he had to forgo all work, but at other times he could do quite a little. The resulting alternation of creative thought and enforced idleness was upsetting, and insomnia began to attack him again. When it did, if his knee permitted a little walking, he would undertake a nocturnal ramble in the Boston Common until his head was calmer and he could go back home and sleep a few hours.

After 1853, Parkman seemed to rally slightly but not to the extent that he could work normally. All he could concentrate on was his one and only novel, *Vassall Morton,* of which the charitable view is that it was therapeutic; for, as he wrote Mary Dwight Parkman, "expression is a relief." It evidently relieved him to put old friends and enemies, as well as various memories and ambitions of his own, into fictional form. But the book today has almost no appeal, and the trifle it has is owing to the fact that a brilliant historian wrote it at a time when his health permitted him to write no history. It feebly elucidates details of his own life, which—to tell the truth—are more viable in his journals and letters. In addition, the novel serves as a soapbox for a historian anxious to say a thing or two about society and politics; but he later said his say again in straight non-fictional prose. Finally, Parkman, like other stoics, knew the moral of *Vassall Morton*—that one learns by suffering—without writing about it; but he wrote about it so didactically that the novel lectures instead of dramatizing and hence fails to persuade many readers.

Parkman's novel, published by Phillips, Samson and Company of Boston, sold badly and did not enjoy a second edition. Parkman was irritated by the poor commercial showing it made; so he did not include it in his collected works. In addition to being of therapeutic value to its author, *Vassall Morton* may have taught him to write later history more pictorially and dramatically than most novelists write fiction.

Within two years, Parkman lost both son and wife; and the year 1858 marks the nadir of his spirit. His survival, fully as much as his stupendous literary production thereafter, is perhaps his most splendid accomplishment. Naturally an invalid whose maladies were in part so close to what modern diagnosticians would consider psychosomatic was immediately rendered dreadfully sick by two deaths in the family; but Parkman rallied. He deposited his two daughters, Grace and Katharine—the older one seven years old; the other, a tiny infant—with his cooperative sister-in-law Mary Bigelow and went to Paris to consult Dr. Charles Édouard Brown-Séquard.

In Paris, Parkman established a comfortable regimen—pleasant hotel, drives in the Bois de Boulogne, omnibus rides, cafés in the evening, and five-minute walks for exercise. He also placed himself in the hands of the eminent physician, who improved his lame knees but could do little for his head beyond report with a twinkle in his eye that he could discern no evidence of insanity (*Letters*, I, 133, 134, 183). If the doctor had followed his patient into Parisian archives as that lame but determined historian arranged for documents to be copied for him, he might have questioned the sanity of a sick man who crossed an ocean for medical advice only to do what he pleased after he had heard it. In fact, a distinguished Philadelphia doctor once wrote Parkman late in life, "I fear that the counsel I gave you could have been of little value to a man who had so thoroughly studied his own case." [24]

Parkman, who studied the doctors, wrote mordantly about them in his early autobiographical letter:

> Meanwhile the Faculty of Medicine were not idle, displaying that exuberance of resource for which that remarkable profession is justly famed. The wisest, indeed, did nothing, commending his patient to time and faith; but the activity of his brethren made full amends for this masterly inaction. One was for tonics, another for a diet of milk; one counselled galvanism, another hydropathy; one scarred him behind the neck with nitric acid, another drew red-hot irons along his spine with a view to livening that organ. Opinion was divergent as practice. One assured him of recovery in six years, another thought that he would never recover. Another, with grave circumlocution, lest the patient should take fright, informed him that he was the victim of an organic disease of the brain, which must needs despatch him to another world within a twelvemonth, and he stood amazed at the smile of an auditor who neither cared for the announcement nor believed it. (I, 182)

By mid-April, 1859, Parkman was able to report to his sister Lizzie that his Parisian doctor was helping him: his eyes were less inflamed, his head was better, and so were his arthritic knees.

And yet, after he had returned to Boston, he found himself still unable to read and concentrate upon historical documents. So he began his pattern of residing at Jamaica Pond in the summer months and then visiting his mother and sisters during the winter ones.[25]

For recreation, and ultimately for intellectual challenge too, Parkman began to grow roses. Since a person of his temperament could not simply order a gardener to stick a few roots into a corner of his property and then hope for the best, Parkman read everything scientific on the subject of roses, hired some strong arms and backs to spade and hoe a plot sixty by forty feet in area, and then carefully spread manure obtained from the floor of a horseshoer. This fertilizer was ideal, he felt, because it combined manure and hoof shavings; it was rich, porous, and light. The lowest layer of this material was spread eighteen inches below the surface, then a mixture of yellow loam and black surface dirt was applied, then more manure, then more mixed soil, finally still more manure—this time carefully mixed with sandy road-scrapings. Sedgwick reports in conclusion, perhaps seriously, "Each act was performed with sacerdotal exactness." [26] Next Parkman supervised the construction of a greenhouse on the plot. When he was able to do so, he would walk jerkily through his garden, overseeing the spade work, sowing seeds, tilling, weeding, and pruning. When intense sunlight hurt his eyes or arthritis kept him off his feet, he would wait until cloudy days came or impatiently propel himself in his wheelchair through his paths. From his chair, he cut the grass himself, and raked, hoed, and weeded among his roses and lilies. And often he would sit in the perfume of his blooms and respond merrily to their riotous colors.

Honors came to him because of his roses and lilies. The Massachusetts Horticultural Society voted him a life membership. During the early part of the Civil War, a fellow Harvard alumnus, before joining a Massachusetts infantry regiment, bequeathed Parkman a huge consignment of bulbs and plants sent to him from Japan. The historian, incapacitated from military duty, gratefully accepted these Oriental flowers and made them flourish in his greenhouse. They comprised the first collection successfully sent straight from Japan to America. In 1862, Parkman went into partnership in an attempt to increase the amount of garden area under his supervision and to market the resulting plants commercially. This business venture failed in spite of the fact that Parkman had inherited from his canny grandfather a measure of mercantile shrewdness which he demonstrated on other occasions. He cultivated and hybridized varieties of the delphinium, iris, lily, peony, phlox, and poppy. He developed a new crimson and white auratum, properly christened the *lilium Parkmanni*, which he later sold to a British specialist for a tidy sum.[27]

But Parkman was most successful and happiest with roses, which Van Wyck Brooks in writing about Parkman aptly notes are the "flower of historians," since George Bancroft, William Hickling Prescott, John Fiske, Henry Adams, and Henry Cabot Lodge also cultivated them in many varieties.[28] Parkman himself is said to have had a thousand different kinds of roses. He won more than three hundred awards because of the aristocratic beauty of some of them.[29] The indomitable rosarian capped his horticultural career by publishing *The Book of Roses* in 1866, by which time his interests became more academic again. From 1867 to 1872 he published twenty-six brief articles in Tilton's *American Journal of Horticulture*. At the same time, his creative ingenuity was beginning to revert to history. Therefore, when in 1871 Harvard appointed him a professor of horticulture in its Bussey Institution, he did not report there often enough to do any actual teaching.

Through the hideous years of the Civil War, during which Parkman continued to be both crippled and active, he found solace in his fragrant avocation. In the words of Charles Haight Farnham, who as his secretary saw the bustling man often wheeling himself amid his blooms, "Horticulture . . . gave him his most intimate contact [after 1846] with nature; it was indeed the only means by which his love came in from the wilderness to a homely and affectionate regard for individual objects." [30] But one should be aware that the gardener never submerged the intellectual. In his *Book of Roses*, the aristocratic Parkman makes a curious but typical remark of interest to the reader of his historical works:

> The art of horticulture is no leveller. Its triumphs are achieved by rigid systems of selection and rejection, founded always on the broad basis of intrinsic worth. The good cultivator propagates no plants but the best. He carefully chooses those marked out by conspicuous merit; protects them from pollen of inferior sorts; intermarries them, perhaps, with other varieties of equal vigor and

beauty; saves their seed, and raises from it another generation. From the new plants thus obtained he again chooses the best, and repeats with them the same process. Thus the rose and other plants are brought slowly to their perfect development. . . .

The village maiden has a beauty and a charm of her own; and so has her counterpart in the floral world,—the wild rose that grows by the roadside. Transplanted to the garden, and, with its offspring after it to the fourth and fifth generation, made an object of skilful culture, it reaches at last a wonderful development. . . . The village maid has risen to regal state. She has lost her native virgin charm; but she sits throned and crowned in imperial beauty.

. . . Thus have risen families of roses, each marked with traces of its parentage. These are the patricians of the floral commonwealth, gifted at once with fame, beauty, and rank. (95–97) [31]

It is surely not fanciful to see in such remarks, with which *The Book of Roses* is replete, the proud Brahmin historian's theory that the only worthy adversaries to do battle for that tough aristocrat of wildernesses, the American forest, should be Champlain, La Salle, Frontenac, Montcalm, Wolfe, Pontiac, and their superb, blue-blooded peers—rich full flowers, all, of generations of fine and fortunate breeding. Furthermore, the passage reveals Parkman's deep-seated bias against sentimental, Rousseauistic agrarianism. The best rose—like the best human being—is the aristocratic end product of rural and urban breeding.

V *The Civil War*

During the Civil War, Parkman was as miserable as Hawthorne, who also remained sick on the sidelines. But Parkman was more active, more positive, keeping himself as informed as Emerson, as creative as Herman Melville, as restless mentally as Henry Adams. Like many other New Englanders—for example, Richard Henry Dana, Jr.—Parkman was dismayed at first that federal control was in the calloused hands of an Illinois railsplitter. A Brahmin of Parkman's Federalist persuasion naturally revered George Washington most, then Alexander Hamilton, and perhaps even Ben Franklin—except for his fussy materialism. He deplored Thomas Jefferson's Frenchified, democratic agrarianism.

In one of his early public letters—"Where Are Our Leaders?" published in the Boston *Daily Advertiser* in January, 1862—Parkman discharged this patrician volley: "Out of three millions, America found a Washington, an Adams, a Franklin, a Jefferson, a Hamilton; out of twenty millions, she now finds none whose stature can compare with these. She is strong in multitudes, swarming with brave men, instinct with eager patriotism. But she fails in that which multitudes cannot supply, those master minds, the lack of which the vastest aggregate of mediocrity can never fill" (*Letters,* I, 145). In a private letter written later the same year, Parkman was more pointedly critical when he called Abraham Lincoln the "feeble and ungainly mouthpiece" of the North (I, 153). Farnham sums up the matter when he says that Parkman "came at last to admire Lincoln, though thinking him generally over-rated,—a man whose undeniable worth and usefulness were due to circumstances more than to inherent ability." [32]

Parkman gave the North the support of his pen in eleven open letters to the *Daily Advertiser.* As soon as he saw that pusillanimous vacillation was at an end and that military conflict was inevitable, he almost rejoiced to have it start: "The rebel cannon at Fort Sumter were the resurrection of our manhood" (I, 157). Soon thereafter he objectively defended an anti-Union British war correspondent who had written in the summer of 1861 an unflattering account for the London *Times* of the First Battle of Bull Run. Parkman courageously wrote: "There may be question as to this factor or that, but there is none that our arms have been disgraced and our courage impugned" (I, 141). In September, he noted the deeper purpose of the North and urged its soldiers to fight treason in the name of right, honor, and safety, so that the United States—like a fighting man—might grow stronger, as Rome, England, and France had, from war.

In an awesome letter, "To the Lingerers" (August, 1862), Parkman vilified the malingerers: "those who, rich or otherwise, of 'Beacon Street' or any other street, sound in wind and limb, with time to spare, and no strong ties to constrain them, can yet linger at home . . . follow[ing], as far as they may, their wonted round of amusement and ease. . . ." He then more positively advised them: "Enlist and fight your way to a commission, those of you who have a lurking spark of manhood . . ." (I, 151, 152). One can almost see Parkman struggling over the wording of such a letter, with his pen in a fist which he often thought should have held a sword instead. And one can perhaps feel that Melville might have been outraged by reading "To the Lingerers." Certainly the beginning of Melville's poem "The March into Virginia" implicitly deplores such sabre-rattling.

> Did all the lets and bars appear
>   To every just or larger end,
> Whence should come the trust and cheer?
>   Youth must its ignorant impulse lend—
>   Age finds place in the rear.
> All wars are boyish, and are fought by boys . . .

Parkman's rebuke "To the Lingerers" and Melville's *Battle-Pieces* indicate a fundamental difference between the two contemporaries, alike though they are in other ways. The historian regarded the Civil War as a road to manhood and to future national greatness; furthermore, prolonged pain had made him indifferent to the prospect of death. On the other hand, the novelist considered the war as hideous loss and tragedy, one more proof of the unchanging sharkishness of life.

Parkman went on with his public letters. In "Why Our Army Is Not the Best in the World" in October, he explained that the North lacked inspiring junior-grade officers: "The leader ought at least to be as good a man as he who follows, and yet many an officer in federal pay might, with great propriety, change places with half the privates who obey his mandates." He added that the chivalric code of the "essentially military" South "compels a man to face wounds and death rather than incur the insupportable stigma of cowardice" (I, 154–55, 159).

In the summer of 1863, Parkman wrote a pair of remarkable open letters contrasting North and South. Patriotically denouncing the Confederacy as a predatory oligarchy, he still admitted that "Through all the illusions and falsehoods with which that fierce and selfish aristocracy has encompassed itself, runs a vein of sound political truth," which is simply that society should choose its best men for its chiefs. Then Parkman poetically contrasted the well-led but impoverished South and the sturdy but ill-advised North: "A head full of fire, a body ill-jointed, starved, attenuated, is matched against a muscular colossus, a Titan in energy and force —full of blood, full of courage, prompt for fight, and confident of victory. Strong head and weak body against strong body and weak head; oligarchy against democracy" (I, 162, 163).[33]

Of Parkman's last two war letters, one deplored the fact that the political machine put brave Brahmins on the battle line to be slaughtered rather than in decision-making positions where their well-trained minds might have been of more use. The other letter elaborated on stories told Parkman by his brother John, who had been captured while taking part in the Union blockade of Charleston and had spent eight months in a Southern prison camp. Parkman bitterly indicted the South for inhumanity to its prisoners of war. Then he evidently realized that the North was not destined to produce any Washingtons, or even any Robert E. Lees; for he wrote no more public letters after the fall of 1864.

Through the years of the war, Parkman fought the slave oligarchy with a bitter pen, but he would certainly have traded it for health enough to measure his valor on the battlefield. He was happy to observe that war galvanized the torpid North into energetic activity, but he was sufficiently aristocratic throughout the generally irrational war years to praise the South for its cavalier daring and to record his hatred of cowardly and materialistic citizens in the North.

VI Back to History

From the time Parkman published *Pontiac* in 1851 until the end of the Civil War, he worked when he could—and often when his physicians said that he should not—on the true beginning of his vast historical project. As has been observed, he was unable to do much research in the mid- and late 1850's: his health did not permit it, and his spirit was more crippled than his body by death in his family. But, during the early months of the war, he seems to have felt invigorated by the example of his soldier-friends. At any rate, for the first time in years he began to work steadily at his historical writing. He may have rushed *Pontiac* into print through fear that he would not live long enough to write the entire history of the English and French in the New World. But now that he felt more durable, he continued in greater earnest to collect his materials and to formulate his historical pattern, which would be to narrate the colossal story chronologically, beginning with the conflict in Florida between the French Huguenots and the Spanish Catholics. At the same time, he studied the career of a slightly later French pioneer farther to the north,

Samuel de Champlain. However, it should be borne in mind that Parkman had comprehensive vision, which enabled him to view the long struggle of European powers for control of America as a unit; consequently, for at least two decades before he published *Pioneers of France in the New World* in 1865, he planned to make that study the initial volume of a multi-volumed series.

A mute reminder that *Pioneers* was the product of a proud historian's Civil War years is contained in its dedication to his kinsmen Theodore Parkman, Robert Gould Shaw, and Henry Ware Hall—"slain in battle." Parkman could accord them no finer tribute than to lay the first volume of his courageously wrought history at their warriors' bier. In his introduction as well, Parkman suggests that he wrote his history at a time of military strife on a national scale: "The subject to which the proposed series will be devoted is that of 'France in the New World,'—the attempt of Feudalism, Monarchy, and Rome to master a continent where, at this hour [January 1, 1865], half a million of bayonets are vindicating the ascendency of a regulated freedom. . . ."

Then, like a playwright, Parkman marshalls his antagonists: "Feudalism still strong in life, though enveloped and overborne by new-born Centralization; Monarchy in the flush of triumphant power; Rome, nerved by disaster, springing with renewed vitality from ashes and corruption, and ranging the earth to reconquer abroad what she had lost at home." Parkman also identifies the victim in his drama, the priceless virgin forest: "These banded powers, pushing into the wilderness their indomitable soldiers and devoted priests, unveiled the secrets of the barbarous continent, pierced the forests, traced and mapped out the streams, planted their emblems, built their forts, and claimed all as their own." Next he spelled out the *raison d'être* of the human struggle soon to transpire in this wilderness: ". . . Liberty and Absolutism, New England and New France. The one was the offspring of a triumphant government; the other of an oppressed and fugitive people: the one an unflinching champion of the Roman Catholic reaction; the other, a vanguard of the Reform." Finally, Parkman suggests a kind of naturalistic—perhaps even Calvinistic—Continental drama: "Each [England and France] followed its natural laws of growth, and each came to its natural result" (*Pioneers*, I, xcv-xcvi).

It would be a mistake, however, to read Parkman's history as a statement of delight at the victory of English Protestantism, democracy, and industrialism over French Catholicism, despotism, and feudalism.[34] The fact that British Protestant democracy defeated French Catholic monarchy in the late nineteenth century in America did not mean that Parkman was overjoyed—nor would he have been pleased had the opposite occurred. Parkman declared himself unequivocally in a letter to a Canadian colleague in 1875: "My political faith lies between two vicious extremes, democracy and absolute monarchy, each of which I detest the more because it tends to react into the other. I do not object to a good constitutional monarchy, but prefer a conservative republic, where intelligence and character, and not numbers, hold the reins of power" (*Letters*, II, 82). Professor R. W. B. Lewis concludes that Parkman "favor[ed] neither the French nor the English, neither the Jesuits nor the Indians, neither Montcalm nor Wolfe. . . . Parkman had no difficulty in being dispassionate about the outcome, because the outcome was not what interested him personally. What interested him was the struggle, not its resolution. What interested him was struggle in general—as the condition of life." Lewis also calls Parkman's histories "an account of a series of great assaults upon the forest and its inhabitants." [35] Lewis' statements are brilliant and provocative; but, as shall be seen, they need periodic qualification.

It is obvious that the many journal entries in which Parkman expresses his adoration of the vast forest and its raw power prove that nature was his love and that only those who could meet its challenges were heroic. In the process of grappling for a continent, the French and the English sent many men to America who became heroic. The drama of their struggle was Parkman's subject. His struggle with sickness and other adversities, while he wrote his histories, was hardly less dramatic.

CHAPTER *3*

Productive Years, 1866-1893

THE STORY OF Parkman's last decades is not full of wild rambles in the forests of New England or through Western Europe or along the Oregon Trail, nor is it marred by so much uncertainty and pain as were the years of his maturity and middle age. It is, instead, the account of a "ripe scholar" (Parkman's own term [1]) who continued to shake off persistent attacks by a dozen maladies in order to complete the historical edifice begun with his *Pioneers of France in the New World*. Progress was steady, partly because, while Parkman was writing *Pioneers*, he was also assembling much of the material necessary for the later volumes and had actually started parts of some. By 1865 he had written almost a third of *The Jesuits in North America in the Seventeenth Century*, about half of what he later called *La Salle and the Discovery of the Great West*; in addition, his notes for *Count Frontenac and New France under Louis XIV* were partly sorted for composition, and much else was gathered together [2]—all pointing toward the capstone, which would be *Montcalm and Wolfe*. The story of these years includes, therefore, remarkably regular publication—and in addition honors and treasured professional friendships and, of course, inevitable professional feuding. Through it all, Parkman usually displayed predictable stoicism, equanimity, and confidence.

I "... Get at the Truth"

When the Civil War had ended, one of Parkman's first accomplishments was to go to Washington, D.C., and Richmond with five hundred dollars from the Boston Athenaeum to purchase Confederate newspapers and other documents. Among other items, Parkman brought back a complete file of the Richmond *Examiner* with not a corner torn. Owing partly to his efforts, the Athenaeum's Confederate collection is superb.[3] In addition, Parkman visited a few battlefields and would have spent more time in the South but for a brief attack of poor health.

In 1866, Parkman was so much better and also had been making such progress with his next volume of history—*Jesuits*—that he began regularly to visit Montreal and Quebec. He rejoiced in the hearty companionship of his sister Caroline's Ulsterman husband John Cordner, the Montreal minister, and also in the professional camaraderie he richly merited with Canadian historians, Catholic and otherwise. His many Quebec colleagues, including Judge Henry Black, Judge George O'Kill Stuart, and the brilliant antiquarian Sir James Macpherson Le Moine of the Quebec Literary and Historical Society, aided Parkman both in his documentary research and in his topographical verifications. As Sedgwick writes, "In the company of these gentlemen Parkman would wander over the battlefields from Cap Rouge on the west to the Falls of Montmorency on the east, examining the historic spots, such as Sillery, a little village on the north bank of the [St. Lawrence] river, famous as possessing the oldest house in Canada, and in the brave days of old crowned with a French battery." [4]

A list of admirers of Parkman would have included most of Canada's historians and men of letters. His closest Canadian friend was Abbé Henri-Raymond Casgrain (1831–1904), whose distinguished pioneering work in Canadian history Parkman usually read gratefully and reviewed favorably. Casgrain wrote Parkman in March, 1866, and thereby began what Wade calls "one of the most interesting historical correspondences on record." [5] Casgrain, a member of a distinguished French-Canadian family whose seigneury was at Rivière Quelle, near Ile-aux-Coudres on the lower St. Lawrence, had been educated at Quebec and had tried medical school for a couple of years. He had then studied for the priesthood, been ordained, and taught Canadian literature at Laval University in Quebec; he then became sick and partially blind, and therefore had to forgo further teaching. [6] Parkman was older, but his prolonged sicknesses had cost him more lost time than the abbé's had; the result was that, when the two began to exchange letters, they were able to pace each other professionally. In their letters, each historian reveals himself to be committed to his own point of view and yet at the same time not only tolerant of the other's position but also determined that nothing intellectual should ever destroy their warm friendship. On one occasion, midway through their voluminous correspondence, Parkman answered some professional criticism from Casgrain by gently generalizing thus: "I have always recognized, in your writings, *la main amie derrière le critique*" (*Letters,* II, 119). Earlier, when Parkman had sent Casgrain a copy of his *Jesuits,* his note had read in part as follows: "Remembering that I am a heretic, you will expect a good deal with which you will be very far from agreeing" (II, 20). The good abbé, who tolerantly bridled at the word "heretic," replied that he would give Parkman "le nom plus doux de *frère séparé.*"[7]

After *Jesuits* came *La Salle and the Discovery of the Great West,* research for which drew Parkman to the Middlewest again for the first time since he had followed the Oregon Trail with his cousin Quin Shaw. In 1867, when the historian visited Fort Snelling, south of Minneapolis, getting there took him in July and August through Iowa, Illinois, and Wisconsin, along the Illinois River, and out to St. Louis again, where he found his idol Henry Chatillon "much broken down & by no means so rich as reported" (II, 16). Aside from talking with his former guide to the Oglalas, the most satisfying experience for Parkman that summer was verifying the location of an Illinois Indian village by using evidence from his reading of French manuscripts and maps. He interviewed long-time residents of Utica, Illinois, which he judged to be near the site; and, by describing to them a rock and a prairie view which he had never seen but had read about, he was able to equate the French explorers' Aramoni River with the Vermilion River, a branch of the Illinois River, and their place called Le Rocher—Fort St. Louis—with the cliff now called Starved Rock, and to pinpoint the vanished village of the Illinois tribe between Starved Rock and the mouth of the Vermilion.[8]

As was the case after his momentous Oregon Trail trip, Parkman became very sick after his Starved Rock exploration: "1868 was a year of exceptional suffering, rendering all work impossible," his secretary C. H. Farnham recorded.[9] Casgrain, who had done research in Paris the previous spring and summer, now reported to his sick Yankee colleague that Pierre Athanase Margry, officer in charge at the Archives de la Marine et des Colonies in Paris, had assembled a monstrous mass of documents dealing with old Northwest and colonial New York history. Since Parkman was chafing at enforced idleness anyway and since Paris had always improved his spirits in the past, he decided in November to try its intriguing boulevards, cafés, and archives for another season. By mid-January, 1869, he was writing from Paris to his sister Lizzie: "I am getting on very well indeed, and am far better than when I left home" (*Letters*, II, 27). It is characteristic of this considerate man that he took time to ask Lizzie to send a few American and Canadian postage stamps to add to the philatelic collection of his concierge's little daughter.

Still in Paris late in February, Parkman wrote Lizzie disarmingly: "Don't let the doctor think that I am doing anything but amuse myself, for I am not. I meet a few people incidentally but am very stiff in declining overtures" (II, 31). As if to prove his idleness, he sent Tilton's *Journal of Horticulture* a lengthy note describing the beautifully planned gardens of Paris and the mildness of its winters. However, he could never be truly idle and in reality was trying his best (but unsuccessfully) to pry La Salle's letters out of Pierre Margry's grasp. This goateed little scholar had unearthed historical documents for Lewis Cass, the American minister to France, in the 1830's, and later for New York historian John Romeyn Brodhead. When such work began to intrigue Margry, he became a government archivist. Amassing hordes of unique manuscripts, he was seized by an ambition to publish them all personally and hence was adamant in refusing Casgrain and then Parkman much access to them.

Parkman had long, lively, witty talks with Margry on the subject of their common interest and, as Sedgwick says, "freely forgave him" for his jealous stewardship of government papers. In addition, as Wilbur R. Jacobs, the editor of Parkman's letters, reminds us, "Margry's manuscript volumes [of copies of documents] are protected for posterity while some of the collections he used have been exposed to hazards of fire and neglect." Critics closer to Margry were, however, not so tolerant and laudatory; some called him a faithless filcher.[10] For his part, Parkman—ever a realist and a historian incapable of being sidetracked—ultimately persuaded fellow scholars in America to join him in beseeching the United States Congress to appropriate ten thousand dollars to publish Margry's six-volume *Découvertes et établissements des Français dans l'ouest et dans le sud de l'Amérique Septentrionale (1614–1754), Mémoires et Documents Originaux* (Paris, 1876–88). Parkman had published his own *Discovery of the Great West* in 1869 and therefore was abliged to revise it nine years later—then calling it *La Salle and the Discovery of the Great West*—in the light of Margry's tardy revelations (*La Salle,* I, vii-ix).

It is typical of Parkman that instead of cajoling and browbeating, he helped a man who seemingly deserved little but criticism.[11] Parkman was interested in only one thing—accessible facts to make history more honest and complete. When John Gilmary Shea, an intelligent, self-educated American Catholic historian whose work on Catholic missions among the Indians Parkman found excellent and thorough, ventured to deplore Margry's anti-Jesuitical writings, Parkman temperately replied that "He does not like the Jesuits, but is a most zealous Catholic. . . ." After discussing his attitude toward La Salle and the Jesuits, Parkman opened the door farther by adding: "Should evidence turn up showing me to be anywhere in error, in fact or judgment, I shall recant at once, as I care for nothing but to get at the truth of the story" (*Letters,* II, 37, 38).

Margry was not the only French person with whom Parkman was annoyed. Through his friend and mentor George Ticknor, a former Harvard professor of Romance languages and a historian of Spanish literature, Parkman met Count Adolphe de Circourt, a French diplomat and dabbler in history. By letter this man innocently introduced Parkman to Countess Gédéon de Clermont-Tonnerre, a member of the distinguished Vaudreuil family, which had been influential in the settlement of New France. Parkman naturally rushed to meet such a woman. They evidently got along well, and a little later Parkman, back in Boston, received a note from her which opened negotiations for a French translation of both his *Pioneers* and *Jesuits.* He rather grandly replied: ". . . I expect no pecuniary return from the translation. . . . You may say to M. Didier [the publisher] . . . that I renounce all *droits d'auteur sur la traduction"* (II, 43). One cannot understand why this canny Boston merchant's grandson was not willing to accept a percentage of the receipts from French sales of his histories and thus bring back to America a fraction of his professional expenses in Paris over the years.

Much later, when Parkman again wrote the countess, he deplored in his coldest and least characteristic diction the nature of her so-called *traduction* of his *Jesuits:*

I am unable to regard it as in any proper sense a translation at all. Large and essential parts of the book are omitted. The arrangement of the rest is in some parts entirely changed, sentences are in some places interpolated and sometimes suppressed, often in such a way as to make me appear to express views contrary to those of the original. My name is put on the title page of a book which is not mine, either in form or substance, and no intimation is anywhere given that any alterations have been made. (II, 111)

Parkman tactlessly praised the recent German translations of his *Pioneers, Jesuits,* and *The Old Régime in Canada* by Dr. Friedrich Kapp, a skillful linguist, historian, and politician.

II   *The 1870's*

The year 1870 brought Parkman a renewal of insomnia, which made it impossible for him to do much but revise *Pontiac.* For weeks at a time he slept at most only two hours nightly, often less or none at all. The following May brought him face to face at last with his friendly Canadian confrere Abbé Casgrain, after they had failed four times to meet earlier. The brilliant abbé stayed at Jamaica Pond with his happy American host, and the two toured Harvard, talking with Louis Agassiz—the influential professor of natural history with whose daughter, Ida, Parkman was briefly and unrequitedly in love [12]—and then with the popular poet Henry Wadsworth Longfellow, whose *Evangeline,* about the Acadians, treated a subject which later caused Parkman and Casgrain to have a prolonged dispute. Their time together in Boston was brief but pleasant and memorable, and Casgrain later wrote that "Les politesse exquises dont je fus l'objet de sa [Parkman's] part et de celle de sa famille [mostly Lizzie] ont laissé en moi des souvenirs qui ne sont pas effacés." [13]

Although Parkman had hoped to rendezvous with Casgrain in Quebec in the summer of 1871, family misfortunes, including the sickness of his mother, kept him close to Boston except for a brief research trip to Nova Scotia and New Brunswick, one which was truncated because of his mother's death in August. Of her death, Parkman wrote Casgrain: ". . . a life of rare affection, disinterestedness, and self-devotion came to its close on earth" (II, 53). If the statement implied certainty of that life's continuance

in another sphere, the implication owed more to Parkman's respect for his Catholic colleague's faith than to any of his own.
Although he began as the obedient son of a Unitarian minister, he
quickly made his love of nature and of action a mode of faith and
then gradually adopted agnosticism as a silent creed. Farnham
in an often-quoted passage has reported about Parkman: "His
attitude is shown by this bit of intimate conversation with his
sister Eliza. One day when they were rowing on Jamaica Pond
she said: 'If I should be asked about your religious beliefs, it
seems to me I might say that you are a reverent Agnostic.' 'Yes,
that's about it,'" Parkman answered.[14]

Casgrain was liberal enough to respect the integrity of the
non-religious Parkman, but he was Catholic enough to note a bias
against supernaturalism in all of his friend's historical writings.
A year after meeting Parkman in person, he published a generally
flattering biographical sketch of him, which, however, contained
the following opinion: "Mr. Parkman's work is the negation of all
religious belief. The author rejects the Protestant theory as well
as Catholic dogma; he is an out-and-out rationalist. We perceive
an upright soul, born for the truth, but lost without a compass
on a boundless sea. Hence these aspirations towards the true,
these flashes of acknowledgment, these words of homage to the
truth, followed, alas, by strange fallings off, by fits of fanaticism
that are astounding." [15]

After the forthright abbé had sent Parkman pre-publication
proofs of his sketch, Parkman wrote a reply that is an object lesson in historical dispassionateness: "I think you know me too well
to doubt that I accept your criticism as frankly as it is given, and
that I always listen with interest and satisfaction to the comments
of so kind and generous an opponent. I only wonder that, in the
opposition of our views on many points of profound importance,
you can find so much to commend. When you credit me with
loyalty and honor, you give me the praise that I value most of
all" (II, 56–57).

Needless to add, the two remained friends. In 1878, when Laval
University, where Casgrain was located, began to think of grant-
ing Parkman a *Docteur ès Lettres,* Casgrain defended his friend's
"out-and-out rationalist" views against some unbelievably ill-tem-
pered ultra-Catholic abuse. Curiously, the leader of the attack was
a Kentucky-born *émigré* to French-Canada and an anti-American

ultramontane in politics, Jules-Paul Tardivel. A sample of his
tirade against Parkman reads: "In a word, he, a Protestant and
an American, has undertaken to write the history of a country
Catholic and French. Not understanding the glorious destiny of
the French Canadian people, he has been unable to raise himself
above the materialist level. He has made some fine phrases, some
well-rounded periods; he has not written a single page of history." [16] Casgrain, as well as Sir James Le Moine, was embarrassed and apologized. But Tardivel won, in spite of Casgrain's
defense of Parkman, who soon had a letter from the rector of
Laval University explaining that the degree must be deferred, not
conferred. Parkman, who remained detached, loyal only to his
position and his friends, wrote Casgrain that the outbreak struck
him as amusing but regrettable insofar as it had embarrassed
Laval, that he more highly prized the proofs of esteem which its
directors had already given him in suggesting the degree than he
could possibly prize the degree itself, and that he hoped they
would be guided solely by university interests (II, 125–26).

While the battle raged for months in French-Canadian journals,
McGill University, which was dominated by Protestant-English
elements in Montreal, entered the fray and gave Parkman an
honorary degree in 1879. His grateful acceptance of it only con-
vinced the fanatical Catholic faction in Canada that he was ir-
rationally anti-Catholic, which he was not. Parkman, who thought
little of such academic baubles, once wrote an editor: "Don't put
LLD to my name. That sort of thing is so cheap and generally
worthless on this continent that it is best to drop it altogether.
Any two penny college can confer it" (II, 146).

In the middle years of the 1870's, Parkman was alternately busy
and debilitated. Three months after his mother had died, his one
and only brother, John, fell over a banister, hit his head on a
coal bin, and died. Because of this misfortune Parkman and his
sister Lizzie drew even more closely together; the following summer the two took a trip to Europe—to England, Switzerland,
Italy, and then Paris, where Parkman could indulge in some long
and partly fruitful chats with Margry, who by now was willing
to give his American colleague bibliographical leads, names of
reliable copyists (who reproduced ten thousand pages of govern-
ment-owned manuscripts for him from the Marine Archives [II,
149]), general information about La Salle, and even a birthday

poem "À Francis Parkman, Auteur des Français en Amérique"—
but still refused access to his unique documents.[17]

After Parkman had returned to Boston in November, 1872, he
immediately urged historians and congressmen—including James
A. Garfield, the future President—to support his proposal to publish Margry's collection of papers by and concerning Sieur de la
Salle, Le Moyne d'Iberville, the La Vérendrye family, Antoine de
la Mothe-Cadillac, and others. Parkman's efforts were hampered
terribly by the hundred-million-dollar Boston fire which two days
after his return leveled much of the city and ruined many of his
wealthy friends. His unselfish cultivation of colleagues, however,
began to bear fruit in a few years. Meanwhile, both before and
after a visit to Evangeline land in Acadia in August, 1873, during
which he took notes on the appearance of Annapolis Basin, the
old fort, Digby, and Goat Island, Parkman was busy on his historical work, *The Old Régime in Canada*, published the following
spring.

As usual, his only really helpful colleague was Casgrain, between whom and Parkman a lively professional correspondence
darted while *Old Régime* was settling into final form. Parkman,
who was uneasy because his latest work would inevitably offend
French-Canadian Catholics, wrote Casgrain that "The papers
which I brought from Paris . . . have proved extremely rich in
information as to the condition of the colony. . . . Their revelations, unfortunately, are not always agreeable. In fact, the condition of Canada under the old régime was simply deplorable" (II,
76). The next winter Parkman wrote Margry about the rumor
that a pair of distinguished Canadians were joining forces to blast
his position: "I await their attack, in all tranquility. I have forti-
fied myself so well with uncontrovertible proof that I am not
afraid of their breaching my lines" (II, 78).

One attack, however, which surely was much less to his liking
than Parkman professed, came from Casgrain himself, to whose
critical review in the *Revue Canadienne* for April, 1875, Parkman replied:

I could take issue squarely on the principal points you make,
but . . . I do not care to enter into discussion with a personal
friend on matters which he has so much at heart. . . . Let me set
you right, however, on one or two points, personal to myself. . . .

You say that I see Canadian defects through a microscope and merits through a diminishing glass. The truth is, I have suppressed a considerable number of statements and observations because I thought, that while they would give pain, they were not absolutely necessary to the illustration of the subject; but I have invariably given every favorable testimony I could find in any authentic quarter. . . . I have space only to tell you how much I value your testimony to my conscientiousness as a writer, and your remarks, too partial I fear, on the literary qualities of the book.

Then Parkman on another sheet of paper penned a postscript in which he attempted to refute a few more points in Casgrain's review; and he closed with these fantastic statistics: "I expect to receive from France about 6000 (or more) pages of entirely, new material on the war of 1755–63. I have received about 3000 of them this winter, and have still several copyists at work in the archives" (II, 81–82, 83).[18] Before he could use the 1755–63 material, Parkman had to turn to Louis de Buade, Comte de Palluau et de Frontenac.

As usual, Parkman was steadily writing his historical volumes in chronological order and at the same time was collecting material enough to require a decade more of study and composition. By August, 1876, he was virtually finished with *Frontenac and New France under Louis XIV* and, therefore, took a pleasant little vacation trip to Lake Champlain and Ottawa. At this same time, he was keeping up his horticultural interests, though in large part only academically and in a less active outdoor way. He completed arrangements to sell an English flower fancier the bulbs of his renowned *lilium Parkmanni*, already mentioned. He published a distinguished little article, "Hybridization of Lilies." He continued to delight in his fragrant blooms whenever he could, but his first and last love was history.

Parkman now set his sights on that phase of the French and Indian War which culminated in the victory of England over France at Quebec in 1759, and he was determined to narrate at least the epic climax of his history. Fearing that death might keep him from presenting both the half-century of conflict—1700 to 1748—and its climax, he deliberately violated chronological order and leaped to events which converged in the titanic clash on the Heights of Abraham. *Montcalm and Wolfe* consumed most of his professional energies during the late 1870's and for some time beyond.

Parkman also had vigor enough to tilt again with his old friend Abbé Casgrain over a new book on the vexing Acadian question. It seems that François E. Rameau de St.-Père in 1877 published *Une Colonie Féodale en Amérique: l'Acadie, 1604–1710*, which Parkman read carefully before Casgrain could write to recommend it. Parkman reviewed it anonymously but with unmistakable *animus Parkmanni* in the *Nation* late in December. Then he fired off an abusive letter about Rameau to Casgrain which closed with a remarkable challenge to the abbé to repair to Boston and peruse Parkman's bulky manuscripts and annotations preliminary to writing an Acadian critique. "You shall have a quiet room to consult them [the documents] in, and bring with you an amanuensis, if unhappily you still require one [like Parkman, the semi-blind Casgrain often required a reader]. The only condition I wish to make is that you will agree that your critique and my reply shall be printed together" (*Letters*, II, 103). Parkman's challenge lay untouched, but at least the honest historian had blown off some steam. As Wade says, "The Canadian critics were beginning to get under Parkman's skin. . . ." [19] The American said as much himself in his 1878 essay "Mr. Parkman and His Canadian Critics," in which he dared his Northern adversaries to back up their vituperation with facts rather than venom. Still, late that summer and again the next he went north once more for research and pleasure—to Lake George, to Ticonderoga, and especially to Quebec, whose natural beauty and gripping past he could never savor sufficiently.

Parkman also had energy enough as the 1870's waned to write three essays against universal suffrage and then woman suffrage, which, when published in the *North American Review*, aroused an already buzzing hornet's nest. Parkman was railed against for being reactionary, but in passage after passage he had scored a frightening number of points. He attacked the falsity of egalitarian democracy—the tyranny of Demos—which created materialistic politicians and allied them to moneyed interests to develop vote-getting city political machines. He pointed a prophetic finger at urban misery and corruption resulting, in his view, from industrialism, massive foreign migration, and party bosses. He insisted that intrinsic inequality among men should be recognized, even exploited, so that heroes of character, intelligence, and will power would be elected to positions of leadership. Deploring complacency and baseless optimism, which in his view were warping the American mind, Parkman was reluctant, nonetheless, to consider the case as hopeless; instead, he sensibly beseeched his readers to agitate at once for one essential change, civil service reform, to eradicate the spoils system.

Parkman then turned to the ticklish question of woman suffrage. Beginning with some foolish prophecies about ballot-wielding maid servants, Delilahs with scissors in Congress, and females voting their husbands off to the wars—all of which he only half believed—he then more soberly attacked classroom prudery, equal rights for women employees, the gradual attrition of the Victorian "double standard," and in fact almost all aspects of American life which tended to defeminize women and take them from what he regarded as their unique sanctuary—the home. As Doughty has admirably summarized Parkman's attitude, ". . . it was . . . hardly as a depreciator of the feminine that Parkman conceived himself to be entering the lists against woman suffrage, but as the defender of reciprocities based on intrinsic differences between the sexes, which, as he saw it, the triumph of feminism would minimize to the impoverishment of both. Difference is his leading theme; and the symbiosis of opposites of which the cultivation of difference is a precondition." [20]

And so, while still focusing on Montcalm and Wolfe, but occasionally permitting himself a sideways glance at the Gilded Age and its unwashed democrats and rampant suffragettes, Parkman hardly noticed that the 1870's had fled.

III   *The 1880's*

Parkman now began to change slightly his social habits. In 1879, after both of his daughters were married, he continued to make his home at 50 Chestnut Street, Boston, where his mother had lived until her death, and to enjoy the company of his sister Lizzie. But he felt the need of more conviviality, in spite of the fact that he had long been a fairly active member of the famous Saturday Club. So he took a major part in forming the St. Botolph Club in Boston and consented to be its first president, starting in 1880. Hardly had the big group begun to meet than abstemious

Edward Everett Hale presented a motion to abolish liquor at St. Botolph's. As often happens with such motions, this one was sent to committee, tabled, and buried; and Hale soon resigned. Parkman, an admirer of *vinum* as well as *veritas*, wrote his share of sugar-and-acid letters to temperance ladies, as well as suffragettes.

For three summer months in 1880 Parkman, with Lizzie, was again in London, ferreting out more historical data—this time finding Montcalm's missing letters to his lieutenant the Chevalier de Bourlamaque in a private library at Cheltenham (*Letters*, II, 247–48)—and then in Paris, doing more research and in addition visiting happily there with his younger daughter, Katharine Coolidge, whose wise and pleasant husband John Templeton Coolidge was beginning a long residence as an art student. In later years, when the Coolidges and their French-chattering children had returned to America and were living in the Wentworth mansion at Portsmouth, New Hampshire, the old historian was summer after summer a frequent and welcome visitor.

Again in 1881 Parkman voyaged to the Old World, but an August cold so affected him in London that he had to decline invitations to dine with James Russell Lowell, then the American minister to England, and with Henry James, who had long been an admirer of Parkman's dramatic brand of historical narrative and who a little later may have used a few of his anti-feminist arguments in adumbrating the character of Basil Ransom in *The Bostonians*.

Just before New Year's Day, 1882, Parkman took time out from his work on Montcalm and Wolfe to send greetings to old Margry. With a good deal of dramatic stoicism, he described himself thus: "I am sitting in my own study, a caribou rug under my feet, beaver skins on the sofa, and portraits of Montcalm, Amherst, and Wolfe over the fire along with a large red stone pipe which a Sioux chief gave me, and the sword of my younger brother, an officer in the war of 1861–65, who, after surviving a thousand dangers was killed by an accidental fall in California" (II, 148).

Sitting in his study, with mementoes about him of his active past and documents enough to assure a fruitful present and future, Parkman was happy as he worked steadily month after month on Montcalm and Wolfe. For diversion, he took a brief trip to the Adirondacks in October. The next fall, when he turned sixty, he considered the fact as a direct challenge from nature, packed some old clothes, took a train to the area south of the White Mountains, and hired a mulish little horse for an eighty-mile trek through mountain passes to inns with roaring fires and good hot whiskey. He relished everything: the sunset over Mount Washington, an onrush of black clouds, even a soaking rain which followed and left him spongy, and the soft snow which filled the road and burdened the trees. Most of all, he delighted in the challenge met. As he gleefully wrote Margry, ". . . though I'm a grandfather of 60, [I] don't find myself any worse off for the adventure" (II, 160).

Through the summer of 1884, Parkman was plagued again by weakened eyesight, just as he was required to read proof on his massive *Montcalm and Wolfe,* successive volumes of which appeared in the fall (II, 160–63). This work is in many ways the climax of his career, although he went on and presented the background to the battle of Quebec in his final work—*A Half-Century of Conflict.*

Montcalm and Wolfe caused his friend Casgrain much anguish, and their letters for the next five years became sharp and bitter. For example, Parkman in November, 1885, crossly replied to the distressed abbé as follows:

You say that you are disposed to be even more severe against my last book [*Montcalm and Wolfe*] than against the "Old Régime." When you used the term "severe" before I was more amused than annoyed and was content to let it pass with a smile, but as you now use it again it may be well to make the situation clear once and for all. "Severe" is a word appropriately used by one in a position of superior knowledge and authority, such as a teacher towards a pupil. In the present case it is curiously inapplicable as I have given incomparably more study to the subject of my last book than any Canadian whatever, living or dead; and of the vast amount of authentic manuscript material used in it no Canadian ever saw a quarter part. The best informed of your writers before he could rationally talk about being severe, or could even pronounce an intelligent criticism on the book, considered as a narrative of facts, would be forced to pursue a good deal of research in the archives of France and elsewhere, besides diligently studying a course of general history, in which subject French Canadian writers are very deficient, though it is necessary to an understanding of the proportions and relations of their own history. (II, 184–85)

To his credit, Casgrain replied temperately, thus mollifying the seething Yankee, but then published *Un Pèlerinage au Pays d'Évangéline* (1887), a five-hundred-page tome, dedicated to the proposition that Parkman was wrong-headed about the Acadians. In the fall Parkman acknowledged receipt of a gift copy, called it "handsome" but also "so large a book on so small a subject," and then launched a volley at it: "The book would inspire more confidence but for the passionate animosity it shows against the actors on our side, and the equally vehement determination to justify those on the other at any cost. You have entirely suppressed the true cause of the removal of the Acadians. . . . You push out of sight the fact . . . that the French government . . . had intrigued for years to stir up the Acadians to revolt, and that in consequence the position of affairs had become, in 1755, such as to demand the most decisive measures. I do not say, such as to justify the deportation . . ." (II, 211–12, 215). Parkman then treated his evidently better-tempered but more partisan adversary to some clever but unfortunate invective.

After a year had passed, Parkman read an article by Casgrain on the Acadian oath of allegiance and began to seeth again. It seems that Casgrain, with protestations of performing a painful duty, accused Parkman of reading but then choosing to ignore certain documents hurtful to his position. "This means [as Parkman interpreted the allegation] that you charge me with disingenuousness in suppressing certain facts . . . I therefore desire to be informed on what grounds you affirm that these papers were known to me . . . and particularly what is meant by your assertion that I had complete copies of them" (II, 225). Casgrain replied that Parkman was pleading ignorance, to which the American weakly retorted: ". . . I do not plead that or anything else" (II, 228). In the light of Parkman's previous boast of comprehensive knowledge of the subject, Casgrain rather clearly won that little duel.

A year later Parkman was still writing the abbé, now in this vein: "If you will look at the *Nation* article again, you will see that you have quoted it incorrectly, and that . . ." (II, 234). But after what Wilbur Jacobs, the editor of Parkman's letters, calls "an abrupt cooling-off period" (II, 168), the two historians quietly reconciled their differences by the expedient of beginning again to praise each other. Parkman's admiration for Casgrain rose higher than ever, ultimately. In his last letter to Parkman, the abbé praised Lake George, which he had just visited, adding that he liked modern America better than Parkman did. The American agreed: "For my part, I would gladly destroy all his works [improvements by the *nouveau riche*] and restore Lake George to its native savagery—which shows plainly that you are a better American than I am" (II, 265).[21]

During this dispute, Parkman was often far better employed. For example, in March, 1885, a visit to South Carolina and Florida enabled him to observe the area in which part of his *Pioneers* had been cast. He immediately revised the descriptive sections of that work dealing with Florida. In the fall he received "three lines" from Henry James, extolling *Montcalm and Wolfe* in a letter running to fully six hundred words. Parkman was immensely pleased, and in his prompt reply the crusty old anti-feminist ventured to predict correctly the outcome of James's *Bostonians,* then halfway through its unpopular serial run in the *Century Magazine:* "Verena [the feminist heroine], I trust, is to return to nature and common sense" (II, 179–80).

In the late spring of 1886, Parkman camped for a month with his secretary and future first biographer C. H. Farnham on the Batiscan River in the Province of Quebec. The younger man was delighted and wrote eulogistically that it was "the first time this lover of wild life had been to the woods in forty years. A delightful companion he was [Farnham continues], interested in all the labors and pleasures of camp life, cheerful and patient under all circumstances. Despite his lame knee, he insisted on helping me complete the roof, the fireplace, and the tables we needed, and in doing what he could of camp work." [22] Parkman also fired a new Winchester rifle at targets, learned to use a bomboo fly rod, tried canoeing again, studied the nearby beavers, and took some Canadian ferns back to his Jamaica Pond greenhouse. A little later, he headed north again, this time to the Rangeley Lakes in Maine, where he delighted in the scene but found most outdoor exercise impossible and even the light too strong. Still, he wrote Lizzie in August: "I think a little of building a log cabin here, with two small rooms for you, if you should want to come for a week, month, or more. It will cost little, and be independent of the rest [of the Rangeley campers]. . . . How does it strike you?" (II, 196). He proceeded with the project but was so sick the following year that he never used the rough little retreat.

Parkman should have been content to stay in his Jamaica Pond quarters and concentrate on *A Half-Century of Conflict;* but, weak though he was now becoming, he undertook to see Spain and to try some German spas. No sooner had he arrived at Madrid in April, 1887, however, than he was afflicted with insomnia and worsening lameness; so he quickly returned to Boston and his work. At about this time he established a pattern of spending part of his summer with his daughter Katharine, her painter husband John Coolidge, and their children. Parkman seems to have been an almost ideal father and father-in-law, from what evidence is available. In a letter he described Coolidge as "an excellent fellow, a man of feeling and intelligence" (II, 203).[23]

As for Charles P. Coffin, his other son-in-law, Parkman found this Lynn native and Boston attorney to be intelligent and congenial also. When he had desired to marry Grace Parkman, young Coffin had presented his respects and his credentials to the doughty historian and had given as a character reference the popular poet John Greenleaf Whittier, to whom Parkman had been old-fashioned enough to write for particulars: "Will you have the kindness to inform me as to his character, tastes, disposition, and capacity. He impresses me favorably; but in a matter of such importance, I wish to get all possible information" (II, 114–15). Coffin had passed inspection and had become Parkman's son-in-law nine months later.

As the 1880's drew to their close, Parkman lapsed into a genial grandfatherly figure; he played with his daughter Katharine's children and their cats, hobbled about with cane and crutch with his Spartan face betraying none of the manifold pains that shot through him, fly-cast when he could, rowed his little boats, and paid calls and received visitors to chat about history and literature. All the while, he husbanded his energy because his monumental historical *opus* was not yet quite complete. Through the 1880's and a little beyond, he continued to work on his final book. Putting its amorphous materials into unified shape was difficult, as he suggests in the following passage of a letter to Casgrain: "I am still engaged on the remaining volume of my series (1700–

1748) which has given me more trouble than any of the others, from the want of unity in the subject, and the difficulty of weaving its complex parts into a continuous narrative" (II, 243). But he continued his patient weaving.

IV *At Last*

The rest of the story of Francis Parkman's life may be briefly told. The lame old historian was as familiar with his materials as an old infantry officer with the varied terrain of an old enemy. He knew the professional tricks of his trade. Seemingly well aware that he would have time to mount his last attack in his own way, he carefully perused his maps, sorted his annotated documents, outlined his steps, and prepared his chapters on early eighteenth-century border conflicts, expeditions, explorations, and sieges.

During the summers, Parkman continued to head for the Wentworth mansion and his voluble little grandchildren. Early in 1892 the talented young artist Frederic Remington was commissioned by Little, Brown and Company to provide "wild-west" illustrations for a new edition of *The Oregon Trail.* He opened a charming correspondence with Parkman, whose replies prove that his heady adventures with Chatillon and the Oglalas, during which he and his cousin Shaw had stalked buffalo and antelope and had ridden their ponies through prairie dust, were deeply imbedded in his memory. By March, he put down his pen with a tired hand; for *A Half-Century of Conflict* was finished. The title referred to the period 1700–48 in the long battle between the French and the English for control of the New World. But it may be that Parkman chose it to hint quietly, even humorously, that ever since his sophomore year at Harvard, back in 1841, he had struggled to master historical materials and physical infirmities and that out of the five-decade conflict with archives and pain had come his *France and England in North America.*

In his preface, he tells his readers proudly but in clipped words that he has collected manuscript material amounting to seventy bound volumes. Then he adds: "The collection was begun forty-five years ago, and its formation has been exceedingly slow, having been retarded by difficulties which seemed insurmountable, and for years were so in fact. Hence the completion of the series has required twice the time that would have sufficed under less unfavorable conditions" (*Conflict*, I, vi).

Of all the compliments which historians, critics, and general readers sent him, the one from Henry Adams must have pleased Parkman most: "You have had the singular good fortune to complete successfully a great work which puts you at the head of our living historians. . . ." Earlier, Adams had commended Parkman's *Montcalm and Wolfe* but had then beseeched its author to "go over all the work. File and burnish. Fill in with all that you can profitably add, and cut out whatever is superfluous. Give us your ripe best, and then swing the whole at the head of the public as a single work. Nothing but mass tells." [24]

Parkman remembered the staggering suggestion. After publishing *A Half-Century of Conflict* in 1892, he set to work revising *The Old Régime* and managed to see it into print in more acceptable form the next year. He had already rewritten and updated parts of *Pontiac*, in 1870; *La Salle*, in 1878; and *Pioneers*, in 1885. If he had lived longer, he would probably have revised the entire series. But he could surely be pardoned for spending his last summer with the Coolidges at Portsmouth: there would be time in the fall to return to his *Jesuits*, to consult documents suggested to him by his peppery colleagues Casgrain and Margry, and to file and burnish alleged rough spots to make the entire work more unified.

In the fall of 1893, however, Francis Parkman ended his allotted three score and ten years, at least twenty of which had been blighted by terrible sicknesses. The final assault began shortly after his seventieth birthday. He had recovered from pleurisy and phlebitis a few months earlier; but now appendicitis afflicted him, and soon peritonitis set in. He rallied only briefly.[25] The last journal entry he ever made is characteristic: "*Jesuits,* 257, correct '*evening* mass' " (598).

CHAPTER *4*

Oregon *Trail,* Pontiac, *Vassall Morton,* and *Book of Roses*

IN SPITE OF AFFLICTIONS, Parkman wrote eleven books, some in more than a volume each; in addition, he produced sketches, editorials, articles, reviews, and miscellaneous items; and he was also an assiduous journal and letter writer. His first important publication was *The California and Oregon Trail,* 1849, rechristened three years later *Prairie and Rocky Mountain Life: or, The California and Oregon Trail.* For the 1872 edition, it was called *The Oregon Trail,* by which title it is known today.

The first historical work by Parkman was *The History of the Conspiracy of Pontiac,* 1851. Uncertain health then followed, and he wrote *Vassall Morton,* 1856, and *The Books of Roses,* 1866. But, during the early years of the Civil War, he had returned to historical research. The result was: *Pioneers of France in the New World,* 1865; *The Jesuits in North America in the Seventeenth Century,* 1867; *The Discovery of the Great West,* 1869; *The Old Régime in Canada,* 1874; *Count Frontenac and New France under Louis XIV,* 1877; *Montcalm and Wolfe,* 1884; and, finally, *A Half-Century of Conflict,* 1892. Parkman revised and enlarged *Pontiac,* calling it *The Conspiracy of Pontiac and the Indian War after the Conquest of Canada,* 1870. *The Great West* he revised as *La Salle and the Discovery of the Great West,* 1878; he further revised it slightly in 1893. He revised and enlarged *Pioneers* in 1885 and *The Old Régime* in 1893.

The chronological order of the events which these historical works depict is as follows: *Pioneers* (the Spanish in Florida, early sixteenth century; the Huguenots in Florida, late sixteenth century; Chaplain and his fellow pioneers in Canada and New England, late sixteenth and early seventeenth centuries); *Jesuits* (the

Jesuits and American Indians, seventeenth century); *La Salle* (La Salle's explorations of the Great Lakes area and the Mississippi Valley, late seventeenth century); *The Old Régime* (sixteenth- and seventeenth-century feudal chiefs in Acadia, seventeenth-century Canadian missions, and Canada as an exploited French colony in the seventeenth and eighteenth centuries); *Frontenac* (New France under Frontenac, very late seventeenth century); *A Half-Century of Conflict* (border warfare, Acadia, and France in the West, early eighteenth century); *Montcalm and Wolfe* (the French and Indian War, mid-eighteenth century); and *Pontiac* (Indian resistance in the 1760's).

I The Oregon Trail

The Oregon Trail is valuable for several reasons. First, it accurately reports the real-life experiences of a daring, intelligent young man on a trek from St. Louis and Fort Leavenworth to Fort Laramie and its environs, and back via Pueblo, in the key year of 1846, which is called by Bernard DeVoto "The Year of Decision." [1] As such, it is a source book for historians, though not a very helpful one. Readers should not find fault with Parkman, then in his early twenties and not yet a professional historian, for neither sensing that he was a part of vital Western history in the making nor stopping his adventures to take notes for posterity on emigrant trains, British-American animosities generated by the Oregon question, Mormon mores, militancy in the Southwest because of the Mexican War, frontier politics, and the like. It should be remembered that Parkman went to the West to study Indians, have fun, and try to improve his health.

Second, *The Oregon Trail* is valuable as autobiography. Those who think of Parkman as a semi-blind historian know also from his Western book that he was a vigorous and manly fellow to whom the plains and the Rockies spelled freedom and the East, restraint. Third, this vital work is enduring, organic art. It has natural form, distinctive style, bracing theme and message, and intriguing mythic overtones. In spite of numerous compositional faults, it serenely bears comparison with other American travel books.

The Oregon Trail has the commonest structure imaginable—one suggested by the experiences which it recounts. Parkman begins in the East, with which he is familiar. As he moves west, he crosses the threshold into the unknown, where he survives tests and becomes experienced. Finally, when he returns home, he is wiser, no doubt; sadder, perhaps; changed, certainly. The form of the narrative is arch-like, sonata-like, trifoliate, as it moves from introduction (Chapters I-III) to main body (Chapters IV-XXV) and then to conclusion (Chapters XXVI-XXVII).

Numerous balances exist in the work. Obviously the first three chapters balance against the last two. Less obviously, the central chapter (Chapter XIV, with thirteen chapters preceding it and thirteen following) describes the goal of the whole hazardous journey and is called "The Ogillallah Village." Early in Chapter X Parkman writes: "I proposed to join a village [of Indians], and make myself an inmate of one of their lodges; and henceforward this narrative, so far as I am concerned, will be chiefly a record of the progress of this design, and the unexpected impediments that opposed it" (Trail, 122). The center of the book records his success.

In addition, other balances are evident, and Chapter XIV is the pivot. In Chapter IV, Parkman and his party jump off in an initially fruitless search for the Oregon Trail; in Chapter XXIV, they chase buffalo with such murderous success that they must camp for days to dry the meat. In Chapters V and VI, they find the Big Blue and the Platte rivers; in Chapter XXI, they first sight the Arkansas. Chapter VIII is notable for their ridicule of the Oregon-bound Britishers; in Chapters XXI and XXII, they ridicule new members of their train—four disillusioned men returning east. Chapter IX describes Fort Laramie; Chapter XXI, Bent's Fort. In Chapter XII, Parkman records his frustration that the Sioux in the area of La Bonté's Camp have decided against making war on the Snakes; in Chapters XVIII and XIX, he is similarly frustrated in his attempts to hunt deer and sheep. Finally, in Chapter XIII, Parkman bids Shaw farewell and goes without him to the Indian village; in Chapter XIX, the two friends meet again at Laramie.

The book falls into thirds of roughly equal length. The first nine chapters take Parkman and Shaw from civilization to Fort Laramie (Chapters I-IX). The next ten chapters concern Parkman's efforts to find and observe the Indians and then his return to Laramie (Chapters X-XIX). The last eight chapters describe the men's return trip east (Chapters XX-XXVII). Other readers may detect other symmetries; still others may feel that too much should not be made of perhaps unintentionally counterpoised chapters.

More important than simple structure is Parkman's style, which is a complex combination of Realism and Romanticism. The young man traveled west with a professional purpose: to take a close look at redskins beyond the white man's civilization. He knew that the sequence of clashes between the two ways of life would soon spell doom to the primitive, and he wanted to study the Indians before it was too late. Observing their camp life, rituals, hunting techniques, and—if possible—warfare would enable him more accurately to treat Pontiac; the half-century of conflict before that chief's conspiracy; and the Indian enemies and allies of Champlain, La Salle, Frontenac, and other white men in the New World.

Parkman wasted little sentiment on the victims of processes which cannot be helped. For example, when he was traveling with the Oglalas, he once paused to examine the teeming life in a clear pool of water:

> A shoal of little fishes of about a pin's length were playing in it, sporting together, as it seemed, very amicably; but on closer observation I saw that they were engaged in cannibal warfare among themselves. Now and then one of the smallest would fall a victim, and immediately disappear down the maw of his conqueror. Every moment, however, the tyrant of the pool, a goggle-eyed monster about three inches long, would slowly emerge with quivering fins and tail from under the shelving bank. The small fry at this would suspend their hostilities, and scatter in a panic at the appearance of overwhelming force.
>
> "Soft-hearted philanthropists," thought I, "may sigh long for their peaceful millennium; for, from minnows to men, life is incessant war." (295)[2]

Throughout the book, Parkman repeatedly descends to the ground level, so to speak, to give a realistic, apparently unfeeling report. He includes names and descriptions of real persons, place-names and distances, weather reports, dates, and the appearance and smell of his subjects. For example, at one point, when staying just outside Laramie, he writes:

That camp is daguerrotyped on my memory,—the old tree, the white tent, with Shaw sleeping in the shadow of it, and Reynal's miserable lodge close by the bank of the stream. It was a wretched oven-shaped structure, made of begrimed and tattered buffalo-hides stretched over a frame of poles; one side was open, and at the side of the opening hung the powder-horn and bullet-pouch of the owner, together with his long red pipe, and a rich quiver of otter-skin, with a boy and arrows; for Reynal, an Indian in most things but color, chose to hunt buffalo with these primitive weapons. In the darkness of this cavern-like habitation might be discerned Madame Margot [Reynal's squaw], her overgrown bulk stowed away among her domestic implements, furs, robes, blankets, and painted cases of raw hide, in which dried meat is kept. (128)

Later, while hunting with the nomadic Indians, Parkman moved through country which made him write as follows:

Often, even to this hour, that scene will rise before my mind like a visible reality,—the tall white rocks; the old pine-trees on their summits; the sandy stream that ran along their bases and half encircled the village; and the wild-sage bushes, with their dull green hue and their medicinal odor, that covered all the neighboring declivities. Hour after hour the squaws would pass and repass with their vessels of water between the stream and the lodges. (240)

Those who lament the absence of anthropological data in *The Oregon Trail* commit the age-old critical blunder of downgrading a good book for not being a different book. It should go without saying that, if Parkman had been differently trained or motivated, his depiction of the Indians would have been different. He might have psychoanalyzed or sentimentalized them; instead, he simply examined them from his own point of view, and his youthful New England hauteur shaped the lens through which he viewed them. The following passage about the Indians at Fort Laramie is a typical one:

They were bent on inspecting everything in the room; our equipments and our dress alike underwent their scrutiny, for though the contrary has been asserted, few beings have more curiosity than Indians in regard to subjects within their ordinary range of thought. As to other matters, indeed, they seem utterly indifferent. They will not trouble themselves to inquire into what they cannot comprehend, but are quite contented to place their hands over their mouths in token of wonder, and exclaim that it is "great medicine." With this comprehensive solution, an Indian never is at a loss. He never launches into speculation and conjecture; his reason moves in its beaten track. His soul is dormant; and no exertions of the missionaries, Jesuit or Puritan, of the old world or the new, have as yet availed to arouse it. (108)

That sort of generalization could be matched for shallowness by many others in the book but does not in any sense weaken the impact of innumerable pictorial and dramatic passages. For three examples: "His ugly face was painted with vermilion; on his head fluttered the tail of a prairie-cock . . . ; in his ears were hung pendants of shell, and a flaming red blanket was wrapped around him" (123). "He never arrayed himself in gaudy blanket and glittering necklaces, but left his statue-like form, limbed like an Apollo of bronze, to win its way to favor. His voice was singularly deep and strong, and sounded from his chest like the deep notes of an organ. Yet after all, he was but an Indian" (160). And

The Indians were gathered around him [a dead buffalo], and several knives were already at work. These little instruments were plied with such wonderful address that the twisted sinews were cut apart, the ponderous bones fell asunder as if by magic, and in a moment the vast carcass was reduced to a heap of bloody ruins. The surrounding group of savages offered no very attractive spectacle to a civilized eye. Some were cracking the huge thigh-bones and devouring the marrow within; others were cutting away pieces of the liver and other approved morsels, and swallowing them on the spot with the appetite of wolves. The faces of most of them, besmeared with blood from ear to ear, looked grim and horrible enough. (223)

We accept Parkman and his credentials, and feel that with Walt Whitman he is entitled to say, "I was the man, I suffer'd, I was there." The tableaux and the noisy film clips have verisimilitude here. At the same time, Parkman the Eastern tenderfoot is clearly present, calling his subjects ugly, childishly gaudy, wolfish, horrible, only occasionally Apollo-like, and himself civilized.

Parkman was Romantic as well as Realistic, though to a lesser degree. He lauded sturdy individualism and untainted nature, and he responded to the call of the remote and the wild. When he got out west, he admired—even half envied—the rugged mountain men, the intrepid trappers, and even an occasional Indian, for example, Mahto-Tatonka, of whom he writes: "No chief could vie with him in warlike renown, or in power over his people. He had a fearless spirit, and an impetuous and inflexible resolution. His will was law. He was politic and sagacious. . . . In a community where, from immemorial time, no man has acknowledged any law but his own will, Mahto-Tatonka raised himself to power little short of despotic" (157, 158). Parkman was probably never ambitious to lead a tribe of Indians, but surely his resolve to be at the head of American historians was strengthened by observing the fearless will of Indian chiefs and is implicit in his praise of it here.

One of the most delightful Romantic elements in *The Oregon Trail* is the nature description. Parkman is adept at depicting storms, the vastness of the prairies, mountain grandeur, and sunsets etched in blood and ink. Here is one example, which includes several of these elements:

> At last, towards evening, the old familiar black heads of thunderclouds rose fast above the horizon, and the same deep muttering of distant thunder that had become the ordinary accompaniment of our afternoon's journey began to roll hoarsely over the prairie. Only a few minutes elapsed before the whole sky was densely shrouded, and the prairie and some clusters of woods in front assumed a purple hue beneath the inky shadows. Suddenly from the densest fold of the cloud the flash leaped out, quivering again and again down to the edge of the prairie; and at the same instant came the sharp burst and the long rolling peal of the thunder. A cool wind, filled with the smell of rain, just then overtook us, levelling the tall grass by the side of the path. (48)

Like Byron, one of his favorite authors, Parkman seems to have taken a rainstorm as a personal challenge.

Romantically, as Parkman was returning to civilization, he grew more depressed. After the final epic chase of the buffalo, then the cutting up and drying of the meat, he and his party followed the Arkansas River almost sadly back to the settlements. Parkman seemed to be holding back his horse, glancing over his shoulder at this Western chapter in his life as it was closing, and sniffing civilization with repugnance: "On every side we saw tokens of maturity and decay where all had before been fresh with opening life. . . . We hailed these sights and sounds . . . by no means with unmingled pleasure. Many and powerful as were the attractions of the settlements, we looked back regretfully to the wilderness behind us" (409).

At the same time, Parkman makes it painfully clear that he fancies himself more than a match for almost every specimen of manhood in the West. The average emigrant is vile, his British traveling companions are uncooperative, Fort Laramie idlers are illiterate, the mountain men and traders are uncouth and brutish, the Mormons are dreadful, the typical ex-soldier is hangdog while the usual volunteer going to the Southwest is slovenly, and so on. Parkman would even have the reader regard him as the equal of the most ferocious Indians. One of the Oglalas with whom he traveled was Mad Wolf, the volatile Arrow-Breaker of whom he writes: "I had always looked upon him as the most dangerous man in the village; and though he often invited me to feasts, I never entered his lodge unarmed" (267). This passage seems pretentious: if Mad Wolf had wanted to slit his throat one dark night, what could Parkman have done? He was the only white man within miles except for a few unreliable *engagés,* and he was crippled with dysentery.

Aside from his cousin Shaw, the only person for whom Parkman has unqualified praise is Henry Chatillon, their guide and hunter. Romantic-looking with his athletic figure and white blanket coat, broad felt hat, moccasins, fringed deerskin pants, knife, bullet pouch, powder horn, and rifle, Chatillon cut the sort of figure that Parkman wanted to emulate while in the West. In addition, Chatillon was knowledgeable about prairie, forest, and mountain life; bore adversity with a Spartan calm; was an expert horseman and hunter; was thoroughly at home among the Indians; and, to his Eastern tenderfoot employers, was loyal and kind. Half a century later, when Parkman had occasion to write his illustrator Frederic Remington, he noted the following: "If I were asked to name the most striking combination of strength and symmetry I have ever seen, I should say Henry Chatillon. . . . [He had] a figure so well knit and well moulded that awkwardness was impossible to it . . ." (*Letters,* II, 252). But, while

Parkman aimed to emulate this man physically, he knew that Chatillon as an illiterate was obviously his intellectual inferior.

The surface of Parkman's narrative, then, vibrates because of the tension created by his contrary pulls toward Realism and Romanticism. Parkman sought to present a daguerrotype of real savages in the real West, to show without falsifying or moralizing that life out there was red in tooth and claw. Simultaneously he extols a Romantic ideal: courageous manhood in tune with gaudy nature. Meanwhile, beneath the surface of his prose lies more tension. One catches glimpses of a patrician woodsman, a Puritan primitive, an academician who loves the outdoors. It would be valueless to press this matter too far, as Kenneth Rexroth eloquently but irresponsibly does when he says that Parkman out West "met his Id, and it was too much for him. The memory of . . . the naked Sioux belles disporting themselves in the Missouri prostrated him for the rest of his life." [3] Like it or not, Parkman's Ego was too much for his Id; in addition, the only thing which could "prostrate" Parkman was death itself. Nor would it be correct to postulate that he was caught between two worlds, one dead and the other powerless to be born, that is, he was caught between his love for America's past and his vision of her still pure West, for he was not so much self-divided as anxious to have the best of two ways of life. *The Oregon Trail* records his rather complete success in doing so in the summer of 1846. He might have continued to combine the Brahmin and the naturalist but for sickness.

It should be noted that *The Oregon Trail* is a youthful piece of writing, much inferior stylistically to Parkman's later works. In it one finds rather hackneyed similes and metaphors, pretentious literary double negatives, dangling modifiers, and characters and terms introduced early and sometimes defined only later. The following images are taken from the first third of the book: the prairie is "ocean-like" (*Trail*, 10; see also 35, 55); a Leavenworth trader has a "lynx eye" (26); clouds are once like "light piles of cotton" (48); sleet and hail are "like a storm of needles" (68); a ravine winds "like a snake among the hills" (72); lizards dart "like lightning over the sand" (83); and Indian children swarm "like bees" (96). Literary double negatives and near doubles from the middle third of the book include these: "His warlike ardor had abated not a little" (139; see also 183, 249); "it was not impossible that the other villages would prove as vacillating" (169); "His couch was by no means an uncomfortable one" (246); "one of those fits of sullen rage not uncommon among Indians" (267); and "it was not rendered totally unserviceable" (279).[4] Although dangling modifiers are more common in the first part of *The Oregon Trail,* the following, taken from the last nine chapters, are representative of the lot: ". . . being unable to find water, our journey was protracted to a very late hour" (309); and "having no tobacco of his own, we used to provide him with as much as he wanted" (378).[5]

Either because Parkman was very familiar with their names or because he himself was confused, he amateurishly introduces his companions and Indian friends. For example, early during his stay with the Indians but before he joins the Oglala village, he says that four trappers came to their camp; and he gives their names as Morin, Saraphin, Rouleau, and Gingras (147). But the last two of them he has already named (140, 141). Saraphin he fails to describe until six chapters later, along with Rouleau (260–61), in a catch-all section called "The Trappers." A more confusing instance involves the Indian named Mahto-Tatonka: initially, he is identified as a brother of Chatillon's squaw, then as a younger brother, then as Bull-Bear—the translation of Mahto-Tatonka, which name he inherited from his father, a leading Oglala chief (130–31, 145, 148)—then as the nephew of a patriarch first called "the Nestor of his tribe" (156) and later Le Borgne (157). Only a very careful reader can assimilate such casually dispensed information.

Examples of Parkman's use of little-known terms without defining them, and later using them again and then defining them, are not frequent but do occur often enough to make a carping reader wish that the author had had a better editor. For example, Parkman says in Chapter V that his muleteer Deslauriers was "anxious to conform in all respects to the opinions and wishes of his *bourgeois*" (43). In Chapter VII, he mentions Rapin and calls him "the *bourgeois,* or 'boss,' of Fort Laramie" (74–5).[6] The same delay is evident with *shongsasha,* a mysterious element which is mixed with tobacco and smoked; it is first mentioned in Chapter VIII (101), but not until Chapter XIV does Parkman define it as red willow bark (208). As for *bois de vache,* which periodically dots the narrative as it does the prairies, Parkman leaves that euphemism for buffalo dung to be translated by the ingenious.

A final aspect of Parkman's style worth mentioning is his ebullient sense of humor. It is frequently leveled at the Indians, often at Deslauriers and Tête Rouge, and occasionally (but never critically) at himself.[7] One notes the Mark Twain-like verbal felicity in the following picture of an ugly squaw:

> The moving spirit of the establishment was an old hag of eighty. Human imagination never conceived hobgoblin or witch more ugly than she. You could count all her ribs through the wrinkles of her leathery skin. Her withered face more resembled an old skull than the countenance of a living being, even to the hollow, darkened sockets, at the bottom of which glittered her little black eyes. Her arms had dwindled into nothing but whip-cord and wire. Her hair, half black, half gray, hung in total neglect nearly to the ground, and her sole garment consisted of the remnant of a discarded buffalo-robe tied round her waist with a string of hide. Yet the old squaw's meagre anatomy was wonderfully strong. She pitched the lodge, packed the horses, and did the hardest labor of the camp. From morning till night she bustled about the lodge, screaming like a screech-owl when anything displeased her. (151)

The following almost mock-epic description closes with a magnificent periodic sentence worthy of Henry James:

> A vicious-looking squaw, beside herself with rage, was berating her spouse, who, with a look of total unconcern, sat cross-legged in the middle of his lodge, smoking his pipe in silence. At length, maddened by his coolness, she made a rush at the lodge, seized the poles which supported it, and tugged at them, one after the other, till she brought down the whole structure . . . clattering on his head, burying him in the wreck of his habitation. He pushed aside the hides with his hand, and presently his head emerged, like a turtle's from its shell. Still he sat smoking sedately as before, a wicked glitter in his eyes alone betraying the pent-up storm within. The squaw, scolding all the while, proceeded to saddle her horse, bestride him, and canter out of the camp, intending, as it seemed, to return to her father's lodge, wherever that might be. The warrior, who had not deigned even to look at her, now coolly rose, disengaged himself from the ruins, tied a cord of hair by way of bridle round the jaw of his buffalo-horse, broke a stout cudgel, about four feet long from the but-end of a

lodge pole, mounted, and galloped majestically over the prairie to discipline his offending helpmeet. (174–75)

Tête Rouge is repeatedly the target of Parkman's barbs because of his ineptness, inappropriate good spirits, cowardice, voracious appetite, and naïveté. Deslauriers fares little better, for Parkman pictures him as meditating on his mistress while half asleep and at another time as diving so resolutely into the wagon for his gun that "everything but his moccasins disappeared" (362).

Although Parkman seldom pokes fun at himself, one does find this refreshing touch: "At last I fell into a doze, and awaking from it found Deslauriers fast asleep. Scandalized by this breach of discipline, I was about to stimulate his vigilance by stirring him with the stock of my rifle; but compassion prevailing, I determined to let him sleep a while . . ." (62). With mock-solemnity Parkman alludes to his own "character and dignity," which he can make evident to the Indians by serving them dog for supper (211). With mock self-abasement he decides not to intrude his "unhallowed presence" into the Strong Hearts' midnight fire dance (316). He is even stoic enough to spoof his own nearly mortal sickness and—equestrian though he was—his inability to ride a mule down a forty-five-degree slope full of trees. Speaking of himself, he gives a humorous how-to-fail recipe:

> Let him have a long rifle, a buckskin frock with long fringes, and a head of long hair. These latter appendages will be caught every moment and twitched away in small portions by the twigs, which will also whip him smartly across the face, while the large branches above thump him on the head. His mule, if she be a true one, will alternately stop short and dive violently forward, and his positions upon her back will be somewhat diversified. At one time he will clasp her affectionately, to avoid the blow of a bough overhead; at another, he will throw himself back and fling his knee forward against her neck, to keep it from being crushed between the rough bark of a tree and the ribs of the animal. (275–76)

The Oregon Trail is an archetypal journey narrative. Parkman is a typical Eastern tenderfoot naïvely undertaking a trek which is almost too much for him. He eagerly leaves his comfortable home, presided over by generous parents and devoted sisters; is ferried across strange rivers; and jumps off into unknown, dangerous terrain, to be blasted by storms and baked by pitiless suns. He enjoys the friendship of a traditional helper figure in Chatillon, of whom early in the narrative one reads: "He was a proof of what unaided nature will sometimes do. I have never, in the city or in the wilderness, met a better man than my true-hearted friend, Henry Chatillon" (16). If the hero cannot directly confront the legendary beast of the West—the grizzly bear—he can at least rejoice that Chatillon is reputed to have killed thirty such monsters. The adventurer and his group are slowed down by most of the men who accompany them, but they find Laramie, their first goal. Then the hero leaves his friends and passes a lonely test—village life with the Oglalas. He is debilitated by a mysterious malady, which can sap his strength but not his courage. A laughing devil figure in the form of the Indian chief called The Hog tries in vain to barter a daughter for the pure hero's horse. The adventurer tries to find among all the strangers at least one friend somewhat like himself, but little comes of the effort. "He [The Panther] had not the same features with those of other Indians. Unless his face greatly belied him, he was free from the jealousy, suspicion, and malignant cunning of his people. For the most part, a civilized white man can discover very few points of sympathy between his own nature and that of an Indian. With every disposition to do justice to their good qualities, he must be conscious that an impassable gulf lies between him and his red brethren. . . . Yet, in the countenance of the Panther, I gladly read that there were at least some points of sympathy between him and me" (292–93). After threading his way through a mountain pass, the hero finds his friends again, picks up with other wanderers, meets success in his last big test—slaughtering the shaggy buffalo—and then follows a friendly river back to the old threshold again. When the imaginative reader of this book listens for mythic overtones, he can hear several.

Finally, *The Oregon Trail* (1847–48, 1849) bears favorable comparison with several other American travel accounts, notably Washington Irving's *Tour on the Prairies* (1835), Richard Henry Dana, Jr.'s *Two Years Before the Mast* (1840), Herman Melville's *Typee* (1846), and Mark Twain's *Roughing It* (1871) and "Old Times on the Mississippi" (1875). Parkman was as much an Eastern gentleman as Irving but much tougher physically. Irving explored east-central Oklahoma late in 1832 and wrote *A Tour on the Prairies* to tell about it. Both Irving and Parkman feel superior to their companions, at whom they often jibe. Each has a frontier ideal, for Irving's equivalent of Chatillon is the half-breed woodsman Pierre Beattie. Both use loose diary form but vary from it, especially Irving, to include recollected yarns toward the end. Parkman's book is less smoothly written but is infinitely more serious and rewarding. Irving was simply having a one-month lark.

Melville's *Typee*, like *The Oregon Trail*, is a three-part book involving escape from the author's kind, life among aborigines, and finally a compulsive but almost sad return. Melville has a crony in Toby to match Parkman's cousin Shaw, but both authors are left alone with their natives. Parkman reports on his dark-skinned friends both more fully and more critically than does Melville, who, in fact, criticized Parkman's superior attitude toward the savages in a *Literary World* review of *The Oregon Trail* on March 31, 1849. Each is dragged down by mysterious debilitation—Melville, by an infected leg; Parkman, by dysentery. In resisting The Hog's daughter, Parkman remained a better Brahmin than Melville, who had his Fayaway. The persona of *Omoo* is the slovenly friend of Dr. Long Ghost, while Ishmael of *Moby-Dick* is the enraptured friend of immortal Queequeg. Thus, Melville wrote with more abandon than Shaw's cousin, who all the same did write of Chatillon in terms which remind one of Melville's praise of his friend Jack Chase of *White-Jacket*.[8]

Two Years Before the Mast by Dana resembles *The Oregon Trail* in structure, painterly effects, rhetoric, humor, and tone. Dana left Harvard with weakened eyes, as did Parkman, to go to California in search of health, adventure, and freedom from a restraining Boston family. On the voyage and at work ashore, he found his manhood tested; he made friends reasonably well— his *beau idéal* was the fascinating English sailor Tom Harris— and yet, like Parkman, he remained partly aloof because of his pride. On his return journey, Dana was suddenly attacked by a violent toothache which was every bit as serious as Parkman's malady. Once home again, Dana studied law and then entered a profession as exacting as Parkman's.

Twain was no Easterner when he studied the Mississippi River to become a steamboat pilot or when he later "roughed it" in the West. But his adoration of the river, his regret that commerce would change it, and his youthful exhilaration at plunging into the virgin West—especially Hawaii—ahead of the ruinous white man's advance make him resemble Parkman in a few significant ways. Twain is more willing than the author of *The Oregon Trail* to heap humorous abuse on himself as he describes a neophyte gaining experience, and he is as good as any American author at painting the lovely Mississippi and the fresh West. Finally, his epic hero Horace Bixby—master pilot—is a rough cartoon equivalent of Parkman's Chatillon.

The Oregon Trail, then, is one of a distinguished parade of nineteenth-century American travel books, each of which in similar and unique ways shows an articulate person responding to new terrain and to challenging events with uneasy sensitivity and vigor.

II   The Conspiracy of Pontiac

The Conspiracy of Pontiac and the Indian War after the Conquest of Canada was the first venture by Parkman into history, and it provides a good introduction to the professional work upon which his reputation now stands. It summarizes a good deal of what he later wrote about in greater detail; for example, it briefly recounts the defeat of General Braddock and reviews in a few pages the work of La Salle. It might be validly argued that *Pontiac* is the overture to Parkman's opus, because it contains most of the themes developed fully in later works.

The most important sentence in *Pontiac* is the following from its first preface: "It aims to portray the American forest and the American Indian at the period when both received their final doom" (*Pontiac*, I, x). This statement implies that Parkman regarded the vast, brooding American wilderness as one hero of his drama. Many evocative passages combine into symphonic praise of the forests and their waters beyond Oswego, Fort Pitt, Sandusky, and Detroit. Early in the second volume, Parkman remarks that "It is difficult for the imagination adequately to conceive the extent of these fresh-water oceans [the Great Lakes], and vast regions of forest, which, at the date of our narrative, were the domain of nature, a mighty hunting and fishing ground, for the sustenance of a few wandering tribes. One might journey among them for days, and even weeks together, without beholding a human face" (II, 88). Elsewhere, describing the French-Canadian fur traders, Parkman writes that "Those who had once felt the fascinations of the forest were unfitted ever after for a life of quiet labor . . ." (I, 53). On occasion, white captives of the Indians had to be forcibly "rescued" by Colonel Henry Bouquet and his men and returned to the benefits of "civilization" in Carlisle and Philadelphia back in the East.[9] Parkman writes sadly at the outset of his history that the Indian "will not learn the arts of civilization, and he and his forest must perish together" (I, 48). Although there is no overt irony here, it is obvious that Parkman saw in the doomed forest his own happiest home, for "The wilderness, rough, harsh, and inexorable, has charms more potent in their seductive influence than all the lures of luxury and sloth. And often he on whom it has cast its magic finds no heart to dissolve the spell, and remains a wanderer and an Ishmaelite to the hour of his death" (III, 112).

The Conspiracy of Pontiac is in thirty-one chapters, each a hewn cube in a structure which forms a unified and harmonious whole. The history begins with a long, anthropological discussion of factional Indian tribes east of the Mississippi River, with the many subdivisions of the Iroquois stronger and more friendly to the British than were the various Algonquin strains, of which the Ottawa Pontiac was a member.[10] Then Parkman contrasts the French and the British in the New World: the French established missions, forts, and fur-trading posts, while the British colonized and farmed, thus slowly expanding their American population. Collision was inevitable; and Parkman tersely summarizes its military aspects, including the bloody ambush of Braddock on the Monongahela River in 1755, the fall of Quebec in 1759, and the surrender of Canada by the French at Montreal the following year. Meanwhile, white woodsmen began putting intolerable pressure on the redman in the Western wilderness. The British took possession of the French posts in the area, including the strategic one at Detroit. Impolitic attitudes of the British there and elsewhere angered the Indians, especially Pontiac, who late in 1762 accordingly plotted a concerted uprising for the following May. However, not even that great tactician could organize his inevitably inefficient, insubordinate fellow chieftains. Nonetheless, he convened all available warriors at the River Ecorces, southwest of Detroit, harangued them, led a war dance, and enflamed their discontent. But his plan to infiltrate the fort at Detroit misfired because of the alertness of Major Gladwin (spelled "Gladwyn" by Parkman), the British commander. The long siege then began.

The second volume is devoted to Indian successes on the Western border and the white backlash in the East. Pontiac gathered additional forces, including the Christian Wyandots, before the white garrison at Detroit. When Lieutenant Cuyler was dispatched from Niagara to reinforce the post, he was driven back; and during this time eight Western forts fell: Sandusky, St. Joseph, Michilimackinac, Ouatanon, Miami, Presqu'isle, Le Boeuf, and Venango. Pontiac's long siege of Detroit continued. Captain Dalyell ("Dalzell" in Parkman), sent from Niagara to Gladwin's aid at Detroit, finally arrived, obtained permission to mount a counterattack at night, but was butchered at Bloody Ridge northeast of the fort. In writing of these events, Parkman makes use of the *Travels* of Alexander Henry, a trader in the Michilimackinac region, which was the scene of a massacre by the Ojibwas. Parkman then turns his focus upon the frontier forts and settlements in what is now western Pennsylvania. To relieve the hard-pressed frontiersmen and their terrified families, Colonel Bouquet marched with a smoothly disciplined little army from Carlisle to relieve Fort Pitt. He was ambushed at Bushy Run, west of Fort Ligonier; but he turned defeat into victory by a classically executed feint. Meanwhile, in spite of Sir William Johnson's diplomatic maneuvering to the northeast, hostile Senecas from the Six Nations (The Five Nations plus the Tuscaroras) executed a horrible ambuscade of British forces at the Devil's Hole near Niagara. Parkman now turns his attention to the mid-South and discusses the desolation of the Virginia and Maryland frontiers, due in part to the disharmony of those colonies and Pennsylvania, whose Quakers were quick to defend the Indians with rhetoric and slow to aid the frontiersmen with weapons. When Pontiac saw that he was not going to capture Detroit, he raised the siege there. Meanwhile, border ruffians from Paxton, north of what is now Harrisburg, rioted, massacred some harmless Conestoga Indians, and threatened their red brethren, the Moravian converts, east of them.

The short third volume moves to the murder of Pontiac. First, Parkman must tell of the borderers' march on Philadelphia, which, after a good deal of paper warfare, was saved. Then he discusses one of the most inept British officers of the epoch, Colonel Bradstreet, who led an expedition from Albany far into the territory of the Delaware and Shawanoe Indians. They deceived him into consummating a treaty, which Bouquet ridiculed and which General Thomas Gage repudiated. The *coup de grâce* to Pontiac's hopes was delivered by Bouquet, whose army penetrated to the Muskingum River in November, 1764, and forced the Indians to deliver up hordes of white prisoners and to pledge peace in the future. It remained for the white man only to defeat the Illinois Indians, who held the last stronghold east of the plains. Pontiac tried to rally the Western tribes; but the French in the area, the center of which was St. Louis, could no longer support them. The British, under Johnson's deputy George Croghan, began to dominate the entire mid-continent from Detroit to New Orleans. Pontiac journeyed to Oswego to make formal peace with Johnson in July, 1766, three years after which, almost anticlimactically, the once-dreaded Ottawa chief was assassinated in Cahokia, just east of St. Louis, probably by a Kaskaskian Indian of the Illinois.

The six appendices which follow this account are mostly contemporary historical documents useful in substantiating various details of the exciting narrative. At one point Parkman almost expresses the frustration of the exact historian who is limited by his materials but must not fictionalize. He remarks that a prisoner-release scene was "an exhibition of mingled and contrasted passions, more worthy the pen of the dramatist than that of the historian; who, restricted to the meagre outline of recorded authority, can reflect but a feeble image of the truth" (III, 104). However, Parkman's history has many of the virtues of good drama and better novels.

Howard Doughty analyzes the stylistic and structural techniques which the historian uses in *Pontiac*. He praises Parkman for his grasp of theme, his skill in handling dramatic narrative, his fusion of subjective and objective elements, and his skill in synthesizing the scientific and the literary to produce gripping history. He praises the historian's ability to support valid generalizations with specific details, notes Parkman's incremental metaphor of the British as an oncoming tide, and even indicates the occasional use of rhythm, assonance, and rhyme in the charged prose. In addition, Doughty demonstrates his awareness of Parkman's skill in handling setting and narrative scene, in which are dramatized the clash of a savage with a so-called civilization. He briefly mentions the "moral chiaroscuro" evident on both sides of the conspiracy, points out Parkman's "spacial vision" which evokes "the geography of the whole continental heartland," and stresses the almost cosmic counterpoint of the forest wilderness in opposition to the archetypal city. Doughty is alive to Parkman's ready admission that nature is also dual: it combines fabulous riches and venomous snakes. Pontiac, product and epitome of that duality, symbolizes "Romantic primitivism" and, as such, has many virtues which Parkman extols; but on the other hand, the Indian chief blocked, either treacherously or childishly, the way of progress and civilization. Doughty notes, as many critics and general readers have done, that Pontiac is the titular hero of the book and yet is not "as individually distinct and as realistically drawn as . . . Bouquet."[11]

Doughty's analysis leaves little to be added, but one might offer for reflection the theory that in this history Parkman is partly Manichean, as was, for example, Melville in *Moby-Dick*, published two months after *Pontiac*. Parkman develops an enormous series of matched opposites, beginning with the Iroquois and the Algonquins, continuing with the British and French in all their permutations, and including good nature and evil, replete with largess, lavish and poisonous. Moreover, there are evil tribes among the good Iroquois. And obviously Parkman, who is a truthful historian, must criticize the conduct of many Britishers in the New World. Thus, Braddock, Sir Jeffrey Amherst, Colonel Bradstreet, and innumerable Quakers come in for opprobrium in varying amounts. On the other hand, although his spirit generally opposes the French in this epoch, Parkman has many laudatory things to say about some of them. Champlain, Father Isaac Jogues, La Salle, Frontenac, and Montcalm only head a long list of heroic Frenchmen. However, most of the illustrious Frenchmen characterized have adverse traits which Parkman includes in his portrayals. It almost seems that his subtle intention is to suggest that, to be meaningful, any driving purpose must encounter its opposite, within or outside.

As Howard H. Peckham rightly and most recently has observed, Parkman's *Pontiac* "in no sense is . . . a biography of Pontiac." [12] For whole scores of pages, especially in the middle of his history, Pontiac is forgotten or is at most a lurking shadow to the west of the map under immediate consideration. Moreover, Pontiac is imperfectly heroic. A better hero is Henry Bouquet, whose vision, courage, and, to Parkman, "address" are superior throughout to those of Pontiac himself. What we have in Pontiac is, at bottom, a doomed human symbol of the doomed wilderness. The final image in Parkman's history bitterly depicts his chief's unlocatable resting-place: "Neither mound nor tablet marked the burial-place of Pontiac. For a mausoleum, a city has risen above the forest hero; and the race whom he hated with such burning rancor trample with unceasing footsteps over his forgotten grave" (*Pontiac,* III, 189).

Although Parkman's first historical work is generally a superb piece of writing, it is marred by some stylistic infelicities. The historian is occasionally obliged to shift his point of view awkwardly, as when he says, "And now, before launching into the story of the sanguinary war which forms our proper and immediate theme, it will be well to survey the grand arena of the strife, the goodly heritage which the wretched tribes of the forest struggled to retrieve from the hands of the spoiler" (I, 153). Similar are such statements as "I return to the long-forgotten garrison of Detroit" (II, 243) and "To return to our immediate theme" (III, 144). A bit stilted as well, at least to the modern ear, are such negatives as" it was not less necessary" (I, 81), ". . . the not wholly unreasonable statement" (II, 156), "his detachment [was] not a little reduced" (III, 143), and the like.

Humor, which is rare here, is usually in the form of heavy sarcasm. Speaking of Quaker sympathy toward "the benighted race" of Indians, Parkman notes that "This feeling was strengthened by years of friendly intercourse; and except where private interest was concerned, the Quakers made good their reiterated professions of attachment" (I, 87). Later he writes of drunken redskins outside Detroit: ". . . two Indians, in all the valor and vain-glory of drunkenness, came running directly towards the fort, boasting their prowess in a loud voice; but being greeted with two rifle bullets, they leaped in the air like a pair of wounded bucks, and fell dead in their tracks" (II, 28). Parkman reports that an old woman, injured during an Indian attack at Greenbrier, "asked one of the warriors if he could cure the wound. He replied that he thought he could, and, to make good his words, killed her with his tomahawk" (II, 223). Captain Morris, Bradstreet's brave messenger, reports laconically that, during one meeting, Pontiac "opened the interview by observing that the English were liars" (III, 58). Puns are so rare in *Pontiac* that one may be pardoned for concluding that they are accidental, as when Croghan received from the Shawanoes "seven intriguing Frenchmen" (III, 163); and, when crushed Pontiac's deputation arrives at Oswego, it is greeted by the "hollow salutation" of Johnson's battery of cannon (III, 176).[13]

Although Parkman may have had his reasons, a weakness of his history is an undue stress on Alexander Henry's miraculous escape from the Ojibwas, on the Paxton rioters, on the Quakers, and on the whole congeries of border warfare. Moreover, most of his iterative imagery here, drawn from the world of nature, with its tides, waves, wild beasts, consuming fire, and so on, seems somewhat hackneyed,[14] especially when set alongside the incredible richness of the figurative patterns which grace Hawthorne's *Scarlet Letter*, Melville's *Moby-Dick*, Thoreau's *Walden*, and Whitman's *Leaves of Grass*, all of which also appeared in the same half-decade as did Parkman's *Pontiac*. But these minor weaknesses pale in the light of his truly splendid accomplishment, *The Conspiracy of Pontiac*, his first venture as the historian of the American wilderness, and man's heroism and inhumanity therein.

III   Vassall Morton

Vassall Morton: A Novel was published in 1856, was never reprinted, and evidently displeased its author in later years since he refused to include it in collections of his works. In the one reference to it in his letters, he wrote a friend in 1856 that during a sickness, which had begun three years earlier, he had been forced to abandon serious study and therefore had "amused myself with writing a story. Possibly you may have seen it and smiled at the publisher's advertisement of it" (*Letters*, I, 113).

Vassall Morton falls into three roughly equal parts. Chapters 1–25 introduce the handsome, manly, intelligent, rich hero Vassall Morton on the eve of his graduation from Harvard, show him falling in love not only with Miss Edith Leslie but also with ethnological studies, and then push him into a European tour— at the insistence of Edith's father, who wants to test the sincerity of the young man's devotion by a one-year separation from the girl. Chapters 26–48 narrate Morton's voyage to Europe and his imprisonment at Ehrenburg when reactionary Austrian officials are induced by the machinations of Horace Vinal, the villainous rival for Edith's hand, to regard Morton as a political radical. This section also presents Morton's escape after four cheerless years in the dungeon, and his impatient return to Edith and his hated enemy Vinal. In the final section, Chapters 49–74, Morton finds that Vinal has married a reluctant Edith, after having informed her that her hero is dead. Incredibly, Morton tries to help Vinal evade Henry Speyer, the international criminal whom the villain has bribed to put Morton into the dungeon and who is now blackmailing Vinal for every cent he has. At the end, after Vinal has been exposed (but not by Morton, who is stoically away on a research tour), he seeks to escape by sea, only to be swept overboard during a storm. Morton returns to Edith, who evidently has been technically faithful to him all these years.

As an artistic composition, *Vassall Morton* is almost a complete failure. To begin with, Parkman ineptly handles both plot and temporal elements. Morton is attracted to Miss Fanny Euston, an accomplished equestrienne and a vivid beauty. Later he sees her again, only to decide that he prefers to remain loyal to the seemingly lost Edith and therefore coolly turns her over to a Harvard classmate whose love for Fanny is somewhat reciprocated. To show that Morton is interested in ethnology, Parkman early in the novel dispatches him on a two-year tour of the West and far south of the border, and even boasts that "A novel-maker may claim a privilege which his betters must forego. So, in the teeth of dramatic unities, let the story leap a chasm of some two years" (*Morton*, 39). Equally clumsy is Parkman's invitation early in his dungeon sequence to the reader to "let the curtain drop for a space of three years" (204). The whole imprisonment episode, which is quite operatic, is awkwardly truncated when a guard, secretly sympathetic with the American hero, helps him escape and leads him through Tyrolian mountain passes which resemble regions of New Hampshire and Vermont. The friendly guard is shot to death; but Morton survives and breaks out of the mountains near Lake Como, where he conveniently encounters a friend

whose life he saved years earlier in the West. This man helps him
to Genoa and then New York.

Once Morton has returned home, the plot becomes even more
embarrassing. For Edith's sake, Morton shields Vinal from Speyer
and obtains what he thinks are Vinal's damning letters instructing
Speyer to report Morton's death, but they are only tracings. The
preservation of Edith's virginity after her marriage to Vinal is
a touchy topic: the villain is made to fall from his horse and
sustain a fractured leg just before his wedding, and Parkman
tells us that "The ceremony was very private. None were present
but two or three friends of Miss Leslie, the dying father [Edith's],
borne thither on a chair, the disabled bridegroom, and the pale
and agitated bride; for that morning, standing before Morton's
picture [dangling participle], a strange misgiving and a dark
foreboding had fallen upon her, and the sun never shone on a
bride more wretched" (316).[15] With startling rapidity, Morton
returns from his burial alive to denounce the villain—thoughtfully
in private after Edith has left their presence but while she happens to be innocently eavesdropping. By this time, the reader is
in little suspense, for he knows full well either that Morton will
continue to agree with Edith that their fate, though wretched
from most points of view, is spiritually edifying, or that the
villain will be melodramatically destroyed and thus release pure
Edith, who has now left his residence. When she has left Vinal,
Morton, once he has learned the truth, rushes home to stand with
her on the shore of her family lake, "crisped by the June wind"
and "under the shadowy verdure of the pines" (412).

Other technical aspects of *Vassall Morton* are also painful for
the modern reader. Often Parkman introduces a character, presents a thumbnail sketch of his background, relates him briefly
to action involving Morton, and then drops him for ten chapters,
if not permanently. For example, Buckland is presented in Chapter 51 as a love-ruined Virginian whom Morton knew at Harvard;
Chapter 52 is a digression devoted to Buckland's story, told in
his own words. Twenty chapters later Buckland, made well by
following Morton's advice, appears in the East Indies, where
he joins Morton on his research travels to India and elsewhere.
A worse example of inept craftsmanship appears shortly after
Morton returns from the Austrian prison and meets his undergraduate crony Dick Rosny, now a major in the army and about

to fight in the Mexican War. He almost convinces Morton that he should join him for the glory and political good that doing so may bring him. But Morton, who has still not communicated with Edith, declines. Soon after a brief passage in which Parkman follows Rosny to his death at Chapultepec, one reads: "About a year after Rosny's departure [we still know nothing more of Edith], Morton chanced to be again in New York . . ." (301–2); and we watch Rosny's coffin wheel past with his name "wrought in white upon the sable drapery" (302), which touches Morton to tears. Parkman, obliged to back up a year, in order to dramatize his hero's approaching reunion with Edith, next writes awkwardly, "To resume. On returning to his hotel after taking leave of Rosny . . ." (303).

Other awkwardnesses include interminable conversations, sometimes for several pages without any indicators to tell the nodding reader who is speaking. The novel is also marred by old-fashioned asides and soliloquies, one of which is reminiscent of Hamlet's. Vinal is discovered poetizing as follows: " 'Drape the skeleton as you will, the bare skeleton is still there. Paint as thick as you will, the bare skull grins under it . . .' " (399). Morton soliloquizes from dungeon depths, thus: " 'God! could I but die the death of a man! De Foix,—Dundee,—Wolfe. I grudge them their bloody end . . .' " (210).

For all its weaknesses and amateurish composition, *Vassall Morton* is, however, rather absorbing. Parkman moves his narrative along, awkwardly to be sure but still with considerable suspense. The melodramatic confrontations of hero and villain, hero and beloved, and villain and blackmailer are all dramatic too. Furthermore, Parkman charmingly describes deep woods and thunder-blasted peaks and the fitful flames of Tyrolian bivouacs. The violent storm which ultimately takes Vinal to his death is as magnificent pictorially as a Turner painting. Noteworthy also are Parkman's skillful patterns of animal, vegetable and water imagery, which knit the novel together. Also apt, for the times, are his little pro-feminine but also anti-feminist lectures.

But the only excuse a person would have today to read *Vassall Morton* would be for possible light on its author's personality. Wilbur Jacobs, editor of Parkman's letters, says that the probable reason Parkman did not want the novel reprinted is that "it is transparent that the hero is Francis Parkman himself" (*Letters,*

I, xlv). Both Parkman and Morton decided in their undergraduate days at Harvard to devote their powerful minds to study
which would necessitate travel, often among aborigines. Morton's
denunciation of American commercial materialism, with its consequent rape of the wilderness, sounds like an editorial by Parkman. Both Parkman and Morton enjoyed vibrating between town
and country. Parkman's illness-bred idleness and isolation are
appropriately symbolized by Morton's literal dungeon. When
Fanny Euston psychoanalyzes Morton, the reader today should
not miss the autobiographical overtones; Fanny says, " 'Out of
this life you were suddenly snatched and buried in a dungeon;
shut off from all intercourse with men; your energies stifled; your
restless mind left to prey upon itself, or sustain a weary siege
against despair. Pain or danger you could have faced like a man;
but this passive misery must to you have been a daily death' "
(355).

The lesson of the novel was probably therapeutic for Parkman
to develop and then ponder. Morton generously tells Edith that
his physical confinement was less a torture than her predicament
of marriage to an unmasked villain. Later he tells her that she is
of the brave stuff which produces women like Joan of Arc. When
they agree that suffering turns in time to virtue which is re-
warded, the novel ends on a nobly high note. But the reader will
probably longest remember Morton caged in a foreign jail as
Parkman's metaphor of himself jailed by semi-blindness, pain,
and insomnia. Then it is that his hero speaks more like the heroic
historian: " 'Whatever new disaster meets me, I will confront it
with some new audacity of hope. I will nail my flag to the mast,
and there it shall fly till all go down, or till flag, mast, and hull
rot together' " (217). Like Morton, Parkman won his way to
success.[16]

IV The Book of Roses

When his health took a bad turn in 1859, Parkman began to
cultivate roses and other flowers—a hobby that won him international recognition. A side effect of this hobby was his curious little
manual *The Book of Roses*, published in 1866. It is in two parts:
"Culture of the Rose" and "Description of the Rose." The first
part has four chapters; the second, three and a supplement.

The first chapter of "Part One," devoted to open-air culture, discusses planting roses, pruning them, training them to climb and to run; such enemies of the rose as mildew and insects; and how to deal with them. In his introduction, Parkman explains that his purpose "is to convey information" (9). He does so, in prose which is direct and unadorned:

> The slug is a small, green, semi-transparent grub, which appears on the leaves of the rose about the middle of June, eats away their vital part, and leaves nothing but a brown skeleton, till at length the whole bush looks as if burned. The aphis clings to the ends of young shoots, and sucks out their sap. It is prolific beyond belief, and a single one will soon increase to thousands. Both are quickly killed by a solution of whale-oil soap, or a strong decoction of tobacco, which should be applied with a syringe in the morning or evening, as the application of any liquid to the leaves of a plant under the hot sun is always injurious. (33)

Chapter Two discusses details of pot culture, and Chapter Three presents the five modes of propagating roses: by layers, cuttings, budding, grafting, and suckers. Chapter Four encompasses miscellaneous matters: how to raise new varieties of roses, to improve climbing roses, to build tall-stemmed bushes as standards, to deal with the New England frost, and to plant rose bushes in groups.

Part Two begins philosophically with a discussion of the advantages of "intermarrying" vigorous varieties of roses, including that "village maiden," the wild roadside rose, to produce new forms of imperial beauty and grace. Parkman scorns the miniaturizing techniques of Oriental horticulturalists: "By artificial processes of culture, roses have been produced, beautiful in form and color, but so small, that the whole plant . . . might be covered with an egg-shell. . . . The culture that refines without invigorating, belongs, it seems, to a partial or perverted civilization" (98). Chapter Five continues with a description of the commoner rose groups: Provence, moss, French, hybrid China, damask, alba, Austrian brier, sweet-brier, Scotch, double yellow, Ayrshire, sempervirens, multiflora, boursault, banksia, and prairie (each of which varieties blooms once a season). China, tea, Bourbon, hybrid perpetual, perpetual moss, damask perpetual, moisette, musk, Macartney, and microphylla (all of which are perpetual) are also discussed. Chapter Six is concerned with summer roses;

Chapter Seven, with autumnal roses. Finally, a supplement sturdily lists, in addition to those previously discussed, 579 more varieties of roses.

Although rose-fanciers can still glean valuable information from Parkman's delightful little handbook, this work is more valuable for the light it throws on its author. Even in the garden, he was an uncompromising philosopher on the subject of man and man's checkered history. One can almost see him there—remorselessly pruning a defective bud, consigning to oblivion a whole scraggly bush, but also pausing to glory in the end-product of nature and of man's noble patience. He must often have compared an especially rich bloom—blood-red or perhaps baroque—to Pontiac, to La Salle, to Bouquet, or to a few of his other touchstones of human greatness.

With his historical research bearing fruit in *Pontiac* and his physical maladies held in check again, Parkman was now ready to forget fiction, devote only glances at his roses, and resume the work which would earn him professional immortality.

CHAPTER *5*

Pioneers, The Jesuits, La Salle, and The Old Régime

B ETWEEN PUBLICATIONS OF *Vassall Morton* (1856) and *The Book of Roses* (1866), Parkman's strength began to return and with it his determination to resume writing history. The results, seven titles, streamed through the press as inexorably as his beloved St. Lawrence River through its rocky channels. *Pioneers of France in the New World* appeared in 1865. Two years later *The Jesuits in North America in the Seventeenth Century* was published. Then, after two more years, *The Discovery of the Great West* appeared—later to be called *La Salle and the Discovery of the Great West.* Five years passed, and then *The Old Régime in Canada* was issued. After three more years appeared *Count Frontenac and New France under Louis XIV.* Seven slow years followed, then came *Montcalm and Wolfe.* Eight years then preceded publication of the final work, *A Half-Century of Conflict,* in 1892. A year later Parkman died.

These seven works comprise more than four thousand pages of text, exclusive of front and end matter. With *Pontiac,* the total approaches five thousand pages. The whole canon reads like a tremendous, historically oriented *War and Peace.* Over and over, Parkman chafes at the inadequacy of his sources—fertile though many of them are—expresses or implies sorrow that he is not a novelist free to dramatize and provide dialogue, and makes up for professional limitations by lavishly describing his epical setting, the continental wilderness of North America. His drama is one of good pitted against evil, but it is never couched in simple terms. Spanish conduct in Florida the historian saw mostly as pure villainy, but even in that arena Spanish energy and ingenuity come in for some praise. Furthermore, the French there were brave and resolute but incredibly shortsighted; moreover, they were ruinously divided into Catholic and Huguenot. In what became Canada, the French were again divided, so that cross and sword became twin emblems that were occasionally uncooperative; and both were once in a while shamefully disguised under a welter of beaver skins. Parkman also has two opinions of the shrewd Jesuits, as well as of the British who ultimately contested French encroachments south of what later became the Canadian border. The inevitable clash occurred, with its culmination at Quebec. Both Montcalm and Wolfe were at least slightly split personalities, and their Indian allies and foes were more than slightly so.

As will be seen, R. W. B. Lewis' poetic dictum—that Parkman sided with neither the French nor the English—needs detailed and periodic qualification.[1] The historian loathed all sixteenth-century Spanish officials. But he admired the French Huguenots for their seriousness and honor, the French explorers for their tough perseverance, inscrutable Indian stoicism and savage primitivism, the Jesuits' curious mixture of severe good and canny opportunism, British colonial policy and democratic decency, and New England Puritan energy but not its intolerance. On the other hand, Parkman despised Spanish treachery, Catholic hypocrisy, French absolutism, British stolidity, Indian perfidy and cruelty, and man's inhumanity to man and—just as important—to nature. The entire drama is thus intricate, complex, and full of shadings of good and evil, heroism and cowardice, honor and dishonor, and spoliation of the wondrous but sometimes vicious wilderness, which fortunately could become innocent again more easily than irreversibly dishonored human beings could.

I   Pioneers of France in the New World

Pioneers of France in the New World is a long prologue to the drama of France and England in North America, just as *Pontiac* is its agonizing epilogue. The French had made a fatal mistake almost at the outset by siding with the Algonquins in their war with the Iroquois. Parkman describes Champlain's joining an Algonquin war party in a raid against its Iroquois enemies in 1609. When he loaded his arquebuse with four balls, killed two enemy chiefs, and wounded another, "Thus did New France rush into collision with the redoubted warriors of the Five Nations. Here was the beginning, and in some measure doubtless the cause, of a long suite of murderous conflicts, bearing havoc and flame to generations yet unborn. Champlain had invaded the tiger's den; and now, in smothered fury, the patient savage would lie biding his day of blood" (*Pioneers*, II, 178).

But the Indians had also made an enormous initial mistake: they had neglected to kill every white men who had set foot on their native land. Another mistake, almost as bad, was the loss of their own legendary ability to live in ecological balance with nature; instead, they became dependent on the white man for beads, cloth, rum and brandy, firearms, gunpowder, and lead. Poignantly, when Pontiac first began to exhort his Indian allies to unite to fight the common white foe, a Delaware prophet in support "enjoined them to lay aside the weapons and clothing which they received from the white men, and return to the primitive life of their ancestors. By so doing [he added], and by strictly observing his other precepts, the tribe would soon be restored to their ancient greatness and power, and be enabled to drive out the white men who infested their territory" (*Pontiac*, I, 187). But, by then, it was at least a century too late for the Indians to do so.

The first Englishmen in the New World had also made grievous mistakes, almost as soon as they had arrived. Unerringly, Parkman centered attention upon the primary one: ". . . at the outset, New England was unfaithful to the principle of freedom. New England Protestantism appealed to Liberty, then closed the door against her; for all Protestantism is an appeal from priestly authority to the right of private judgment, and the New England Puritan, after claiming this right for himself, denied it to all who differed with him. On a stock of freedom he grafted a scion of despotism . . ." (*Pioneers*, II, 255–56). A century and a half later, the first British at Pontiac's Detroit were little changed. Whereas the French regularly bribed their Indian neighbors with weapons and trinkets, the British in 1760 shortsightedly decided to save such an expense: ". . . the intentions of the English were soon apparent. . . . [T]he presents which it had always been customary to give the Indians . . . were either withheld . . . or doled out with a niggardly and reluctant hand . . . When the French had possession of the remote forts, they were accustomed

. . . to supply the surrounding Indians with guns, ammunition, and clothing, until the latter had forgotten the weapons and garments of their forefathers, and depended on the white men for support. The sudden withholding of these supplies was, therefore, a grievous calamity" (*Pontiac*, I, 180–81). Starvation was the result, which in turn engendered hatred and a consequent desire for revenge.

Meanwhile, how had the wilderness fared? For what must be the purpose of making nature partly symbolic, Parkman repeatedly depicts it in autumn. Of course, certain historically important events occurred in the fall, as for example when Jacques Cartier visited the Indian village of Hochelaga, the future site of Montreal, in 1535. "The morning air was chill and sharp, the leaves were changing hue, and beneath the oaks the ground was thickly strewn with acorns" (*Pioneers*, II, 28). And when Pontgravé left Champlain to hold Quebec through the winter of 1608–09, one reads that the ". . . shores and hills glowed with gay prognostics of approaching desolation,—the yellow and scarlet of the maples, the deep purple of the ash, the garnet hue of young oaks, the crimson of the tupelo at the water's edge, and the golden plumage of birch saplings in the fissures of the cliff. It was a short-lived beauty. The forest dropped its festal robes. Shrivelled and faded, they rustled to the earth. The crystal air and laughing sun of October passed away, and November sank upon the shivering waste, chill and sombre as the tomb" (II, 158). It is not too outlandish to equate the pure air and happy sun with the doomed Indians, soon to fall like the hectic-colored leaves. Nature, unlike the vanished redskin, however, could renew itself. Parkman, who writes poetically of the return of spring to Quebec, begins by saying that "This wintry purgatory wore away" and continues by describing the crash of melted "icy stalactites," the clamor of returning geese, blossoms of the water willows, and young grass gilded spottily by marigolds (II, 161).

The picture of early seventeenth-century America which one derives from *Pioneers* is that of "the shaggy continent, from Florida to the Pole, outstretched in savage slumber along the sea, the stern domain of Nature . . ." (II, 119). Parkman prepares one well for this portrayal, for in his Introduction to the work he writes beautifully that "A boundless vision grows upon us; an untamed continent; vast wastes of forest verdure; mountains silent in primeval sleep; river, lake, and glimmering pool; wilderness oceans mingling with the sky. Such was the domain [he adds sardonically] which France conquered for Civilization" (I, xcviii).

Pioneers is in two unequal parts. The first, which is shorter and more gruesome, deals with the unsuccessful attempts of the French Huguenots to establish a settlement in what is now Florida. The second concerns Champlain and his associates, and their heroic attempts to carve a foothold for themselves in what is now Canada. Parkman states at the very beginning that "The story of New France opens with a tragedy" (I, 3). From the start, politics and religion were against any success that Calvinism might have had in Florida, both because French Catholics opposed the Huguenot plan for it and because violently Catholic Spain claimed Florida. Moreover, the indigenous Floridians, the local Indians, were already split into rival factions under Satouriona and Outina, illustrious chiefs who controlled the lesser bands. By the close of *Pioneers,* Parkman makes it clear that dire conflicts are yet to come, with Champlain dead, with less able explorers to follow, with Jesuits and Récollet friars on the scene, and with rival commercial interests pouring in men and money—all with the connivance of that arch temporizer, Richelieu.

After a sketch of early Spanish efforts to exploit the New World, including those of Ponce de León at Bimini and elsewhere, Pamphilo de Narvaez's fatal search for Eldorado in Florida, and Hernando de Soto's exploration of the Mississippi River and his burial in it, Parkman presents in more detail Gaspar de Coligny's abortive plan to build a Huguenot colony in Florida under the leadership of Nicolas Durand de Villegagnon. The historian's method here is excellent: first, a sketch presents the gigantic, shadowy political and religious forces contending in the background; second, a portrait of each particular human contestant follows; third, a sigh is given for the lush terrain which must be ravaged by the white rivals. At each stage, Parkman makes clear the range of his major historical sources and the degree of their reliability. Thus, at first one has a contrast of Spain and France, then careful character studies of their major fighters, a depiction of Florida, and interspersed citations of and comments on contemporary memoirs, letters, and maps, later biographies of the principals, and even personal observations from firsthand experience in the geographical areas scorched by war.

When Villegagnon failed, Coligny dispatched Jean Ribaut to try a second Huguenot colony, which, however, was quickly wrecked by mutiny. René de Laudonnière was next in 1564, and he came so close to succeeding—in spite of attempted sedition, native unrest, and famine—that Spain felt obliged to stop his pretensions in Florida. Therefore Pedro Menendez de Avilés, an almost matchless figure of satanism in a century notable for ferocity, entered the scene. Parkman regards Menendez as a microcosm of sixteenth-century Spanish reactionary absolutism. King Philip II commissioned him to proceed to Florida and level Laudonnière's Fort Caroline there. Employing butchery on a grand scale, Menendez in 1565 succeeded all too well; and Parkman's account of the slaughter is nauseating. Poetic justice would demand that Menendez, who took French prisoners by lying to them and then ordered them stabbed to death in droves, should meet his punishment in proper storybook fashion. And no one would have been more anxious than Parkman to report a gruesome finish for what he calls "this pious butcher" (I, 126); but Parkman was a historian, not a novelist. Therefore, since Dominique de Gourgues' brilliant private campaign against Menendez did not enjoy complete success, the historian had to content himself with anti-Catholic sarcasm: "There is reason, then, to believe that this pious cut-throat died a natural death [in 1574], crowned with honors, and soothed by the consolations of his religion" (I, 180).

At the end of the first volume of *Pioneers,* Parkman prepares to shift his focus from the completely evil Spaniards in the South to the partially good French pioneers in Canada: "And foremost on this bright roll of forest chivalry stands the half-forgotten name of Samuel de Champlain" (I, 181). Shortly after Menendez had ruined French Protestant hopes in Florida, Champlain began to plant French Catholic hopes in Canada. He dominates the entire second volume, near the end of which appears a skillful summary of his character:

Long toil and endurance had calmed the adventurous enthusiasm of his youth into a steadfast earnestness of purpose; and he gave himself with a loyal zeal and devotedness to the profoundly mistaken principles which he had espoused. In his mind, patriotism and religion were inseparably linked. France was the champion of Christianity, and her honor, her greatness, were involved in her fidelity to this high function. Should she abandon to perdition the darkened nations [the Indians] among whom she had cast the first faint rays of hope? (II, 276)

The second volume is an account of Champlain's valiant struggles, which were sometimes aided but as often impeded by his so-called allies.

Preceding Champlain were John Verrazzano, Jacques Cartier, Sieur de Roberval, and the Marquis de la Roche—all of whom had failed in different ways to make a firm beginning on which French conversions and commerce might be built. Behind the failures were political, mercantile, and religious squabbles. But none of these differences deterred Champlain, who, after exploring in the West Indies and Mexico for two years around the turn of the century, found his true destiny in New France. His story thereafter is a puzzling sequence of Atlantic crossings which are relieved by lengthy and arduous sojourns in little Canadian settlements and among the Algonquins. After enough adventures to satisfy ten forest-piercers, Chaplain died at Quebec at the age of sixty-eight in 1635. Parkman rightly considers Champlain half-forgotten but makes it clear that he was one of the most important Europeans ever to set foot on American soil.

The seventeen chapters of the volume devoted to Champlain may be divided into four almost equal parts. The first four chapters make a unit describing the failures of early French pioneers, including Champlain himself until 1607. The next four chapters concern the efforts of the first Jesuits in Acadia and end with the defeat of their hopes at the hands of Captain Samuel Argall. The next four chapters relate Champlain's success in quelling a conspiracy at Quebec, his discovery of the beautiful lake now bearing his name, his decision to join the Algonquin war party, and then his failure to find the river which a foolish liar told him flowed north to the sea which washed the Far East. The last five chapters tell of his exploration of Lake Nipissing and his discovery of Lake Huron, the ruinous hostility of rival fur companies, the surrender of Quebec to British forces in 1629, and Champlain's death a few years later. Curiously, the British failed to follow up their conquest but instead soon restored New France to the French crown, once France paid Charles I of England a promised dowry to his queen, who was the daughter of Henry IV of France. Thus, Parkman concludes, for "about two hundred and forty thousand dollars . . . Charles entailed on Great Britain and her colonies a century of bloody wars" (II, 272–73).

Much can be said about the sparkling style of *Pioneers*. Sweeping movement alternates with memorable scene. Parkman's favorite verb seems to be "pierce," which he uses repeatedly to suggest the fated thrust of civilization into the wilderness. Varied landscapes are destined to be changed by the advent of the on-pressing white man. Almost regardless of the subject discussed, Parkman draws figurative imagery from the realm of dangerous, angry nature, Thus, metaphorical use is made of cloud, fire, flame, fog, frost, gulf, hound, shadow, smoke, storm, and wolf. In one provocative image Parkman suggests the fear of La Saussaye and his men as they approach fogbound Mount Desert: "They sailed to and fro, groping their way in blindness, straining their eyes through the mist, and trembling each instant lest they should descry the black outline of some deadly reef and the ghostly death-dance of the breakers" (II, 126). Sea and shore are not at war in Parkman; but intrusive man may, and sometimes should, be crushed between them.

The tone of *Pioneers* is often ironic, sardonic, mordantly humorous. Scores of examples might be chosen. Parkman laughs at the vanity of human wishes: "Ponce de Leon found the island of Bimini, but not the fountain [of youth]" (I, 11). The historian amusingly criticizes certain Indians for cowardice: they "were rushing on again with a ferocity restrained only by their lack of courage" (I, 88). He ridicules Ribaut's strategy by remarking that it "seems as well conceived as it was bold, lacking nothing but success" (I, 115). The pretensions of monarchy are scorned when Parkman tells of a man who named himself "feudal lord of half a continent in virtue of two potent syllables, 'Henri,' scrawled on parchment . . ." (II, 74). He laughs at an aged Indian for adopting the monogamous ways of his French visitors by calling his abstemious intentions "hardly a superlative merit in a centenarian" (II, 117). Argall is rebuked when Parkman, annoyed that the man should hold Virginia in a rigorously theocratic grip, adds, "Nor was he less strenuous in his devotion to mammon" (II, 146).

Almost mock-epic in effect are numerous double-barreled epithets, and what they are meant to describe is usually clear without definition: "clerical truants" (I, 107), "greasy potentate" (II, 25), "centenarian sagamore" (II, 94), "birchen flotilla" (II, 96), "naked auditory" (II, 169), and finally "celestial artillery [thunder]" (II, 237).

A few puns add to the humor. Of inquisitorial French monks and priests Parkman states with a straight face that "Their all was at stake . . ." (I, 21). Similarly, the Spanish are said to have "roamed sea and land, burning for achievement, red-hot with bigotry and avarice . . ." (II, 7). There are other puns, but they are worse and may be accidental, as when Laudonnière's peppy men are said to be "in various intercourse with the tribes far and near . . ." (I, 74).

To suggest that the events which Parkman discusses occurred long ago, he occasionally uses a kind of weary, outmoded diction. He writes of Champlain's zeal as early as 1598: "Here much knowledge was to be won and much peril to be met" (II, 59).[2] To depict a fine, early settler in New France, Parkman writes: "The ardent and adventurous baron was in evil case, involved in litigation and low in purse; but nothing could damp his zeal" (II, 99). Related to this semi-archaic language are Parkman's often wistfully poetic lines: "Floating idly on the glassy waste, the craft lay motionless" (I, 46); ". . . the young Huguenot nobles, whose restless swords had rusted in their scabbards since the peace" (I, 49); ". . . on the farther side the flat, green meadows spread mile on mile, veined with countless creeks and belts of torpid water, and bounded leagues away by the verge of the dim pine forest" (I, 53–54); "They strewed the ground with boughs and leaves, and, stretched on that sylvan couch, slept the sleep of travel-worn and weary men" (I, 55); "With slowly moving paddles, they glided beneath the cliff whose shaggy brows frown across the zenith, and whose base the deep waves wash with a hoarse and hollow cadence; and they passed the sepulchral Bay of the Trinity, dark as the tide of Acheron,—a sanctuary of solitude and silence: depths which, as the fable runs, no sounding line can fathom, and heights at whose dizzy verge the wheeling eagle seems a speck" (II, 153); and, finally, ". . . his

evening meal was livened by the rueful music of the wolves"
(II, 238).

Parkman, discussing the journal of murdered Étienne Brulé,
says that "As we turn the ancient, worm-eaten page which pre-
serves the simple record of his fortunes, a wild and dreary scene
rises before the mind . . ." (II, 238). Parkman's own pages are as
evocative.

II   The Jesuits in North America

The narrative which Parkman unfolds in his *Jesuits in North
America in the Seventeenth Century* is epic, dramatic, pictorial,
and tragic. National types are pitted against one another before
a natural backdrop of titanic dimensions. French forces and
also Indian tribes, and to a lesser extent Dutch and English
groups, are in conflict. Since national traits cannot quickly change,
the outcome is inevitable doom, both for the French missionaries
and for their Indian converts and enemies. The ultimate ruin of
the hopes of the Jesuit missionaries sets the stage, in turn, for
later conflicts. Therefore, the fated drama seems unending.

The battle lines were complex when, from about 1632 until
1670, the Jesuits attempted to Christianize the Indians southwest
of Quebec. On one side were the following: a handful of French
missionaries, soldiers, laborers, and nuns; many Huron Indians
and some Algonquins; and a few sympathetic Dutch settlers and,
to the south of Quebec, the nearly neutral British in Boston. On
the other side were the fierce Iroquois; their commercial allies,
the Dutch at Fort Orange (now called Albany); and numerous
anti-Catholic English in Massachusetts and elsewhere.

All contestants were self-defeating to some extent. The Jesuits
were so ruinously concerned with baptizing dying infants and
old warriors that they took suicidal chances, failed to encourage
their Indian allies to take proper military precautions, paid too
little attention to agriculture, and neglected to see that the New
World could produce the means—for example, furs—of supplying
them with equipment necessary to advance their missionary work.
Secular French governors at Quebec and Montreal were jealous
of one another. Most of the French soldiers and laborers were
brave and industrious, but the fur trade lured too many of them
westward and away from the Catholic church and Christian
morals. Finally, the few women at Quebec and adjacent forts saw

as their purpose the conversion of Hurons, not population increase. A curious symbol of these hardy and well-meaning women was Marie de l'Incarnation, who abandoned her fatherless son in France, became an Ursaline, and migrated to Canada in 1639 to help convert heathen infants. A better symbol of devotion to the next world was the life and martyrdom of Father Isaac Jogues, who, after escaping the Iroquois with scars of mutilation, returned voluntarily to them after writing a friend, "Ibo et non redibo [I shall go and not return]" (*Jesuits*, II, 118). He ecstatically endured torture which he knew would end with death and decapitation.

Parkman rightly praises Father Jogues as "one of the purest examples of Roman Catholic virtue which this Western continent has seen" (II, 125), but the historian is also right, in the main, to make the impracticality of the Jesuits and their co-workers the butt of irony and invective, as when he labels the priests "commissioned interpreters of the Divine Will" (I, 131). When a group of nuns on their way to Canada are about to drown, Parkman notes that "It is scarcely necessary to say that they were saved by a vow to the Virgin and St. Joseph" (I, 274). A certain flagellating zealot wore a belt which pierced him with a thousand sharp points; this torture, the historian notes, "filled his confessor with admiration" (II, 4). Parkman enjoys reporting that a French lay sister at Quebec used to ask her chickens and cows if they loved God; when they refused to answer, she killed them (I, 19). Deploring vows of celibacy, the historian notes that it is "the state to which Holy Church has always ascribed a peculiar merit" (II, 83). His Protestant bias becomes clear when he criticizes the missionary Joseph Marie Chaumonot: "the grossest fungus of superstition that ever grew under the shadow of Rome was not too much for his omnivorous credulity, and miracles and mysteries were his daily food . . ." (II, 193–94).

It must be immediately added that Parkman, who could appreciate stoical courage and philosophical firmness, praises the Jesuits for having such manly ingredients. On the last page of his *Jesuits* he writes of these men that "Their virtues shine amidst the rubbish of error, like diamonds and gold in the gravel of the torrent" (II, 275). One of his most eloquent paragraphs describes the success of Father Gabriel Druilletes, who not only converted to Christianity a band of Montagnais Indians in what is now

Northern Maine but even induced them to pray for the forgive-
ness and conversion of the Iroquois, their traditional enemies:
"Those who know the intensity and tenacity of an Indian's hatred
will see in this something more than a change from one superstition to another. An idea had been presented to the mind of the
savage to which he had previously been an utter stranger. This is
the most remarkable record of success in the whole body of the
Jesuit *Relations* [their annual reports]; but it is very far from
being the only evidence, that, in teaching the dogmas and ob-
servances of the Roman Church, the missionaries taught also the
morals of Christianity" (II, 139).

The French were not the only split personalities in New
France, for the Hurons and Iroquois were also self-divided. The
savage Huron hosts of the newly arrived Jesuits soon vacillated
between acceptance of some of their tenets and murderous rejec-
tion. Some were converted, but many Hurons decided that the
French heaven would not do for them because it did not offer
good hunting. They wondered at such civilized wonders as the
clock, which they alternately regarded as a god—calling it "captain" and asking what it ate—and wanted to destroy as the cause
of famine and disease. The powerful Iroquois were the scourge
of both Hurons and Algonquins; and, in addition, they usually
tracked down, killed, and ate every Frenchman they could find.
Yet on one occasion, when they had captured three priests, they
tomahawked only one of them, mutilated but then tolerated another, and actually adopted the third into their tribe. Furthermore, the Mohawk, Oneida, Onondaga, Cayuga, and Seneca
components of the Iroquois could by no means always agree on
policy. In fact, if a Mohawk Pontiac had appeared in 1640 to
convince his allies to unite, not only the French but also the
British and Dutch could easily have been driven from the New
World; and the history of mankind would have been different.

Concentrating upon the dualistic nature of the Indians, Parkman explains why they were doomed from the moment represen-
tatives of Europe first appeared: "The Indians melted away, not
because civilization destroyed them, but because their own ferocity and intractable indolence made it impossible that they should
exist in its presence. Either the plastic energies of a higher race
or the servile pliancy of a lower one would, each in its way, have

preserved them: as it was, their extinction was a foregone conclusion" (II, 140).

Jesuits is built of big blocks of prose which do not always fit
together neatly. The long introduction summarizes in too much
detail the divisions of native tribes and their ways. The opening
chapter introduces the first Jesuits who came to Canada. The
second chapter is devoted to St. Ignatius Loyola, the vital force
behind them. These two chapters might have been reversed, except that Parkman probably wished to begin dramatically and
pictorially, and then present the theology behind the activity at
Notre-Dame des Anges in 1634. Chapters I, III, IV, V, and VI are
a unit telling of Father Paul Le Jeune, his associates, and their
early missionary efforts. Chapters VII, VIII, X, and XI combine
to show how slow the Indian was to change, how impermanent
many of his apparent mutations were, and yet how dogged the
Jesuits continued to be. Intercalary chapters function to move
the narrative along a roughly chronological line to the year 1636,
at which time Charles Huault de Montmagny, the new governor,
and various Ursaline women arrived.

The second part of *Jesuits* is composed of more chapters than
the first, but most of them are rather short. Again one finds a kind
of haphazard counterpoint: Chapters XV and XVIII tell about
the establishment of Villemarie de Montreal, a trio of religious
communities; but Chapters XVI, XVII, XIX, and XX concern the
failures of Fathers Jogues, Joseph Bressani, and Anne de Noüe
and of such Indian leaders as the wily Iroquois Kiotsaton to
establish peace. Chapters XXI and XXII are loose episodic nar-
ratives about the escape of women prisoners from the Indians.
The next two chapters also ramble, but with Chapter XXV Parkman returns to his main narrative to tell about the 1648 build-up
of Sainte Marie, which was a mission, a residence, and also a fort.
The last nine chapters, culminating in Chapter XXXIV, detail the
hideous story of the torture and deaths of several devout priests,
the ruin of the Huron remnants, the abandonment of Sainte
Marie, and the escape of the French from Isle St. Joseph back
to Montreal. Parkman shifts from French to Iroquois to show
that, no matter what the missionaries planned, their adversaries
pursued them like furies.

The historian ends by explaining that Jesuitical success in New
France would have meant the transplanting to American soil of

European absolutism. Just as Parkman prefers French rationalism to mysticism, Mohawk courage to Huron softness, so does he inevitably strike here for Anglo-Saxon liberty over any vestigial remains of Continental feudalism.[3] But he generously pauses to pay tribute to the manly virtues of fortitude and endurance on both sides. Many heroes emerge, and not the least is the sadistically tortured Father Jean de Brébeuf and the Oneida war-chief Ononkwaya, who crawled to attack his tormentors after they had scorched him and then cut off his hands and feet.

Jesuits has many stylistic and technical splendors. Parkman conveys an exciting sense of suspense. He frequently dramatizes events by inviting the reader to walk with him into Quebec, to paddle along the St. Lawrence River, to push aside the birch flap of a Huron wigwam, and so on. He skillfully alternates detailed scenes viewed close up and panoramic pictures necessarily looked at from a distance. His similes and metaphors are graphic, if occasionally a bit hackneyed according to the standards of modern explicators. One of his most effective recurrent literal images concerns fire, whether used to warm the interior of a Huron house of many families, to light nocturnal speakers, to destroy a captured village, or to torture a prisoner of war. In fact, *Jesuits* concerns so much diabolical activity at night that Doughty, after quoting two particularly Dantesque descriptions, concludes that "The image of Hell on earth which makes its first appearance in these passages is the central, organizing image of the book, literally and constantly present to the Jesuit imagination as the figure par excellence of the circumstances of the Canadian mission, and set forth by Parkman . . . in . . . scenes of torture, burning, and violent death, which are such a prominent feature of the book, as they were of Jesuit experience, in their capacity both as witnesses and victims."[4]

Another notable stylistic feature in Parkman's *Jesuits* is his ironic, low-keyed humor. The fact that this piquant spice flavors the first half of the work more than it does the second may help to account for the reader's slight fatigue after about the twenty-second chapter. A few examples of humor will suffice, as when Parkman describes the undainty eating habits of a band of Montagnais whom Father Le Jeune visited: "All shared the feast together, his entertainers using as napkins their own hair or that of their dogs . . ." (I, 103). An Indian convert enjoyed a stay in

France but then returned to Canada, "where, to the scandal of the Jesuits, he . . . relapsed into his old ways, retaining of his French education little besides a few new vices" (I, 104). After discussing a certain French woman's sham marriage for church gain, and Jesuitical connivance involved, Parkman concludes that "All agreed that the glory of God was concerned" (I, 263). Finally, the historian complains that he has little information about the Mission of Sainte Marie and adds that "now, for once, one must wish that Jesuit pens had been more fluent" (II, 185).[5] Other targets for humor are Indian marital habits and notions of heaven, and some of the less rational elements of Catholicism. Parkman often seems a little too certain that white, Anglo-Saxon Protestantism is a *sine qua non* of the nineteenth-century historian.[6]

Like most of his other books, *Jesuits* is marred by Parkman's habitual odd negatives, by delayed and inconsistent definitions and identifications, by repetitions which may have been the result of his necessarily painful method of composition, and by occasionally stilted introductions of new topics. But these are minor matters, and the study remains an invaluable, vigorously written explanation of the failure of brave French Jesuits to convert to Catholicism the Huron and Algonquin Indians of the New World.

III   *La Salle and the Discovery of the Great West*

His book about Réné-Robert Cavelier, Sieur de la Salle, is one of the finest sustained pieces of writing Parkman ever accomplished, because La Salle was an admirable archetype to the historian, who at the end of his study called the explorer "a grand type of incarnate energy and will" (*La Salle*, II, 217). Assuredly Parkman is another example of the type, for the crippled writer who vowed that he would continue until he was "made cold meat of" was surely like the intrepid explorer—that "pioneer of western pioneers" (I, 198), as Parkman calls La Salle—to whom adversities like debt, conniving politicians and merchants, storms and winter ice, sickness, and a thousand miles of trackless forest and prairie were only stimulants to an inflexible purpose.

At the same time, *La Salle* is a study about which it seems both difficult and needless to say much in detail. In it, Parkman follows his subject's career as explorer and trader south of the Great Lakes in the 1670's, his return to France to obtain a monopoly of all trade in the Mississippi Valley, his voyage down the Mississippi River in 1682 to the region which he named Louisiana, his landing with a couple of hundred colonists in Texas by mistake, and finally his men's mutiny and his murder in 1687. In *La Salle*, Parkman again demonstrates his mastery of source material, his smooth and suspenseful narrative technique, and his dramatic and painterly effects as he takes the reader along with the explorer on his almost unbelievable trips. Parkman is half in love with his subject—a man of one purpose, to gain immortal honor by finding the Mississippi and colonizing it for the glory of France.

Parkman approves of La Salle's friends, who included King Louis XIV and his marine minister, the powerful Marquis de Seignelay; La Salle's patron, the Prince de Conti; Count Frontenac, governor of Canada after Courcelle; Henri de Tonty, the courageous, loyal, one-handed explorer whose deeds in the Mississippi Valley rival La Salle's; and comic Father Louis Hennepin, who was articulate and brave—especially when one listens to his side of the story—until he tried to steal glory from La Salle. And Parkman disapproves of La Salle's enemies, including the crafty Jesuits, Frontenac's successor Le Febvre de la Barre, most of the Iroquois, disloyal and mercenary Frenchmen, and of course the murderous Duhaut, who killed La Salle when he was only forty-three years old.

True to his temper, which was Manichean or perhaps only Realistic here, Parkman complicates his narrative by turning coin after coin from obverse to reverse. For example, one should consider Sieur de Beaujeu, the naval officer in charge of La Salle's ill-starred flotilla in 1684. Beaujeu, who hated his assignment, judged La Salle insane to think it could succeed. Therefore, Parkman treats the crusty officer harshly; yet the honest historian includes so many thoroughly sensible passages from Beaujeu's own reports that the reader is tempted to take sides against La Salle. Parkman does too but only tentatively; for his final assessment, a brilliant psychological analysis, includes a quotation from Henri Joutel, La Salle's brave associate (but also a liar), who writes as follows of his adored leader. "'His firmness, his courage, his great knowledge . . . and his untiring energy . . . would have won at last a glorious success for his grand enterprise, had not all his fine qualities been counterbalanced by a haughtiness of manner which often made him insupportable, and by a harshness towards those under his command which drew upon him an implacable hatred, and was at last the cause of his death'" (II, 174).

Parkman uses this splendid vignette as a challenge to produce an even better conclusive comment. First, he contrasts La Salle with the central subjects of his two immediately previous historical studies: "The enthusiasm of the disinterested and chivalrous Champlain was not the enthusiasm of La Salle; nor had he any part in the self-devoted zeal of the early Jesuit explorers." Second, he discusses La Salle's seriousness and restlessness, his shyness in society, his reserve, distrust, and egocentricity. Third, he adds that La Salle "contained in his own complex and painful nature the chief springs of his triumphs, his failures, and his death." Parkman concludes with some dazzling prose, in which he lauds his subject's "Roman virtues" and images the man as standing "like the King of Israel, head and shoulders above" his enemies, "a tower of adamant, against whose impregnable front hardship and danger . . . emptied their quivers in vain." The Melvillean prose flows on. "That very pride which, Coriolanus-like, declared itself most sternly in the thickest of the press of foes, has in it something to challenge admiration. Never, under the impenetrable mail of paladin or crusader, beat a heart of more intrepid mettle than within the stoic panoply that armed the breast of La Salle. To estimate aright the marvels of his patient fortitude, one must follow on his track through the vast scene of his interminable journeyings . . ." (II, 174–75, 176).[7]

Parkman's style in *La Salle* is noteworthy. The historian builds his effects by massive contrasts, for La Salle is opposed almost universally. Furthermore, within a given entity there are warring factions. Parkman renders graphic his major points by superb description, as in the scene in which Father Jacques Marquette dies at Kaskaskia in 1675: his past, the present natural setting, and his grieving companions combine into a single fine etching. Many passages contain muted writing of exemplary charm, and two examples are: ". . . in the morning they embarked again, [and] the mist hung on the river like a bridal veil, then melted before the sun, till the glassy water and the languid woods basked breathless in the sultry glare"; and, much later, "The sun set, and the wilderness sank to its savage rest. Night and silence brooded over the waste, where, far as the raven could wing his flight, stretched the dark domain of solitude and horror" (I, 64, 208).

This poetic tone is often lightened by humor. Usually the butts are the Jesuits and the slovenly, thieving Indians and their curious religious beliefs. The object of the historian's most unremitting fire is Father Hennepin, who was "the reverse of spiritual" and whose adventures—"imaginary and real" (I, 131, 187)—he details. Neither La Salle nor Tonty is ever portrayed in a humorous light.

Parkman is unconsciously very self-revealing in *La Salle*. It is obvious that he admires his hero's ally Frontenac and looks forward to writing about him. Parkman also worships the natural beauties he describes, for example, Niagara. He seems to be almost mystically magnetized by Starved Rock. Over and over, as in *Jesuits* earlier and in *A Half-Century of Conflict* later, he individualizes his study of La Salle by inserting recollections of his own adventures in the West. When he writes as follows of the French explorer in adversity, the New England historian surely has himself in mind as well: "Where weaker men would have abandoned all in despairing apathy, he turned anew to his work with the same vigor and the same apparent confidence as if borne on the full tide of success" (I, 202). He must also be thinking of himself when, more comprehensively, he generalizes that ". . . a trained and developed mind is not the enemy, but the active and powerful ally, of constitutional hardihood. The culture that enervates instead of strengthening is always a false or a partial one" (I, 198).

Unfortunately, Parkman betrays his anti-Catholic bias in these pages, just as he did in *Jesuits*. This prejudice has been sufficiently stressed; but it might be added in passing that, when he is discussing various reports concerning La Salle's death, he ventures to doubt the version of the Récollet friar Anastase Douay, who saw the killing; prefers the account of Joutel, who was not present but only interviewed witnesses; and even says that Joutel had "the best means of learning the facts" (II, 177).

Like Pontiac, Champlain, Fathers Jogues and Brébeuf, and Sieur de la Salle, Parkman remained true to the vision which made his long, unaging youth one incandescent glow. In a mov-

ing passage involving two French idealists of a later time, Willa
Cather has one say to the other: " 'To fulfill the dreams of one's
youth; that is the best that can happen to a man. No worldly
success can take the place of that.' " [8] In a moving eulogy of a
confrère whose life of pain death cut short, Henry James wrote
that he had died "in time not to be old—early enough to be . . .
young and late enough to have drunk deep of the cup." [9] La Salle
too pursued his dream, drank deep, and died before anything
withered. Parkman conveys it all, in a narrative which he could
never quite match until he wrote of Wolfe.

IV   The Old Régime in Canada

The Old Régime in Canada is more complicated and less exciting than *La Salle;* in fact, it is dull even when compared to
Jesuits. Its complexity is partly due to the fact that Parkman
makes it an anthology of essays on Acadia, on Jesuit missionary
endeavors after Father Brébeuf's martyrdom, on Bishop François
Xavier de Laval-Montmorency's pious tyrannies, and on French
political and social problems in colonizing Eastern Canada. The
book often fails to excite the reader because throughout its entire
chronological span, from the 1630's until 1763, there is no hero
like La Salle for Parkman to identify with and dramatize. By
comparison to La Salle, Charles Saint-Étienne de la Tour and
Charles de Menou d'Aunay Charnisay are operatic figures; [10] and
Bishop Laval is impossibly cold and devious. Furthermore, the
third part of *Old Régime* is mostly generalized social history in
essay form.

Old Régime has twenty-four chapters. The first three make up
a semi-detached introduction entitled "The Feudal Chiefs of
Acadia," and concern the bitter rivalry of La Tour and D'Aunay
for control of pathetic Acadia in the 1640's. The reader feels
little but relief when both rivals fail. Their entire story seems un-
real, especially when the widow of D'Aunay marries his arch-
enemy La Tour, not for love but to protect her family.

The second section has nine chapters, is called "Canada a
Mission," but tells several unrelated stories. It begins by plunging the reader into the most Gordian of ethnic tangles. It seems
that in 1653 the Onondagas, a member of the Iroquois Five
Nations, suddenly professed to want peace with the French. In

reality, they wished simultaneously to make war more easily on their Indian enemies the Eries and to betray and butcher the Jesuits if they accepted an invitation to establish a mission at Lake Onondaga. Meanwhile, the Mohawks, even though as another of the Five Nations they were nominal allies of the Onondagas, became jealous of their Iroquois brethren and resented their overtures to the French. Under Father Dablon, the Jesuits, half-tempted by the likelihood of martyrdom, accepted the invitation and journeyed to the lake; but they finally escaped from their would-be cannibals. Next Parkman tells of the establishment of a Sulpitian nunnery at Montreal, which discomfited jealous Quebec. Then he tells of the suicidal preventive raid, on seven or eight hundred Iroquois advancing toward Quebec, by young Daulac des Ormeaux and his small band at the Long Saut Rapids in the spring of 1660. Clearly, New France was in mortal danger in the 1650's.

The second half of the second section is dominated by Laval. Parkman dislikes this brilliant first bishop of Canada but tries to remain objective. Like the reader, Parkman seems almost spellbound as he watches Laval outmaneuver opponent after opponent to emerge champion of Catholic Canada. Again, the historian begins with another Gordian knot, the two strands of which may be labeled Gallican and Ultramontane. To simplify, in 1657 the nationalist forces in France backed the Sulpitian Abbé de Queylus when he was named by the Archbishop of Rouen to be vicar-general of Canada; but the papist forces in France supported pro-Jesuit Laval after Pope Alexander VII had named him to be vicar apostolic for Canada. Soon after the rival ecclesiastics went to Canada, a struggle broke out; and, by the early 1660's, Laval was the victor. Next, rather like a chess master, Laval met and defeated the following adversaries in order: Vicomte d'Argenson, governor of Canada, who favored state over church and was forced to resign in 1660; Baron Dubois d'Avaugour, the next governor, who criticized Jesuit hypocrisy and was recalled in 1663; Jean Péronne Dumesnil, an agent of the Company of New France, who discovered bookkeeping irregularities and was browbeaten and forced to run for his life back to France in 1663; and then Saffray de Mézy, the following governor, who, though rashly zealous, was so sincerely anxious for reform that

Laval induced France to recall him, but who died in Quebec in 1665.

The long third section, "The Colony and the King," has twelve loosely related chapters. It begins picturesquely in 1661 at Fontainebleau, where the new king, Louis XIV, has emerged resplendent and decided to intervene in Canada and make it a royal colony. His intentions were of the best, but Parkman is so sturdily Anglo-Saxon and so freedom loving that, in his view, King Louis's absolutism doomed France in the New World. The historian's repeated point in this whole section is that King Louis smothered growth in his colony by making it a welfare state. This long section ends in 1763, following the British military victory over New France. Of this event, Parkman writes provokingly thus: "A happier calamity never befell a people than the conquest of Canada by the British arms" (*Old Régime*, II, 204).

The dozen chapters of the last section include straight history and essays on socio-economic affairs in New France. The section is important for historical sociologists; but, as narrative history, it represents a falling off from *Pontiac*, much of *Pioneers*, parts even of *Jesuits*, and all of *La Salle*. For one finds few dramatic confrontations and even fewer pictorial scenes. Parkman continues to be master of his material, but he turns with a sigh of relief, for example, from repeating his opinions concerning the Jesuits to a depiction of the freedom of the *coureurs de bois*, whom he must officially deplore but whose wild life he partly envies. The most remarkable passage in all of *Old Régime* begins as follows: "Though not a very valuable member of society, and though a thorn in the side of princes and rulers, the *coureur de bois* had his uses, at least from an artistic point of view; and his strange figure, sometimes brutally savage, but oftener marked with the lines of a dare-devil courage, and a reckless, thoughtless gayety, will always be joined to the memories of that grand world of woods which the nineteenth century is fast civilizing out of existence" (II, 113).

The other high point in the third section appears at the close when Parkman contrasts New France and New England. France encouraged an unmanly dependence in its colonists upon the mother country, whereas England weaned the child and let him grow into sturdy, free manhood. Parkman puts the contrast in a memorable image: "The cement of common interests, hopes, and duties compacted the whole people [of New England] like a rock of conglomerate; while the people of New France remained in a state of political segregation, like a basket of pebbles held together by the enclosure that surrounds them" (II, 200).

Old Régime is notable for skillful use of graphic contrast, for a few bright patches of vigorously dramatic narrative, and for an intermittent revelation of the personality of the tough old author. Parkman presents history best when he can pit one person or force against another in dramatic terms. La Tour clashed with D'Aunay. Boston was split by theological and political quarrels, as La Tour learned when he visited that city. The Iroquois league was rent. The French opposed the Dutch. In Montreal, Jesuit feuded with Sulpitian, while France itself was divided into Jesuit and Jansenist factions. Ecclesiastical and secular squabbles often threatened to wreck Quebec: as Parkman states on one occasion, "the crozier and the sword began to clash, which is merely another way of saying that he [Argenson] was governor when Laval arrived" (I, 166). In time, King Louis sought to suppress Laval. Hard-working rural curés, on the job often with snow-shoes, were quite different from black-robed Jesuits in town. Only a few threads of closely twisted drama stand out in this work. Examples include La Tour's 1643 interview with Governor John Winthrop in Boston; Father Dablon's silent, nocturnal escape from the treacherous Onondagas in 1658; the tragic slaughter of brave Daulac and his forces at the Long Saut; the Marquis Prouville de Tracy's devastating attack on the Mohawks; and the bracing depictions of *coureurs de bois* at odds with their hostile environment. Noteworthy also is Parkman's presentation in Chapter XX of quotations from letters sent to France by complaining governors and intendants. The dramatic section reads like commentaries for a documentary film.

Once again, Parkman is occasionally humorous. He says that the beavers once took advantage of internecine Indian warfare to multiply and hence create more beaver skins. He adopts the seventeenth-century French point of view and with a straight face rebukes Bostonians for heresy. Comically heavy diction suggests the Indian habit of courteously overeating: ". . . even their ostrich digestion was sometimes ruined past redemption by the excess of this benevolent gluttony" (I, 90). An understandable bias against Louis XIV comes through in the following clever

comment: "The vigorous mediocrity of his understanding delighted in grappling with details" (I, 231). Indians who pretend
to be drunk so that they can commit crimes with impunity are
called "false claimants to the bacchanalian privilege" (II, 124).
Finally, Parkman cannot resist this wry aside when describing
a priest in Laval's Quebec seminary who kindled a kitchen fire
which unfortunately spread and destroyed the whole building:
"His success surpassed his wishes" (II, 187).

Old Régime has many touches in which the author reveals his
personality. Father Poncet's account of his escape from the Iroquois contains "This incessant supernaturalism" (I, 61). As for
Laval, ". . . there can be no apology for [his] means, subversive
of all justice" (I, 202). Parkman expresses his love of autumn in
an immensely long passage which opens as follows: "October had
begun, and the romantic wilds breathed the buoyant life of the
most inspiring of American seasons, when . . ." (I, 253). And he
may have been thinking of himself when he depicted a rheumatic
citizen of Beaupré as "grinning with pain" (II, 165).

Much more might be said of *Old Régime*. The scarcity of its
rhetorical negatives might be commended; but one may cite this
example: the ". . . population . . . gazed on them [Daulac's band]
with enthusiasm, not unmixed with an envy which had in it
nothing ignoble" (I, 129). Present in some abundance are neat
epithets, of which this phrase for one-eyed Major La Fredière is
the best: "the military Polyphemus" (II, 172). Dramatic similes
and metaphors involving fire, wolves, shadows, and hornets vivify
several scenes, particularly the refreshing outdoor ones. But, in
spite of its occasionally bright style, the work is often unexciting.
Parkman's fixed discontent with Catholicism begins to pall; the
Acadian sections seem tangential; worst of all, the whole book
lacks either dramatic or organic structure and is surely the least
vigorous part in the entire series.

Pioneers of France in the New World (1865), *The Jesuits in
North America in the Seventeenth Century* (1867), *La Salle
and the Discovery of the Great West* (1869), and *The Old Régime*
(1874) were now behind Parkman. Yet to be written were *Count
Frontenac and New France under Louis XIV*, *Montcalm and
Wolfe*, and *A Half-Century of Conflict*. In these volumes, the
aging historian would offer startling proof that he had been equal
to the herculean task he had set for himself in his youth.

CHAPTER *6*

Frontenac, Montcalm and Wolfe, and A Half-Century of Conflict

AFTER HE HAD FINISHED writing *Old Régime*, published in 1874, there was no let-up for Parkman, whose next
book, *Count Frontenac and New France under Louis XIV* (1877)
was probably easier to write than much of his previous work.
In collecting material for *Jesuits, La Salle,* and *Old Régime,* he
had assembled and set aside for later use quantities of information which went into *Frontenac.* Parkman had introduced his
readers to Count Frontenac in *La Salle,* in which he had written
at one point of the governor and the explorer: 'There were points
of likeness between the two men. Both were ardent, bold, and
enterprising. The irascible and fiery pride of the noble found its
match in the reserved and seemingly cold pride of the ambitious
burgher. Each could comprehend the other; and they had, moreover, strong prejudices and dislikes in common. An understanding, not to say an alliance, soon grew up between them" (I, 85).
   Those parts of *Old Régime* constituting a sociological treatise
depicted various problems from the 1650's to decades beyond
Frontenac's death in 1698. Throughout *Frontenac,* Parkman contrasts French and English New-World policies, which were so
different that they guaranteed continued trouble. Immediately
after Frontenac's death, some of his aims were temporarily
achieved; but renewed and more bloody conflict soon followed,
lasting half a century and culminating in titanic battle on the
Heights of Abraham, the fall of Quebec, and the fall of Canada.
The final page of Parkman's *Frontenac* points toward the last
two titles of his series—*Montcalm and Wolfe,* and A *Half-Century
of Conflict.*

I   Count Frontenac and New France under Louis XIV

Early in *Frontenac*, Parkman comments on his hero at the age
of fifty-two as he exchanges his courtly military life in France
for the ardors of Canada: "A man of courts and camps, born and
bred in the focus of a most gorgeous civilization, he was ban-
ished to the ends of the earth, among savage hordes and half-
reclaimed forests,—to exchange the splendors of St. Germain
and the dawning glories of Versailles for a stern gray rock,
haunted by sombre priests, rugged merchants and traders, blan-
keted Indians, and wild bush-rangers" (I, 17–18). Early in the
second volume, one finds Frontenac with his officers eighteen
years later in 1690, at a meeting in Montreal where he exhorts
Huron and Ottawa allies from Michilimackinac: "Now ensued a
curious scene. Frontenac took a hatchet, brandished it in the air,
and sang the war-song. . . . His predecessor [the Marquis de
Denonville] would have perished rather than play such a part in
such company; but the punctilious old courtier was himself half
Indian at heart, as much at home in a wigwam as in the halls
of princes. Another man would have lost respect in Indian eyes
by such a performance. In Frontenac, it roused his audience to
enthusiasm. They snatched the proffered hatchet, and promised
war to the death" (II, 23).

Here again one has a typical Parkman hero, a strong man of
divided characteristics and impulses who is like Champlain,
Father Jogues, La Salle, and Pontiac, among others. It seems
strange, therefore, that a recent biographer of Frontenac should
write that "Even Francis Parkman, a staunch advocate for Frontenac and the historian who has done more than any other to
create the generally accepted estimate of him, had difficulty in
defending Frontenac's sorry record in civil affairs." [1] Of course,
the records of Parkman's *beaux idéals* include some of their sorry
chapters. In a summation of the character of Frontenac, Parkman
honestly presents in clever dialogue form passages of oratorical
eulogy and sardonic criticism of the dead governor; and then he
observes that his subject was petty, formalistic in his religion,
and barbarously cruel in war, but also vigorous and able, loyal
to friends, and never obliged to retreat. The historian then concludes with a typical image: "greatness must be denied him; but

a more remarkable figure, in its bold and salient individuality and sharply marked light and shadow, is nowhere seen in American history" (II, 217).

Frontenac is composed of five roughly equal blocks. The first, comprising Chapters I-IV, introduces the reader to Frontenac and to his intriguing but uncooperative wife, in France; transports him to Quebec as governor; throws him into conflict first with Perrot, governor of Montreal, and then with the intendant Duchesneau; and finally sees him recalled to France in 1682 and replaced after a decade of stormy service. The second section, Chapters V-IX, is devoted to a recital of the unsuccessful efforts from 1682 to 1689 of the next two governors, La Barre and Denonville, to restrain the Iroquois, their bellicose buffer which screened them from the Dutch and English at Albany and in New England, respectively. The next part covers Chapters X-XIV and brings back Frontenac, who carried war into the South in 1690 but who was soon attacked in turn, first inefficiently by Sir William Phips of Massachusetts and then gorily by the Iroquois, whose strength unsettled Frontenac's Indian allies in the West.

The next four chapters, XV-XVIII, are a necessary grab bag without much organization; but they tell about Frontenac's problems with his Jesuit critics in Quebec, about intermittent warfare in Acadia, and about the geographical and political differences between New France and New England—all with a loose forward chronological movement from 1690 to 1697. The fifth and final block, Chapter XIX-XXI, describes Frontenac's attack in 1696 on the Onondaga and Oneida segments of the Five Nations, King Louis's peace order following the Treaty of Ryswick in 1698, and Frontenac's death the same year. Parkman closes by assessing the work of his subject and by showing that the seeds of new conflict have been sown that will surely sprout, regardless of temporary quiet in Europe.

Like may of his subjects, Parkman is often of two minds: he admires Frontenac but does not hesitate to dramatize his disfiguring pettiness. And yet one so thoroughly likes Frontenac that one forgives him and calls him only human. With respect to New England, Parkman is also of two minds: he lovingly uses place names from Massachusetts, his revered home state, and proudly introduces persons important to its past as they begin to figure in his present narrative; but he writes candidly at one point about "The government of Massachuetts, with its usual military fatuity" (II, 157). Moreover, Parkman regularly downgrades the illustrious Cotton Mather, whom in one footnote he rebukes for "tell[ing] the story in his usual unsatisfactory and ridiculous manner" (II, 145). It would seem that, while trying to remain impartial and to give credit and debit where both are due, Parkman favors New England slightly. He is pro-American when he writes of Phips's brave officers Major John Walley and Captain Ephraim Savage, for example, during the 1690 attack on Quebec, and later of the forbearance of the New Englanders after the cowardly attack two years later by the French on the settlements of York and Wells. Earlier, in fact, Parkman can hardly conceal his delight when Colonel Thomas Dongan, governor of New York, outmaneuvers Denonville in their epistolary war of 1686–88. Indeed, so dismayingly have the reader's shifting loyalties been taxed that he would hardly know which side to cheer for if *Frontenac* were historical fiction instead of almost novelistic history.[2]

Curious also is the shift in the historian's opinion of the Iroquois, who in *La Salle* were bloodthirsty frustrators of his hero's plans for opening the West. It seems quite a reversal for Parkman to praise the Iroquois when they rebuked their English allies for pacifism in 1694: "Nothing [says the historian] could be more just than these reproaches; and if the English governor [Fletcher of New York] had answered by a vigorous attack on the French forts south of the St. Lawrence, the Iroquois warriors would have raised the hatchet again with one accord" (II, 179). In 1701 the Indian allies of the French honorably returned their Iroquois prisoners and extracted a promise from their fierce foes for like consideration; but, when the Iroquois broke that pledge, Parkman is insufficiently critical: "Callières [Frontenac's replacement] yielded . . . and took an empty promise in return. It was a triumph for the Iroquois, who meant to keep their Indian captives, and did in fact keep nearly all of them" (II, 233).

Since *Frontenac* involves extensive discussion of political and military policy, it is not distinguished by much descriptive writing; one finds, therefore, few epic panoramas. Three glorious exceptions, all in the second volume, are Parkman's depiction of Phips's first sight of Quebec in 1690, Frontenac's panoplied foray six years later into the stronghold of the Onondagas in command of twenty-two hundred men, and the colorful funeral of the Rat, a wily Huron chief. Such events evoke Parkman's splendid painterly talents, but they are evinced infrequently in this work.

Also of less concern to Parkman in *Frontenac* than elsewhere are the continuing efforts of the Jesuits at conversion to Catholicism of whatever Indians they could persuade. But, when Parkman has an opportunity to advert to this subject, he does so with relish; he writes once, for example, of such activities in Acadia: "The French missionaries are said to have made use of singular methods to excite their flocks against the heretics. The Abenaki chief Bomaseen, when a prisoner at Boston in 1696, declared that they told the Indians that Jesus Christ was a Frenchman, and his mother, the Virgin, a French lady; that the English had murdered him, and that the best way to gain his favor was to revenge his death" (II, 153).[3] Much preferring the milder Récollet friars, just as Frontenac did, Parkman sweepingly brands the Jesuits as "the apostles of carnage" (II, 152). Time and again he makes religious zealots a major target for his derisive humor, especially when in the second volume he has more opportunity to ridicule their missionary bellicosity. When Bishop Laval prays for the defeat of Phips's reluctant armada, "it is not surprising that the head-winds which delayed the approach of the enemy . . . should have been accepted as proof of divine intervention" (II, 53). All the same, the next summer "an army of caterpillars . . . set at naught the maledictions of the clergy" (II, 67).

Parkman also pokes fun at unpreparedness, inability, and pretentiousness, especially in the military. One reads that "lighted hand-grenades down the chimney, . . . exploding among the occupants, told them unmistakably that something was wrong" (I, 139); "thirty young volunteers . . . sallied out to find the enemy. They were too successful . . . They were met by a fire so close and deadly that half their number were shot down" (I, 240–41); "The Puritan gunners wasted their ammunition in vain attempts to knock it [the Quebec cathedral spire] down. That it escaped their malice was ascribed to miracle; but the miracle would have been greater if they had hit it" (II, 45); and " 'The expedition,' says Frontenac, 'was a glorious success.' However glorious, it was dearly bought; and a few more such victories would be ruin" (II, 88).

As usual, Parkman makes his dramatic narrative move by

highlighting opponents, large and small, in confrontation. Thus, Frontenac, who was himself self-divided in several ways, is opposed by the Jesuits, Perrot, Abbés Salignac de Fénelon and d'Urfé, Duchesneau, and New York's Earl of Bellomont. The Illinois Indians fight against the Seneca branch of the Five Nations; the Iroquois against the tribes around Michilimackinac; La Barre, briefly, against La Salle and then against Dongan, who soon is pitted against Denonville; King Louis XIV against King James II of England; the French against the English traders at Hudson's Bay; the Boston citizenry against Sir Edmund Andros; the French army against the Jesuits in Canada; Indian energy against Indian indolence; Perrot against the Baron de Saint-Castin; New England against Canada; and, after Frontenac's death, Callières against the intendant Champigny. Parkman wraps up innumerable subsumptions in this all-encompassing final comment: "An invalid built the Bourbon monarchy, and another invalid battered and defaced the imposing structure,—two potent and daring spirits in two frail bodies, Richelieu and William of Orange" (I, 193).

Once again, Parkman betrays occasional carelessness in composition, which it seems almost too petty to mention. But his pronouns do become confused once in a while, as in the following: ". . . the Jesuit Milet, who had been captured a few months before, adopted, and made an Oneida chief, used every effort to second the designs of Frontenac. The authorities of Albany tried in vain to induce the Iroquois to place him [Milet] in their hands. They [the Iroquois] understood their interests too well, and held fast to the Jesuit" (I, 205–6). Parkman has nine danglers and an expected quota of "not withouts," "not a littles," "not unfittings," "not unlikes," and the like. But, by this time, one should regard such constructions as a not altogether unpleasant mannerism in a writer who, in *Frontenac*, has realistically depicted a credible human being, an admirable leader, flawed but vigorous and memorable. Parkman's portrait of the tough count is part of a well-planned gallery, on the last and best-lighted wall of which is a stupendous diptych, *Montcalm and Wolfe.*

II   Montcalm and Wolfe

If Parkman had had better health, he would have turned from *Frontenac* to the composition of *A Half-Century of Conflict*. But, since he was uncertain how many years of productivity might remain, he decided to write the last phase of his historical epic at once and then, if permitted, turn back to the penultimate section. When speaking of *Montcalm and Wolfe* in his preface, he says that "The plan of the work was formed in early youth; and though various causes have long delayed its execution, it has always been kept in view. . . . These . . . volumes are a departure from chronological sequence. The period between 1700 and 1748 has been passed over for a time. When this gap is filled, the series of 'France and England in North America' will form a continuous history of the French occupation of the continent" (I, ix).

The frontispieces of the three volumes of *Montcalm and Wolfe* in the Champlain Edition are of the Marquis de Montcalm, a view of Quebec, and General James Wolfe. Here, in graphic symbolism, one finds the crux of the history: French absolutism, as represented and defended with bravery but also with classical limitations by Montcalm; British liberty on the move, at sea and in the expanding colonies, attacking with intrepid imagination (Wolfe); and the austerely beautiful point at rocky, water-girt Quebec where the opposing forces met.

Parkman lavishes praise on Louis de Montcalm and does him justice. He had his faults, as did La Salle and Frontenac before him; but he was courageous, resourceful, loyal, and warm. He was fatally opposed by smaller men, most notably the gasconading liar the Marquis de Vaudreuil, governor-general of Canada, on whom Parkman pours measure after measure of scorn. Also contributing to the ruin of Montcalm's military plans were Canada's corrupt intendant François Bigot and his thief-henchman Joseph Cadet, the commissary-general of Canada. After the fall of their country, these three men with other vultures were returned to France, thrown into the Bastille, and later tried. Only Vaudreuil was acquitted—unjustly.

Aiding Montcalm were many brave and loyal Frenchmen, including Louis Antoine de Bougainville, Chevalier de Bourlamaque, and Chevalier de Lévis, all of whom usually fought fiercely to stave off defeat. The French cause was fanatically aided by priests like Father Louis Joseph Le Loutre, the vicar-general of Acadia and a missionary to the Micmac Indians; by Canadian bush-rangers and partisans like Saint-Luc de la Corne and Marin and Charles Langlade, all of whom lived with the Indians so long that they combined most of their vices with mere remnants of a few Gallic virtues; and finally by many misguided and short-sighted Indians, most notably the vicious Abenakis.

A roll call of Englishmen and American colonials without whom Wolfe's audacious plan to take Quebec would have failed would be too long to give here. At the outset, typical squabbles among all the forces opposed to New France created a terrible threat. London itself could not agree on a master strategy until William Pitt rose head and shoulders above all others, saw all, and ordered all. He recognized, as Parkman puts it, that the Seven Years' War "was a contest for maritime and colonial ascendency" (*Montcalm*, III, 247); and he planned accordingly. He promoted and supported able officers like Wolfe, Admiral Edward Boscawen, General Jeffrey Amherst, Brigadier John Forbes, Admiral Charles Saunders, and Brigadiers Robert Monckton, George Townshend, James Murray, John Prideaux, and William Haviland. As for Americans, one has, among many others, cool young Colonel George Washington, Lieutenant Colonel John Winslow, the Moravian missionary Christian Frederic Post, tough Major Israel Putnam, and the daring ranger Captain Robert Rogers.

Both sides had their failures too. Vaudreuil was a curse to New France, as were the commercial leeches whom he helped to grow rich. Although most of the regular French officers and men were resolute and obedient, Parkman probably overstates his thesis that French absolutism made it easier for French arms to prevail, at first, over the disorganized British and American forces fighting for liberty. Should the supposedly disciplined French army at Quebec have retreated, even when surprised, in the face of Wolfe's lightning attack? When the battle at the Heights of Abraham began, Wolfe commanded fewer than thirty-five hundred men. Montcalm, if obeyed, could have pushed forward twice that number of French, Canadians, and Indians in a counterattack. And after the fall of Quebec, should Lévis, admirable though he usually was, not have consummated his planned counterattack of that city, then occupied by the British?

After all, he had a force of more than eight thousand men, whereas Murray had barely three thousand fit for duty. Military failures too, because they had to be, were most of the native Canadians; for they were caught between two grinding forces, not merely in the Quebec area, where their homes were threatened with British fire if they fought beside Vaudreuil but where they faced summary execution if they did not, but also elsewhere, as in Acadia earlier. Parkman depicts the typical native Canadian of the time as necessarily helpless because he was priest-ridden, listless, and illiterate.

Nor were the British colonials universally bright and brave. At first, each colony was the scene of bickering between the indigenous population and the royal governor. Moreover, the separate colonies were jealous of one another and at first refused to unite against their common foe. To make matters worse, British officers regarded themselves as superior to the colonial troops, even after the butchering of Braddock and his confused redcoats should have taught all observers a lesson.

The most pathetic group of combatants may well have been the Indians. Semi-converted in some areas by the French, cheated part of the time by the *coureurs de bois* and other Frenchmen having more official status, rendered dependent upon European goods, coddled and bribed by Sir William Johnson, periodically enflamed by French brandy and New England rum, and persuaded by both sides to make war on their own kind, they were the real victims—along with their big woods, gorgeous waters, and waving plains.

For nature was destined to be a victim. No sooner were the St. Lawrence River and its rapids found and Lake Ontario, Lake Champlain, and Lake George explored than their shores were dotted with missions, trading posts, and forts, and their waters became military routes. The main use of the aggrieved forests in eighteenth-century America was to make forts, palisades, fascines, and abatis, which were then splintered by enemy artillery or, if captured intact, burned. Braddock sacrificed millions of trees to hack a road toward Pittsburgh, only to die at the end of it. And, to prevent surprise, both sides habitually cleared all the timber for acres around their wretched wooden forts.[4] Parkman uses a thrilling little image drawn from nature to describe the rapids of the St. Lawrence which Amherst encountered during his 1760 descent to Montreal: ". . . the reckless surges dashed and bounded in the sun, beautiful and terrible as young tigers at play" (III, 217). Everyone knows that when ruthless men see tigers, at play or otherwise, they must kill or capture them.

Montcalm and Wolfe is the crowning achievement of Parkman's life of research. The historian shows great competence in handling his abundant sources. In the preface, Parkman reports that "The papers copied for the present work in France alone exceed six thousand folio pages . . . additional and supplementary to the 'Paris Documents' procured for the State of New York under the agency of Mr. [John Romeyn] Brodhead. The copies made in England form ten volumes, besides many English documents consulted in the original manuscript. Great numbers of autograph letters, diaries, and other writings of persons engaged in the war have also been examined on this side of the Atlantic." He then explains that he copied all of Montcalm's letters to his family and studied the Montcalm-Bourlamaque correspondence. Concerning the mass of "books, pamphlets, contemporary newspapers, and other publications relating to the American part of the Seven Years' War," he adds that "nothing in it of much consequence has escaped me." Finally, he explains that he personally visited "every spot where events of any importance in connection with the contest took place, and . . . observed with attention such scenes and persons as might help to illustrate those I meant to describe. In short [he concludes], the subject has been studied as much from life and in the open air as at the library table" (I, vii-viii, ix).

Most of what Parkman says in this long work is carefully documented with hundreds of footnotes. In addition, at the end of several of the more controversial chapters he appends general bibliographical footnote-essays. On top of all this documentation, he has eleven appendices, often extensive, in which he presents detailed evidence in support of conclusions which might otherwise be seriously questioned. He does not hesitate to state his preference for certain sources over others. But so true is the ring of his authoritative voice that the reader is habitually confident that the historian has consulted everything available for making a judgment.

However, Parkman did not pronounce the last word on every issue. In fact, one modern authority on the subject of Wolfe and

Montcalm is critical of Parkman's work, sometimes on the basis of material unavailable in the 1880's, for minimizing the part the Indians played in the conflict, for abusing British General James Abercromby (nicknamed Mrs. Nabbycromby by his own men), for suggesting that Rogers might once have been a smuggler and a forger, for slurring over Admiral Saunders, and for hero-worshiping Wolfe.[5] All the same, ever since its publication, *Montcalm and Wolfe* has been not only a thrilling narrative but also a document of historical validity.

The work is divided into thirty-two chapters. The first, called "The Combatants," begins in the Old World and contrasts the energetic if inchoate forces for liberty in England with those in Europe, which is stagnating in war. Then Parkman quickly changes the scene to the New World, contested for by France and England in the Ohio Valley, in Acadia, and along the western borders of Pennsylvania and Virginia, but especially around Lake Ontario, Lake George, and Lake Champlain, and along the St. Lawrence (Chapters II-VIII). The main body of the entire history (Chapters IX-XXX) concerns this heartland of waters and forests northeast of Pittsburgh and southwest of Nova Scotia. After the "Fall of Quebec" (Chapter XXVIII) and the "Fall of Canada" (Chapter XXX), Parkman shifts the scene with epic symmetry back to Europe for "The Peace of Paris" (Chapter XXXI) and "Conclusion" (Chapter XXXII).

A list of the key chapters amounts almost to a summary of the main historical events: Chapter IX, "1755, Dieskau" (Crown Point); Chapter XII, "1756, Oswego"; Chapter XX, "1758, Ticonderoga"; Chapter XXI, "1758, Fort Frontenac" (at the northern tip of Lake Ontario); "Chapter XXII, "1758, Fort Duquesne" (the farthest west of the important battles); Chapter XXVI, "1759, Amherst, Niagara"; Chapter XXVII, "1759, The Heights of Abraham"; Chapter XXVIII, "1759, Fall of Quebec"; Chapter XXIX, "1759, 1760, Sainte-Foy" (five miles from Quebec); and Chapter XXX, "1760, Fall of Canada," followed by the peace treaty.

At first, the battles went mostly in favor of the French, through Chapter XV, which ends with the gruesome Fort William Henry massacre. Thereafter, the French went steadily down, until, with the loss of Quebec, all was doomed. In fact, if Amherst, following the capture of Ticonderoga in July, 1759, had pushed northeast immediately, he might have saved Wolfe many losses—and all of his glory. Parkman writes critically of Amherst: "Well pleased, he took possession of the deserted fort [Crown Point], and, in the animation of success, thought for a moment of keeping the promise he had given to Pitt [on June 19] 'to make an irruption into Canada with the utmost vigor and despatch.' Wolfe, his brother in arms and his friend, was battling with the impossible under the rocks of Quebec, and every motive, public and private, impelled Amherst to push to his relief, not counting costs, or balancing risks too nicely" (III, 82). But instead of doing so, Amherst built some new forts where he sat; sent out parties to explore nearby rivers, creeks, and bays; and even started some new roads. Parkman observes with typical sarcasm: "His industry was untiring; a great deal of useful work was done; but the essential task of making a diversion to aid the army of Wolfe was needlessly postponed" (III, 83).

Only after the fall of Quebec, which cost Wolfe his life, did Amherst in the spring of 1760 put his plan into action; but much of it might have succeeded the previous autumn. The plan was to enter Canada from three directions, with Murray ascending the St. Lawrence from Quebec, with Haviland going north from Lake Champlain, and with Amherst himself going down the St. Lawrence from Lake Ontario. The plan succeeded. Murray advanced with almost twenty-five hundred men past a body of troops at Three Rivers, ignoring that post because he knew that, if Montreal fell, Three Rivers would share its fate. In other words, Brigadier Murray was a better tactician than his commanding general. Haviland was soon in contact with Murray. Meanwhile, Amherst was making sluggish progress to the dangerous rapids southeast of Lake St. Louis, where he lost more than eighty men by drowning and almost fifty boats. But by September, 1760, his ponderous force was camped at the walls of Montreal. It was all over but for the signing of Amherst's deliberately severe terms by the properly humiliated Vaudreuil.

Parkman's matchless book has an almost diagrammable symmetry. In spite of the fact that it is in three volumes in many old editions, it really falls into an introductory section and into four roughly equal parts, at the end of each of which is a background chapter. Chapters I-III explain the historical situation and discuss Céloron de Bienville's unsuccessful mission into the Ohio Valley to woo turncoat Indian allies away from trade with the British.

Chapters IV-X take up peripheral battle zones—Acadia, the sources of the Ohio River, western Pennsylvania,[6] Crown Point, and Niagara. Chapters XII-XVII begin with Montcalm's stunning victory at Oswego, continue with his capture of Fort William Henry, and end with a dismal picture of civil corruption in Quebec—which helped spell ruin for the French cause. Chapters XIX-XXIII start with a depiction of the first important English victory, at Louisbourg in 1758, include the last important French military success, at Ticonderoga (also in 1758), and conclude with a picture of New France on the brink of ruin. The fourth and final part, Chapters XXV-XXXII, is the most unified of all; and it dramatically narrates the fall of Quebec, including its prelude and consequences.[7]

Intercalary Chapters XI, XVIII, and XXIV, as well as the first chapter and the last two, provide details of the gigantic historical backdrop against which the main drama is played out. To avoid monotony, Parkman sees that no sequence of more than three successive chapters deals with any one topical unit.[8] The goriest sequence occurs in Chapters V-VII; the most thrilling, in Chapters XXVII and XXVIII, during which Wolfe's morale is symbolized first by the bottom of Montmorency Falls and then the Heights of Abraham to which the hero finally climbs.

Parkman begins by suggesting that France was doomed from the beginning, because of the stupidities of King Louis XV, of whom he writes devastatingly:

> Her [France's] manifold ills were summed up in the King. Since the Valois, she had had no monarch so worthless. He did not want understanding, still less the graces of person. In his youth the people called him the "Well-beloved;" but by the middle of the century they so detested him that he dared not pass through Paris, lest the mob should execrate him. He had not the vigor of the true tyrant; but his languor, his hatred of all effort, his profound selfishness, his listless disregard of public duty, and his effeminate libertinism, mixed with superstitious devotion, made him no less a national curse. (I, 16–17)

Such a man's policies inevitably bred corruption not merely at Versailles and elsewhere in France but also in Quebec, Montreal, and other Canadian governmental, religious, and commercial centers. Therefore, a loyal and resourceful hero like Montcalm was also doomed.

About midway in *Montcalm and Wolfe*, just after a chapter devoted to Bigot, one of the most corrupt Canadian officials, Parkman introduces Pitt, whom next to Wolfe himself the historian most reveres among his parade of personages here. Pitt merits tremendous praise, which includes this stirring tribute: "England hailed with one acclaim the undaunted leader who asked for no reward but the honor of serving her. The hour had found the man. For the next four years [1757–60] this imposing figure towers supreme in British history" (II, 247).

Sadly, at the end of his work, Parkman must bring in George III, who became king of England late in 1760 and who was "a mirror of domestic virtues, conscientious, obstinate, narrow. . . . His ruling passion [Parkman goes on] was the establishment and increase of his own authority. He disliked Pitt, the representative of the people. He was at heart averse to a war, the continuance of which would make the Great Commoner necessary, and therefore powerful, and he wished for a peace that would give free scope to his schemes for strengthening the [royal] prerogative" (III, 237–38). Pitt's enemies united, a peace party grew, and diplomatic machinery was set in motion to end the war. Certain far-seeing Englishmen asserted that with France removed as a scapegoat, thereby exposing British-American differences, the colonies might soon wish to throw off the British yoke. But all of that would be another chapter of history which Parkman had neither the desire nor the strength to write.

The title *Montcalm and Wolfe* suggests that once again Parkman develops his historical narrative by a series of monumental contrasts. The two titular heroes had much in common, obviously, but they represented diametrically opposed ways of life. Yet the historian does not take the easy way of showing that the climax of his vast drama is simply the clash of France and England at the rock of Quebec. As has been seen, France was split, New France was split, and both England and the British colonies in the New World were at odds. Nor did the poor Indians know for certain where their loyalties should lie. And nature was sundered too by the warring factions. On a couple of occasions, Parkman romantically suggests a division almost cosmic, with beneficent nature on one side and evil man on the other. Of a colonial army chaplain briefly off duty, one reads that ". . . he had leisure to reflect on the contrasted works of Providence and man,—the bright lake [Lake George] basking amid its mountains, a dream of wilderness beauty, and the swarms of harsh humanity on the shore beside him, with their passions, discords, and miseries." Later, one reads that the energetic soldiers under Forbes at Rays-town (now Bedford, Pennsylvania) "labored at throwing up in-trenchments and palisades, while around stood the silent moun-tains in their mantles of green" (II, 328, 341).

The style of *Montcalm and Wolfe* is notable for its many pre-dictable touches of humor, its vivid pictorial effects, several apt figures of speech, a few terse epithets, and a few—very few—instances of awkwardness. Targets of Parkman's barbs include New England clergymen, Parliamentary corruption, illiteracy in Virginia, Indian sexual and alcoholic mores, irrationality in Ro-man Catholicism, colonial governors, military "gasconade" (a busy word here), and the Quaker policy of non-violence. Two deadly examples must suffice. Of hated Vaudreuil one reads that "He was courageous, except in the immediate presence of danger, and failed only when the crisis came" (III, 54). And of Madame Pompadour, for whom Parkman's contempt is boundless, one reads that ". . . her fortitude was perfect in bearing the sufferings of others and defying dangers that could not touch her" (II, 250).

Of Parkman's painterly effects, it is sufficient to mention in passing that in *Montcalm and Wolfe* one finds unforgettable pictures of such places and events as Oswego, Beauséjour, Brad-dock's tragic march, the typical New England soldier, winters in Canada, stern Louisbourg under siege, autumn in western Penn-sylvania, and fireships at night on the St. Lawrence.

Most of Parkman's best similes and metaphors here are drawn again from the world of nature. The Duke of Newcastle is likened to a toadstool flourishing in impure Whig soil; Indians, to an ineradicable nest of hornets and to wide-jawed tigers; corrupt Canadian officials, to jackals; a wooden breakwork, to a porcu-pine. Making use of other natural figures, Parkman sees fallen trees in Oswego marshes as the "bones of drowned mammoths, thrusting lank, white limbs above the sullen water" (II, 7); and he describes December winds in Canada as "piercing blasts that scorch the cheek like a firebrand" (III, 178). An imaginative analogy, somewhat Shakespearean in tone, vivifies his notion of Pitt's influence: "As Nature, languishing in chill vapors and dull smothering fogs, revives at the touch of the sun, so did England spring into fresh life under the kindling influence of one great man" (II, 252). Wolfe is beautifully praised, for Parkman writes of the unsleepingly steady purpose of the intrepid British general, who was dangerously sick in August, 1759: "But as the needle, though quivering, points always to the pole, so, through torment and languor and the heats of fever, the mind of Wolfe dwelt on the capture of Quebec" (III, 109).

Parkman also creates several choice epithets. Braddock is the "gallant bulldog" (I, 228). Gaudily attired New Jersey provincials are "gorgeous warriors" (II, 6). The feudal Penn family is "a pestilent anomaly" (II, 24). Quakers are "pacific sectaries" (II, 33). Louis XV is "the pampered Sardanapalus" (II, 249). Brave Brigadier Lord Howe is "this Lycurgus of the camp" (II, 297). Redskin torturers of tough Israel Putnam are even "tawny Philistines" (II, 334).

Grammatical and syntactical irregularities continue to appear, though rarely in a bothersome manner. More than thirty of Parkman's odd negatives appear, of which this one is the oddest: ". . . seeming ingratitude not wholly unprovoked" (II, 12). Of the four or five dangling modifiers to be found, the following is the most startling: "Then, by driving the enemy from Niagara, securing that important pass, and thus cutting off the communication between Canada and her interior dependencies, all the French posts in the West would die of inanition" (I, 199–200). Pronominal use is occasionally so careless that the reader is sometimes genuinely puzzled, as in this instance: "Yet the [French] fireships did no other harm than burning alive one of their own captains and six or seven of his sailors who failed to escape in their boats. Some of them ran ashore before reaching the [British] fleet." And "The French on the ridge had formed themselves into three bodies . . . Two field-pieces, which had been dragged up the heights at Anse du Foulon, fired on them with grape-shot, and the troops, rising from the ground, prepared to receive them. In a few minutes more they were in motion . . ." (III, 53, 139).

As one should expect by now, Parkman reveals much of himself in *Montcalm and Wolfe*. He admires Wolfe, Pitt, Montcalm, and Lévis; and he also has words of praise for other brave men on both sides who did their work well. Perhaps the most dramatically introduced *beau idéal* in all of Parkman, if only because one is aware of his greatness, is the young colonial officer George Washington when he arrived at the wretched French outpost of Fort Le Boeuf, late in 1753,

> . . . when, just after sunset on the eleventh of December, a tall youth came out of the forest on horseback, attended by a companion much older and rougher than himself, and followed by several Indians and four or five white men with pack-horses. Officers from the fort went out to meet the strangers. . . . On the next day the young leader . . . had an interview with the commandant, and gave him a letter. . . . [Legardeur de] Saint-Pierre and the officer next in rank . . . took it to another room to study it at their ease; and in it, all unconsciously, they read a name destined to stand one of the noblest in the annals of mankind; for it introduced Major George Washington, Adjutant-General of the Virginia militia. (I, 137)

Parkman is rarely critical of the Jesuits in this work, probably because they played little part in the military struggles recounted here. He does have one unforgivably vicious footnote, however, about Father Roubaud, missionary to the Abenakis: "The long letter of the Jesuit Roubaud . . . gives a remarkably vivid account of what he saw. He was an intelligent person, who may be trusted where he has no motive for lying" (II, 202). In addition, Parkman offers one comprehensively anti-Catholic criticism of French-Canadians at the end of the whole work: "Civil liberty was given them by the British sword; but the conqueror left their religious system untouched, and through it they have imposed upon themselves a weight of ecclesiastical tutelage that finds few equals in the most Catholic countries of Europe. Such guardianship is not without certain advantages . . . but it is fatal to mental robustness and moral courage; and if French Canada would fulfil its aspirations it must cease to be one of the most priest-ridden communities of the modern world" (III, 259).

In summary, it is likely that Parkman excessively admired Wolfe because both the historian and the general ignored wasting illness to achieve greatness. Parkman's vision was essentially tragic. In one of the most remarkable passages in the entire sweep of his writings, one finds this Shakespearean view of military success: "On the night after the battle [of Lake George, 1755] the yeomen warriors felt the truth of the saying that, next to defeat, the saddest thing is victory. Comrades and friends by scores lay scattered through the forest. . . ." (I, 322). In Parkman, the tragic view and the bitingly ironic were united; perhaps for this reason he often approvingly quotes the wicked barbs of Horace Walpole, one of his favorite commentators. Above the tragic and ironic views, however, Parkman ultimately reveals a Hardy-like cosmic position. Too long to quote in full but begging to be noticed is the stunning passage which opens Chapter XIV. "Spring came at last, and the Dutch burghers of Albany heard, faint from the far height, the clamor of the wild fowl, streaming in long files northward to their summer home." One then follows "the aerial travellers" far above "the seat of war [which] lay spread beneath them like a map" as they fly over the Hudson River, past the ugly forts, and then over Lake George, Ticonderoga, Lake Champlain, with the Adirondacks on the left and the Green Mountains to the right, and beyond them "the White Mountains throned in savage solitude," and then along the St. Lawrence to Montreal. "Here we leave them, to build their nests and hatch their brood among the fens of the lonely North" (II, 140, 141). The entire passage is a thrilling overview, from a point of view almost Olympian, of the military map of most of the Seven Years' War, and it is one of Parkman's most splendid rhetorical achievements.[9]

III   A Half-Century of Conflict

When read after *Montcalm and Wolfe*, *A Half-Century of Conflict* (1892) is probably the most unsatisfactory of Parkman's historical works. The conclusion seems inevitable that the historian was aging and fatigued, for *A Half-Century of Conflict* is a long, ill-organized prologue to *Montcalm and Wolfe*, which was the crowning work of his professional career. *A Half-Century of Conflict* is necessary since it fills the historical gap between *Frontenac* and *Montcalm and Wolfe*, but that period is geographically and chronologically a sprawling one which resists unifying.

A chronological summary of major events and of the numbers of the chapters discussing them would be too protracted, but it would graphically indicate the confusing array of material handled in this work. The earliest event discussed is the 1683 visit of Le Sueur to the Sioux of Minnesota, taken up in Chapter XV. Another pre-eighteenth-century event, Antoine de la Mothe-

Cadillac's assumption of command at Michilimackinac in 1694,
is treated in Chapter II. Two 1700 events mentioned are Le
Moyne d'Iberville's colonizing Biloxi and Le Sueur's exploration
of Louisiana, discussed in Chapters XIII and XV. Events of 1704
are discussed in Chapters III, IV, and VII, the last of which also
narrates a 1710 military victory for New England forces. The
busy year of 1720 figures in Chapters IX, XVI, and XVII; however, the only event which occurred precisely a decade later and
is treated by Parkman is mentioned in Chapter XIV, and the only
1740 event, in Chapter XIII. The year 1724 figures in four different chapters (X, XI, XIII, and XV). No happenings in the following years are mentioned: 1701–02, 1706, 1715, 1718, 1723,
1729, 1733–37, 1741, 1743, and 1748–49.

   This information, however, is somewhat misleading and unfair.
The major and minor events discussed in *A Half-Century of
Conflict* are heterogeneous and are therefore difficult to reduce to
order. Parkman does what he can, and the result is that Chapters
I-III, mostly panoramic background, show the consequences in
America of Queen Anne's War, 1703–13 (or, as it was called in
Europe, "The War of the Spanish Succession"). Chapters IV and
V describe the agony of Massachusetts frontiersmen. The next
four chapters (VI-IX) shift to Acadia. Chapters X-XIII are
separate units, dealing with Father Sebastien Rale, Lovewell's
Fight, the Outagamies (as does Chapter XIV), and Louisiana. In
Chapters XV and XVI, Parkman moves west to discuss early
French explorations. Realizing that these chapters have little to
do with the fifty years of conflict, the nominal subject of his work
here, Parkman in Chapter XVII discusses the rival claims of England and France to portions of the New World. He then devotes
the heart of his book, Chapters XVIII-XXII, to a brilliant nar-
ration and analysis of the daring scheme of bold New Englanders
to lay siege to Louisbourg, which William Pepperrell and Commander Peter Warren took in 1745 and held, mainly because of
misfortunes besetting the Duc d'Anville and his fleet. The last
two chapters (XXIII and XXIV) are devoted first to the tentative
successes of Governor Clinton of New York and Sir William
Johnson in the face of bickering among their constituencies, and
then to the military success of Rigaud [10] in his attack on Fort
Massachusetts in 1746.

Parkman necessarily skips about, giving the reader an anthology of disparate historical essays [11] which prove that sooner or later the French and British must clash on a grand scale. Over and over in *A Half-Century of Conflict,* Parkman offers comments which combine to whisper to the reader, "Wait and soon I will let you read *Montcalm and Wolfe,* which for the sake of historical continuity should be read after the present penultimate work."

As usual, Parkman builds his argument on a series of conflicts. When one considers the impediments thrown in the way of each contesting party, it is a wonder that the Indians are not still in control of their ancestral lands. The Jesuits opposed the French army and also the mild Récollet friars. Governor Joseph Dudley of Massachusetts contended with native Puritans. Whigs and Tories rankled each other in England. Boston was at loggerheads with London. Canada stirred periodically for more liberty. New Yorkers never supported their governors properly. Massachusetts disputed with New Hampshire, Rhode Island, and what is now Maine. The strategic harmony of Pepperrell and Warren was only intermittent. The Dutch north of Fort Massachusetts loved their British neighbors so little that they evacuated the region without warning them of Rigaud's advance.

Fortunately for the future of the Americans, the Indians were also at mortal odds. Of the Five Nations, the Senecas were generally loyal to the French while the Mohawks usually drank with Johnson and sometimes fought beside him. The French had Huron and other Indian allies to help them drive out the Outagamies. In the South and the West, the Choctaws opposed both the Natchez Indians and the Chickasaws, while the Sioux remained the Snakes' foes.

Parkman again provides a quota of humor, but here it seems a little tired, especially in the second half of the work. He pokes fun once more at the non-apostolic Jesuits. He enjoys the racy language of La Mothe-Cadillac's reports to Versailles. He wrings mordant humor out of Indian atrocities, as, for example, when he describes the torture of a white infant: ". . . the Indians hastened its death by throwing hot coals into its mouth when it cried" (*Conflict,* I, 49). Major Benjamin Church was so fat that, while on the trail, "he kept a stout sergeant by him to hoist him over fallen trees" (I, 121). Parkman pokes fun at such traditional authorities as Cotton Mather, Samuel Sewall, and Ben Franklin. He writes that Sewall had an "aged, matronly countenance," that by the 1720's he was "perhaps touched with dotage," and that on one occasion "He rose from his seat with long locks, limp and white, drooping from under his black skull-cap,—for he abhorred a wig as a sign of backsliding,—and in a voice of quavering solemnity spoke . . ." (I, 241). Moreover, Parkman is always ready to ridicule his own New England forebears, including Pepperrell's raw-boned volunteers, Governor William Shirley of Massachusetts, and clergymen out of place in their part-time capacity as chaplains.[12]

A *Half-Century of Conflict* has few memorable pictorial effects. It almost seems as though Parkman were hastening to assemble his notes into as efficient a form as possible, without elaborate literary flourishes. One does find a vivid description of a frontier wedding at Deerfield, a chilly picture of winter in Lovewell territory, a sketch from memory of hot prairies quivering under the sultry sun, the forbidding coastline of Chibucto (now Halifax) which oppressed poor D'Anville, and the stern environs of Fort Massachusetts.

Imagery here is never surprising. Indians are still wildcats, wasps, wolves, cougars, firebrands, and dogs. War is still fire, and the Jesuits still kindle hate and enflame their followers. Louis XIV is still a sun figure. And once, harking back to *Jesuits*, Parkman describes in these familiar terms the oppressiveness of an Indian lodge which sheltered the La Vérendrye party in the West: ". . . they could pass a winter endurable to Indians, though smoke, filth, vermin, bad air, the crowd, and the total absence of privacy, would make it a purgatory to any civilized white man" (II, 30–31).

Parkman could rarely write anything without revealing a good deal about himself. In *A Half-Century of Conflict* he gives one, almost as an *ave atque vale*, several charming personal notes. Thus, the tells that, when he was a boy, he saw at his father's house in Boston one of the grandsons of Eunice Williams, who was kidnaped by Indians from Deerfield and became a squaw. In the 1830's, he saw a war dance by a party of visiting Outagamies on the Boston Common. When he describes the scouting habits of the Bow Indians who are trying to avoid their enemies the Snakes, he adds in a footnote, "At least this was done by a band of Sioux with whom the writer once traversed a part of the country ranged by these same Snakes . . ." (II, 31). His longest personal digression is an excusable but unnecessary one in which he describes a house near Pepperrell's Kittery Point mansion: "Not far distant is another noted relic of colonial times, the not less spacious mansion built by the disappointed [Benning] Wentworth [who wanted to be commander-in-chief in the 1745 attack on Louisbourg] at Little Harbor. I write these lines [Parkman continues dreamily] at a window of this curious old house, and before me spreads the scene familiar to Pepperrell from childhood" (II, 73).

Early in the work, the sturdy old historian dramatically suggests that all of life, whether vegetable, savage, military, political, or—one might add—professional, is a Darwinian struggle. The passage includes the following notable sentence: "This waste of savage vegetation [along the Maine seaboard] survives, in some part, to this day, with the same prodigality of vital force, the same struggle for existence and mutual havoc that mark all organized beings, from men to mushrooms" (I, 34).[13]

Several weaknesses in *A Half-Century of Conflict* require brief mention. Many chapters have too many incidents. Numerous events are too remote from the experience or common knowledge of any reader but the most ardent specialist. The work was probably composed piecemeal, as is suggested by a few glaring repetitions. For example: "The villages [of Hurons and Ottawas at Michilimackinac] . . . were surrounded by a common enclosure of triple palisades, which, with the addition of loopholes for musketry, were precisely like those seen by Cartier at Hochelaga, and by Champlain in the Onondaga country. The dwellings which these defences enclosed were also after the old Huron-Iroquois pattern,—those long arched structures covered with bark which Brébeuf found by the shores of Matchedash Bay, and Jogues on the banks of the Mohawk." Ten chapters later one reads that "The village of the Pottawattamies was close to the French fort [Detroit]; that of the Hurons was not far distant, by the edge of the river. Their houses were those structures of bark, 'very high, very long, and arched like garden arbors,' which were common to all the tribes of Iroquois stock, and both villages were enclosed by strong double or triple stockades, such as Cartier had found at Hochelaga, and Champlain in the Onondaga country" (I, 18,

279). The curious "not without" and "no little" constructions persist. Of the thirty in *A Half-Century of Conflict*, the following triple negative is the oddest: "The French court approved the plan, though not without distrust" (I, 104). Danglers have almost disappeared. Of the four here, the most colorfully blatant is this: "After drifting for a considerable distance, the wind blew him ashore" (I, 266).[14]

If *A Half-Century of Conflict* is the weakest of Parkman's historical efforts, it still has the virtue of completing a noble plan. America had its titanic half-century of conflict before the Seven Years' War. The historian of that agony, and of its vast prologue as well, had also his half-century of personal conflict. He had weathered the storms of sickness and personal misfortune, and his epic history was complete.

CHAPTER 7

Conclusion

FRANCIS PARKMAN IS a timeless example. He was a great historian, a fine nineteenth-century literary artist, and a brave man. For nearly half a century, he assembled primary source materials, read deeply in his subject, went to distant archives and to historic sites important to his work, and painstakingly wrote volume after volume until he had completed his entire historical project. A few months later, he died at the age of three score and ten.

Some critics have found fault with the historical writings of Parkman. They say that he overemphasized his main thesis concerning the inevitability of the progress of liberty-loving Protestantism; that he failed to stress the history of ideas, especially political ones, and did not understand the economic and sociological conditions of the epochs about which he wrote; that he had an anticlerical bias and a prejudice against the French; that he was an élitist with an ingrained distrust of democracy and the common man; and that he built his historical accounts around great white men too exclusively and did not properly treat their enemy the Indian.[1] Others express fear that his subject was too vast to be presented definitively, that his mode and tone dangerously appealed to unrealistic readers, and that he used details excessively and had a generally poor prose style.[2]

Most experts, however, now say that only Henry Adams as an American historian rivals Parkman in charm, force, and durability. Together they divide historiographical laurels between them —Parkman, for being the greatest literary and Romantic historian; Adams, for being the best scientific one.[3] By comparison with Parkman, other nineteenth-century American historians—for example, William Hickling Prescott, George Bancroft, and John Lothrop Motley—seem stiff and dated. Reading their work is often more a chore than a pleasure, whereas Parkman has the excitement of good fiction; in fact, his contemporaries often compared his works favorably to those of Sir Walter Scott, Washington Irving, and James Fenimore Cooper.

Modern critics praise many specific elements in Parkman. They rightly note that he immersed himself in the spirit of his subject, was unusually familiar with the geography of locales which figure in his histories, and in general revealed fine powers of observation.[4] Almost without exception, commentators praise him for his meticulous, energetic, imaginative, and honest use of source material—and in an age when such was not universally the case.[5] Innumerable critics in our century have remarked favorably upon many aspects of his captivating style.[6] But the old historian would probably have relished most the following modern judgments: Joe Patterson Smith says that he was impartial in his handling of both the French and the British; Russel B. Nye admires his treatment of Indians; Michael Kraus lauds his generosity in cooperating with other historians of his time; and Harvey Wish judges him to be highly influential on the latter frontier school of historiography.[7]

More comprehensively, Samuel Eliot Morison and Henry Steele Commager define Parkman's sweeping history of the Anglo-French conflict in the New World as ". . . the most impressive achievement of the age of historical romanticism."[8] Kraus, bridling at the idea of categorizing him in that manner, remarks that "In spirit Francis Parkman belongs to the romantic school of historians with their dramatic presentation of adventurous deeds, and yet his volumes have been so acceptable to the generations who have followed that his place is more than that of a transitional figure."[9] James Truslow Adams simply calls him the "Greatest of all"[10] American historians.

Parkman viewed the clash of France and England in North America as complex and dramatic. The prize was enormous—nothing less than the New World. He also knew that the vast continent was never to be a new Eden, because there could never be a new Adam. The historian recognized and exposed imperfections even in his heroes—Champlain, La Salle, Frontenac, Wolfe, and Pontiac, among others. Furthermore, he knew that nature was an ever-changing challenge to the spirit of man, but that it was also dualistic and often harshly destructive of man's noblest hopes. All the same, he devoutly loved the heroic gesture against the enigmatic, panoramic backdrop. So he focused his histories not usually upon the American forest, the doom of which he said was their subject, but upon the heroes who both loved and exploited that forest.

The resulting story has the sweep and thrill of a prose epic of which France and England in America are its subject. Parkman invites his readers to share in the action, for his own sense of vicarious participation results in a compelling style. He sets his stages dramatically by introducing his personages into vivid, colorful action. He suspensefully varies his pace, by alternating the long view with the close-up scene, with dialogue-like quotation, by shifts of locale. He develops century-long counterpoints, because he sees duality in all things.

⁓Parkman had curiously mixed attitudes. He generally combined reactionary responses to social and political issues of his times with forward-looking stylistic elements. Thus, he wrote of patriotism in the Civil War with the zeal of a mailed crusader. He was austerely patrician in his dislike of the emerging unwashed masses. He deplored the new-fangled notions of universal suffrage, and he thought that a good woman's place was in the home. He subscribed to the old-fashioned Puritan ethic that in work lies one's salvation. Simultaneously, he was ahead of his co-workers methodologically and stylistically. Anyone who builds on Bryon, Scott, and Cooper is of course partly Romantic; but Parkman used many Realistic effects to enable his readers to experience the action instead of merely intellectually taking note of it. Dana did the same thing in *Two Years Before the Mast,* and Ernest Hemingway was to do it better later. But Parkman was the first American historian to render past events with such immediacy. Stylistically, he seems modern much of the time. He adopted a healthy, twentieth-century tone—that of vitalizing, wide-awake irony. He was aware of what shifting his point of view could do to enhance the impact of his account. His writing is above the winds of change. Perhaps he is not so great as Thucydides, Tacitus, Gibbon, or Macaulay; but he comes as close to them in stature as any American historian ever has.

Parkman loved the big woods, and in his youth he gloried in his fine health, horsemanship, and endurance. But for his neurotic sicknesses, the sources of which are still a mystery, he would have combined historical and political writing with a life of

rugged action. It is no accident that Theodore Roosevelt admired
Parkman tremendously. If circumstances had been different, Parkman would undoubtedly have been a cavalry officer in the Union
Army during the Civil War; then, if he had survived, he might
have continued to combine rough, combative, outdoor life with
literary comment on its delights, as did Hemingway. But "the
Enemy," as Parkman called his maladies, prevented this course
of action; and the historical writing which he initially estimated
might take him two decades consumed his last forty-five years.

In spite of his love of the outdoors, in spite of crippling sicknesses, and in spite of the diversity of his materials, Parkman
combined the often inharmonious elements of his life with his
diverse researches to make a unit. If he could not be a woodsman or a soldier, he could write about the forest and war. When
he was too sick either to travel or to read and write, he sat,
listened, and thought. When he was better, he made up for lost
time by furious work. He traveled widely—north a short distance,
west far past the Mississippi River, and south to Florida—and he
read widely about events in Canada, along the Eastern American
seaboard, in Southeastern America, and down the Ohio and
Mississippi valleys. This jumble of events he molded and pressed
into generally unified shape. His histories, from *Pioneers* to *Pontiac,* tell one story, Moreover, they reflect his heroic personality,
as do his other literary efforts as well.

Finally, it may be validly said that Francis Parkman's dream
in November, 1893, of shooting the shaggy bear in the vast American forest shapes itself into a comprehensive symbol of his life.
Parkman grew strong through search and struggle. He went out
to meet the enemy, which he revered, defeated it, and blended
with it. The forest, the strong creatures ranging it, and the lover
and voice of it—all merged.

Notes and References

Chapter One

1. Mason Wade, *Francis Parkman* (New York, 1942), p. 443.
2. Charles Haight Farnham, *A Life of Francis Parkman* (Boston, 1900), pp. 1–2; Henry Dwight Sedgwick, *Francis Parkman* (Boston, 1904), pp. 12–17.
3. Farnham, *Parkman*, p. 2; Wade, *Parkman*, pp. 6–7; Howard Doughty, *Francis Parkman* (New York, 1962), pp. 2–3. Interestingly, Edward Brooks, who was thus Parkman's great-grandfather, was also the grandfather of Henry and Brooks Adams.
4. Quoted in Farnham, *Parkman*, p. 7.
5. Wade, *Parkman*, p. 380.
6. Doughty, *Parkman*, pp. 284–85. Parkman also revered his Lizzie, to whom he wrote (*Letters*, II, 249) late in life: "You are the beau ideal of sisterhood; of which I am always affectionately conscious, though I do not say much."
7. Sedgwick, *Parkman*, p. 203; Samuel Eliot Morison, ed., *The Parkman Reader* (Boston, 1955), p. 7; Wilbur R. Jacobs, ed., *Letters*, I, 173–74 n.
8. *Francis Parkman*, ed. Wilbur L. Schramm (New York, 1938), p. 11; Wade, *Parkman*, p. 324.
9. I owe this provocative comparison between Parkman and Henry Adams to Doughty, *Parkman*, p. 15.
10. Wade, *Parkman*, p. 8; Doughty, *Parkman*, p. 13. The maternal grandfather's estate is translated into the country home of Colonel Leslie in Parkman's novel (see *Morton*, pp. 132–41, and elsewhere).
11. *Parkman*, ed. Schramm, p. 13.
12. *Ibid.*, p. 4. The Jesuit Pierre Biard's *Memoirs* are also written in the third person. La Salle similarly refers to himself, as does the racy Antoine de la Mothe-Cadillac (see *Pioneers*, II, 141; *La Salle*, I, 32, 123; and *Conflict*, I, 24).
13. Sedgwick, *Parkman*, p. 25.
14. *Parkman*, ed. Schramm, p. 4.
15. Sedgwick, *Parkman*, pp. 23, 26.
16. Quoted in *ibid.*, p. 26.

17. Wade, *Parkman*, pp. 3–75, astutely suggests this head-heart synthesizing which occurred in Parkman's youth by calling his first chapters "The making of a Boston Brahmin" and "The Making of a Woodsman."

18. Sedgwick, *Parkman*, p. 18; Wade, *Parkman*, p. 12. For background information on Harvard at this time, see Samuel Eliot Morison, *Three Centuries of Harvard* (Cambridge, 1936), pp. 246–72.

19. Wade, *Parkman*, pp. 14–15.

20. Farnham, *Parkman*, p. 16; Wade, *Parkman*, p. 18; Morison, ed., *Parkman Reader*, p. 19; Doughty, *Parkman*, pp. 24–25.

21. Wade, *Parkman*, p. 18.

22. Doughty, *Parkman*, p. 26.

23. Edward Wheelwright, "Memoir of Francis Parkman," *Publications of the Colonial Society of Massachusetts*, I (1894), 322.

24. Sedgwick, *Parkman*, pp. 27–28.

25. *Parkman*, ed. Schramm, p. 4.

26. Quoted in Sedgwick, *Parkman*, pp. 328–29.

27. See *Morton*, pp. 37–38.

28. Morison, ed., *Parkman Reader*, p. 10.

29. The Notch House is near the present Crawford House and Willey House, in Crawford Notch State Park, New Hampshire. Willey House is the scene of Nathaniel Hawthorne's "Ambitious Guest." Crawford Notch figures in *Morton*, pp. 9–21, and is also mentioned by Parkman in *Conflict*, I, 256, as is the locale of Lovewell's Fight, 1725 (I, 260–68), which fight provides background for Hawthorne's story "Roger Malvin's Burial."

30. Parkman used elements of this climb (*Journals*, pp. 12–15) in his short story "The Scalp Hunter," *Knickerbocker Magazine*, XXV (1845), 297–303, in which the climber falls to his death.

31. See Doughty, *Parkman*, p. 106. Mason Wade, ed., *Journals*, p. 332, less persuasively sees Pamela Prentiss as a prototype of Edith Leslie, heroine of *Morton*. I disagree and feel that Parkman's wife Catherine is Edith's model.

32. This energetic man was Ralph Waldo Emerson's brother-in-law. He was a geologist, chemist, surveyor, and inventor of an early form of the telegraph, and of guncotton and anesthetics (see Wade, ed., *Journals*, p. 333; Doughty, *Parkman*, p. 37).

33. Wade, ed., *Journals*, p. 332, says that Thoreau may have met the Indian Annance at Northeast Carry, in northern Maine, in 1857.

34. Wade, *Parkman*, p. 36. Parkman writes of this region in *Conflict*, I, 37, 222.

35. One of the first camping goals of the hero of Parkman's novel is the "Margalloway" (see *Morton*, p. 18).

36. Later Parkman comprehensively criticized Slade thus: "Ap. 23

[1845] D.D.S. . . . cross, childish, self-willed. He likes people whom he can direct, and who always yield to his selfish will"; *Journals*, p. 296. This comment sounds partly like a criticism of young Parkman.

37. For a detailed analysis of Parkman's personality as it emerges from the pages of his first journal, consult Doughty, *Parkman*, pp. 33–47, which contains a brilliant summary of the experiences of young Parkman at this time, comments on his already incisive prose style, considers his Federalist attitude toward rude frontier personalities encountered in the forest, and suggests the depth of his love for the wilderness.

38. Parkman later wrote in a slightly fictionalized form about his experiences during this trip, in "Exploring the Magalloway," *Harper's Magazine*, XXIX (1864), 735–41. In it, White is renamed Brown. Later, when Parkman wrote *Morton* he obtained onomastic revenge on Henry White: he gave the blackmailer Speyer the first name of Henry and his villain Vinal the pseudonym of White (see *Morton*, pp. 169, 393).

39. Doughty, *Parkman*, p. 64.

40. Farnham, *Parkman*, p. 14; Sedgwick, *Parkman*, p. 56; Wade, *Parkman*, p. 76; Doughty, *Parkman*, p. 104.

41. Wade, ed., *Journals*, p. 87.

42. *Ibid.*, pp. 88–89, 352. What the Indians told Parkman he may have made minor use of in *Old Régime, Frontenac, Montcalm*, and *Conflict*, in all of which the Penobscots briefly appear.

43. See Wilbur L. Schramm, "Parkman's Novel," *American Literature*, IX (1937), 219–20, where Schramm prints parallel passages from Parkman's journal, as quoted by Sedgwick, and *Morton* to show close similarities.

44. This episode also went into *Morton* (see pp. 115–16).

45. Doughty, *Parkman*, p. 78. In his journal, Parkman does not go into the intellectual and emotional background of his decision to observe from the inside something of the monkish mode of life. But years later he did so, in "A Convent in Rome," *Harper's Magazine*, LXXXI (1890), 448–54. In a footnote to *Jesuits*, I, 197, he also mentions his Roman convent experience.

46. This area lies along the escape route of Vassall Morton from the Ehrenburg dungeon to Lake Como (see *Morton*, pp. 243–50).

Chapter Two

1. Thoreau somewhat similarly wrote in his essay "Walking" that "'. . . in Wildness is the preservation of the World"; *The Writings of Henry David Thoreau*, Manuscript Edition (20 vols., Boston and New York, 1906), V, 224.

2. Doughty, *Parkman*, p. 87.

3. Sedgwick, *Parkman,* p. 116. Sedgwick, p. 140, makes this comment, based on a study of Parkman's journal, which sometimes mixes elaborate American history notes and brief law-school schedules: "A poor pennyworth of law to an intolerable deal of border war; this affords a fair measure of the division of his interest between law and history."

4. Wade, ed., *Journals,* pp. 306, 375; Wade, *Parkman,* pp. 206, 208.

5. Parkman casts one scene of *Morton* at Niagara but makes almost no fictional use of the locale (see pp. 110–16).

6. Doughty, remembering Parkman in Rome and anticipating his trip to the Oregon Trail, comments as follows in *Parkman,* p. 112: "As he had taken himself to Rome for light on the life and spirit of Catholicism, so it was the more urgent to make contact with the Indian culture as a living organism. Here, it was evident, there was nothing for it but to push his quest beyond the frontier, to that West of the wild tribes, where on so many other counts, his inclinations had been pointing him." The region of the Onondagas figures in every one of Parkman's historical works. The Detroit area is of special importance in *Pontiac, La Salle,* and *Conflict.*

7. Sedgwick, *Parkman,* pp. 143–44; Wade, *Parkman,* p. 215.

8. Such a brief, almost shorthand note is typical of many in the 1846 journal and must have immeasurably aided Parkman when he wrote *Trail.*

9. Wade, ed., *Journals,* pp. 401–2, suspects that they were British spies heading for Oregon. However, in his Introduction to the Heritage Press edition of *The Oregon Trail* (New York, 1943), p. viii, Wade says that the Britishers "were out for sport and adventure."

10. Wade, ed., *Journals,* p. 620.

11. *Ibid.,* p. 621.

12. Parkman calls upon his memory of these observations to describe the 1742–43 La Vérendrye expedition, in *Conflict,* II, 23–35 *passim.*

13. Sedgwick, *Parkman,* p. 192.

14. Wade, *Parkman,* p. 295.

15. *Parkman,* ed. Schramm, pp. 8–9.

16. *Letters of Charles Eliot Norton, with Biographical Comment,* eds. Sarah Norton and M. A. DeWolfe Howe (Boston, 1913), I, 27–28; Kermit Vanderbilt, *Charles Eliot Norton: Apostle of Culture in a Democracy* (Cambridge, Massachusetts, 1959), pp. 32, 199. But for evidence that the two did not work closely together, see E. N. Feltskog, ed., *Trail,* pp. 60a–62a.

17. Jacobs, ed., *Letters,* I, 99–100 n.

18. Morison, ed., *Parkman Reader,* p. 17. Actually the heroine, Edith Leslie, is more like Catherine herself and is less like an Amazon

than is Fanny Euston, whom Vassall Morton neither loves nor marries.

19. Sedgwick, *Parkman*, p. 217.

20. Farnham, *Parkman*, p. 28; *Letters*, I, 126–27; Jacobs, ed., *Letters*, I, 97, 137 n.

21. Sedgwick, *Parkman*, pp. 223–26.

22. Farnham, *Parkman*, p. 27.

23. Quoted in Sedgwick, *Parkman*, p. 335.

24. Quoted in Jacobs, ed., *Letters*, I, xlv.

25. *Letters*, I, 138; Farnham, *Parkman*, p. 29.

26. Sedgwick, *Parkman*, p. 237. See also *Roses*, pp. 14–15, 24–26.

27. Farnham, *Parkman*, p. 31; Wade, *Parkman*, p. 350; Jacobs, ed., *Letters*, II, 88 n.

28. Van Wyck Brooks, *New England: Indian Summer* (New York, 1940), p. 183.

29. Farnham, *Parkman*, pp. 31, 32.

30. *Ibid.*, p. 33.

31. See the similar anti-democratic, Darwinian comment about forest plants in *Conflict*, I, 34–35.

32. Farnham, *Parkman*, p. 278.

33. Parkman's description of the North reads as if it could have been a model for Robinson Jeffers' mordant poem "Eagle Valor, Chicken Mind."

34. John Fiske, *A Century of Science and Other Essays* (Boston and New York, 1900), p. 222, implies a belief in this interpretation. See also Wade, *Parkman*, pp. 405–6, 445.

35. R. W. B. Lewis, *The American Adam* (Chicago, 1955), p. 170. Once, while they are hiking in New England, Vassall Morton tells Edith Leslie, who is admiring the remoteness of their surroundings from railroads and factories, that "They will follow soon . . . ; they are not far off. There is no sanctuary from American progress" (*Morton*, p. 84). Parkman's preface to the 1892 edition of *Trail* (pp. viii, ix) reinforces Lewis' thesis. In it Parkman deplores the retreat of "Old Ephraim," the truculent grizzly bear, before the modern rifle, and laments that "The Wild West is tamed, and its savage charms have withered." In *Morton*, p. 363, there is even a grizzly bear image: when the villain Vinal sees Vassall Morton at a dance, "He started as if he had found a grizzly bear behind the curtain." Since Morton is an autobiographical figure, did Parkman envisage himself as a denizen of the wilds?

Chapter Three

1. See Francis Parkman, "The Tale of the 'Ripe Scholar,' " *Nation*, IX (December 23, 1869), 558–60.

2. *Parkman*, ed. Schramm, p. 12.

3. Wade, *Parkman,* p. 374.

4. Sedgwick, *Parkman,* pp. 265–66. These places figure prominently in *Montcalm.*

5. Wade, *Parkman,* p. 384.

6. Jacobs, ed., *Letters,* II, 8–9 n.

7. Casgrain to Parkman, *Québec,* 4 février 1868; in Parkman Papers, Massachusetts Historical Society, Boston.

8. See *Letters,* II, 18, and *La Salle,* I, 239–41. This important locale is repeatedly discussed in *La Salle.* There seems to be no extant journal by Parkman annotating this journey.

9. Farnham, *Parkman,* p. 35.

10. Sedgwick, *Parkman,* p. 289; Jacobs, ed., *Letters,* I, 117 n.

11. Parkman makes extensive use of Margry's findings, especially in *La Salle* (see I, vii-ix; II, 255–56). Parkman does later point out a minor error in Margry's work but then goes out of his way to praise his French colleague (see *Conflict,* II, 25, 42). For evidence that Parkman was naïve in accepting Margry's work without ever questioning it, see Jean Delanglez, *Some La Salle Journeys* (Chicago, 1938), pp. 3–22 *passim;* see also William R. Taylor, "A Journey into the Human Mind: Motivation into Francis Parkman's *La Salle,*" *William and Mary Quarterly,* 3rd series, XIX (1962), 221 n. 3, 231 n. 27, 234 n. 41.

12. Doughty, *Parkman,* pp. 207–8.

13. Quoted in Sedgwick, *Parkman,* p. 270.

14. Quoted in Farnham, *Parkman,* p. 312.

15. Henri R. Casgrain, "Biographies Canadiennes," in *Oeuvres Complètes* (Quebec, 1885), II, 316; quoted in Sedgwick, *Parkman,* p. 271.

16. Quoted from *Le Canadien,* 1878, in Wade, *Parkman,* p. 420. See also Jacobs, ed., *Letters,* II, 123 n.; and Doughty, *Parkman,* pp. 309–10.

17. Sedgwick, *Parkman,* p. 290.

18. At one time, Parkman paid twelve cents per hundred words for documents copied in the United States; at another, threepence per hundred words in England (see Sedgwick, *Parkman,* p. 294; *Letters,* II, 90). See also "The Correspondence of Francis Parkman and Henry Stevens, 1845–1885," *Transactions of the American Philosophical Society,* new series, LVII, Pt. 6 (August, 1967), 24–34 *passim,* for random information on Parkman's costs in obtaining research materials.

19. Wade, *Parkman,* p. 416.

20. Doughty, *Parkman,* pp. 333–34. Parkman smuggles in a few anti-feminist remarks in *Jesuits,* I, 20, 22; II, 13, 133.

21. Wade, *Parkman,* pp. 435–40, extensively discusses Parkman's

argument with Casgrain over the Acadian question and their subsequent reconciliation, and prints a translation of Casgrain's last letter to Parkman, whose whole treatment of the Acadians seems best described as careful but ill at ease (see *Montcalm*, Chs. IV and VIII, and *Conflict*, Chs. VI, VII, IX, and XXII). The fate of the Acadians comprises one of the saddest chapters in all of American history. Parkman writes in conclusion (*Montcalm*, I, 294–95) that "Whatever judgment may be passed on the cruel measure of wholesale expatriation, it was not put in execution till every resource of patience and persuasion had been tried in vain. The agents of the French court, civil, military, and ecclesiastical, had made some act of force a necessity. We have seen by what vile practices they produced in Acadia a state of things intolerable, and impossible of continuance. They conjured up the tempest; and when it burst on the heads of the unhappy people, they gave no help. The government of Louis XV. began with making the Acadians its tools, and ended with making them its victims."

The Canadian historian Harrison Bird, *Battle for a Continent* (New York, 1965), pp. 85–86, implicitly vindicates Parkman, whom, however, he does not name, when he writes that ". . . the simple-minded, primitive farming people [the Acadians] fiercely maintained their foible of loyalty to the King Louis who had forsaken them. . . . By 1755, with an outright war imminent, the soldier-governor of Nova Scotia no longer could tolerate the menace of the perfidious Acadians combining with the French forces from Louisbourg . . . Governor Charles Lawrence gave the order for transportation of all the Acadians."

22. Farnham, *Parkman*, p. 37.

23. For a description of the house and its surroundings, see *Conflict*, II, 72–74.

24. *Henry Adams and His Friends: A Collection of His Unpublished Letters*, compiled by Harold Dean Cater (Boston, 1947), pp. 267, 134.

25. Wade, *Parkman*, p. 443.

Chapter Four

1. Bernard DeVoto, *The Year of Decision: 1846* (Boston, 1943).

2. Throughout *Trail*, Parkman sees the wild West as a combination of surpassing beauty and energy, and of horrible processes—exemplified by blood-smeared Indians, ferocious grizzly bears, buffalo carcasses "fermenting under the hot sun" (381), and especially rattlesnakes. In *Pontiac*, his first historical work, Parkman similarly views Indian-dominated nature as paradisiacal and cursed (see Doughty, *Parkman*, pp. 190–93).

3. Kenneth Rexroth, review of *The Parkman Reader,* ed. Samuel Eliot Morison, *Nation,* CLXXXI (July 2, 1955), 14.

4. Parkman would have profited from George Orwell's suggestion in "Politics and the English Language" in *Shooting an Elephant and Other Essays* (New York, 1950), p. 90: "One can cure oneself of the *not un-* formation by memorizing this sentence: *A not unblack dog was chasing a not unsmall rabbit across a not ungreen field.*"

5. Melville is the wildest perpetrator of dangling modifiers in serious American literature. *Omoo* alone has sixty-five, including this one: "Waking the men, the corpse was immediately rolled up in the strips of blanketing upon which it lay . . ." (Ch. XII). Leedice Kissane seems ingenious but misguided when she tries to justify Melville in "Dangling Constructions in Melville's 'Bartleby,'" *American Speech,* XXXVI (1961), 195–200. Danglers are simply illogical, however clear contextually.

6. Parkman provides a careful footnote explaining the word in *Pontiac,* II, 56.

7. Parkman admits making only one mistake during the entire adventure. After dark one evening he fires at a skulking wolf and then confesses, *Trail,* p. 394: "I had missed my mark, and what was worse had grossly violated a standing law of the prairie. When in a dangerous part of the country [dangling elliptical clause], it is considered highly imprudent to fire a gun after encamping, lest the report should reach the ears of Indians."

8. For extended comparisons between Parkman and Melville, see Doughty, *Parkman,* pp. 117, 118, 158–59.

9. See also the story of Eunice Williams in *Conflict,* I, 75, 80, 90–91.

10. This introductory section resembles and functions like William Hickling Prescott's long essay on the Aztecs which opens his *History of the Conquest of Mexico* (rev. ed., 3 vols., Philadelphia: J. B. Lippincott, 1874), I, 1–208.

11. Doughty, *Parkman,* pp. 185, 187, 196, 197.

12. Howard H. Peckham, *Pontiac and the Indian Uprising* (Princeton, 1947), p. ix.

13. Parkman puns most dreadfully when he calls Indian scalpers "hairdressers," in *Montcalm,* II, 66; III, 181.

14. All the same, I cannot agree when David Levin, in *History as Romantic Art* (Stanford, 1959), p. 223, suggests that ". . . the weakness of Parkman's prose lies in his most self-consciously heroic diction and his trite imagery. . . ."

15. One passage of conversation between Vassall Morton and high-spirited Fanny Euston has embarrassing Freudian overtones. He says, "'You are difficult to satisfy. What may I call you? A wild Arab racer

without a rider?'" Then he goes on, "'Or a rocket without a stick?'" To this she answers, "'I have seen rockets; but I do not know what the stick is. What is it? What is it for?'" When he explains that the stick gives balance and aim to the sparkling rocket, she concludes, "'Ah, I see that a stick is very necessary. I will try to get one'" (*Morton*, pp. 75, 76).

16. Parkman surely chose many of his seventy-odd chapter epigraphs with his plight more in mind than Morton's, for example, Satan's powerful lines from Milton's *Paradise Lost*, Bk. I: ". . . to be weak is miserable,/Doing or suffering . . ." (*Morton*, p. 207).

Chapter Five

1. See, for example, Parkman's comments and hints in *Pioneers*, II, 257, 259; *Jesuits*, II, 273–75; *Old Régime*, II, 156, 198; *Montcalm*, I, 215, 269, II, 106; and *Conflict*, I, 299–300, 323. Support for Lewis' thesis may be found in *La Salle*, II, 52; and *Old Régime*, II, 113.

2. With this aspect of Champlain in mind, Doughty, *Parkman*, p. 233, writes: "The leading motif of the book is the passion for knowledge, the Western *libido sciendi* by which, and by the will and courage to implement which, its hero, Samuel de Champlain, is possessed to the full. . . . In sum, . . . what we have to do with in *Pioneers* is the *libido sciendi* of Western man under its fairest aspect—a glowing, disinterested love of knowledge for its own sake, predominant over instrumental considerations, in harmony with nature and with human nature."

3. Russel B. Nye, in "Parkman, Red Fate, and White Civilization," in *Essays on American Literature in Honor of Jay B. Hubbell* (Durham, 1967), pp. 161–63, discusses Parkman's attitude toward a French-Huron victory in North America.

4. Doughty, *Parkman*, p. 257. Doughty might have added that fire is a splendid symbol of the Jesuit impulse in the New World. Fire illuminates, comforts, and destroys. The Marquis de Denonville, when governor of Canada, wrote Colonel Thomas Dongan, governor of New York: "Think you that religion will make any progress, while your traders supply the savages in abundance with the liquor which, as you ought to know, converts them into demons and their lodges into counterparts of Hell?"; quoted in *Frontenac*, I, 133. Parkman surely approved of and may have been inspired by Denonville's image.

5. Levin, *History as Romantic Art*, p. 104, discusses the ironic situation in *Jesuits* which makes the naïve Indians conclude that, since the priests often can find only dying infants to baptize, baptism causes death. Parkman, who of course is not responsible for this irony, obviously relishes it.

6. Clarence Walworth Alvord, in "Francis Parkman," *Nation*,

CXVII (October 10, 1923), 395, accuses Parkman of having an "Anglo-Saxon superiority complex."

7. Doughty, *Parkman*, pp. 282, 283, says that Parkman regards La Salle as "an 'isolato' from real life comparable only to Melville's Ahab as an embodiment of atomic Western individualism . . ."; praises Parkman's final picture as the "culmination" of his "art of tragic portraiture" and as a splendid "mingling of psychological realism and tragic amplitude, of objectiveness of manner and inwardness of feeling, of depth of penetration and breadth of reference . . ."; and sees in Parkman's conclusive statement about La Salle "a crowning example of that nervous, masculine, expressive, and many-leveled prose, which, without the slightest trace of surface peculiarities, nevertheless strikes as idiosyncratic a note as any in our literature." For adverse criticism of Parkman's admiration of La Salle, see W. J. Eccles, "The History of New France According to Francis Parkman," *William and Mary Quarterly*, 3rd series, XVIII (1961), 171–72.

8. Willa Cather, *Death Comes for the Archbishop* (New York, 1927), p. 261.

9. Quoted in Leon Edel, *Henry James: The Treacherous Years* (Philadelphia and New York, 1969), p. 60.

10. Otis A. Pease, *Parkman's History* (New Haven, 1953), p. 37, comments on the "restrained, mock-heroic operetta" qualities of "The Feudal Chiefs of Acadia."

Chapter Six

1. W. J. Eccles, *Frontenac: The Courtier Governor* (Toronto, 1959), p. 155.

2. Eric F. Goldman, "The Historians," *Literary History of the United States*, eds. Robert E. Spiller *et al.*, rev. ed. (New York, 1953), p. 538, complains with some validity that Parkman's work "shifts perspective both within the series and within particular books of the series."

3. One of Parkman's sources for what Levin, *History as Romantic Art*, p. 105, rightly considers to be a "lurid perversion . . . of doctrine" is *Magnalia Christi Americana* by Cotton Mather, whom the historian occasionally ridicules elsewhere (see *Frontenac*, II, 11, 12, 145). Parkman also reports that Jesuit missionaries, especially at and near Michilimackinac, sometimes excited their Indian-convert allies to commit un-Christian atrocities. He tells us that one such missionary persuaded some Hurons to kill and cook an Iroquois prisoner, to render unlikely the ratifying of a treaty to the advantage of the English, Parkman quotes (*Frontenac*, I, 216 n.) the eighteenth-century French authority La Potherie: "Le Père Missionaire des Hurons . . . leur dit que ceux-ci vouloient absolument que l'on mit *l'Iroquois à la*

chaudière . . ." But elsewhere (*Pioneers,* II, 154 n.; *La Salle,* I, 129) Parkman calls some minor comments by La Potherie "fanciful" and "erroneous"; so the authority would seem to be only selectively reliable. For more on the Gallicizing of Christ, see *Montcalm,* I, 71.

4. Doughty, *Parkman,* p. 377, with his usual skill suggests that "Montcalm's [wooden] *cheveaux-de-frise* at Ticonderoga [are] an emblem of the whole great belt of wilderness that guards New France, with whose fate that of the wilderness and the Indian is identified." Of nature's self-healing powers, Parkman once wrote: "Nature is strong in her resources. Give her but the opportunity, and in a soil and climate like those of the greater part of this continent she will renew and create with unbounded fecundity"; review of C. S. Sargent's *Forests and the Census, Atlantic Monthly,* LV (1885), 837.

5. Bird, *Battle for a Continent,* p. 367. But how can Bird defend Abercromby (spelled "Abercrombie" by Parkman), who in 1758 precipitately retreated with about 13,000 men in the face of Montcalm's determined defense of Ticonderoga with fewer than 4,000 men?

6. In reality, neither Braddock's defeat near Fort Duquesne in 1755 nor Forbes's victory there three years later was of central concern in the war. As Doughty, *Parkman,* p. 374, says, ". . . for immediate strategic purposes the Allegheny front was a minor one. . . ."

7. Goldman, "The Historians," p. 530, mentions Prescott's aim to make history resemble romance and drama. On the structure of *Montcalm,* Levin, *History as Romantic Art,* p. 211, writes: "Although Parkman did not divide *Montcalm and Wolfe* into books with separate titles, he did give it a clearly dramatic structure, which invites subdivision into a prologue and five acts." Levin then suggests these divisions: Prologue, Chs. I-VI; Act I, Chs. VII-X; Act II, Chs. XI-XVII; Act III, Chs. XVIII-XXIII; Act IV, Chs. XXIV-XXVIII; and Act V, Chs. XXIX-XXXII. It seems to me, however, that history presented in general chronologically cannot be compared effectively to conventional five-part dramatic structure. In addition, Levin's Prologue seems too long and his first and last acts too short.

8. In another connection, Doughty, *Parkman,* p. 379, praises Parkman's skill in changing his point of view: "Then, with a sudden heightening of immediacy, the focus of the narrative is shifted . . ."

9. Doughty, *ibid.,* p. 377, notes the passage, combines it with others, and makes the following effective point: ". . . the main chapters on this phase of the war [the last French successes] open with a bird's-eye view. . . ."

10. Rigaud de Vaudreuil (called "Rigaud") is not to be confused with his brother the Marquis Pierre Rigaud de Vaudreuil-Cavagnal (called "Vaudreuil"), governor of Canada and Montcalm's political enemy (see *Conflict,* II, 235 n.).

11. Goldman, "The Historians," p. 530, comments on Prescott's similar preference "for a topical rather than a chronological matrix."

12. Ever on the alert for analogies between Parkman's historical writing and other literary forms, Levin, *History as Romantic Art*, p. 98, comments on Pepperrell's rustic army thus: "In two of the best chapters in *A Half-Century of Conflict* Parkman presents the siege of Louisbourg in 1744 [1745] as 'broad farce,' and the New Englanders' pretentiousness is an important ingredient in the comedy."

13. The passage continues, less successfully, by suggesting that in a democracy an unfortunate leveling process goes on which is similar to the choking of saplings in the Darwinian forest. For apt criticism of this analogy, see Levin, *History of Romantic Art*, pp. 134–35.

14. Doughty says that *Conflict* "shows Parkman's prose at its most characteristic in pace, economy, finely shaded incisiveness, and balance between rhetorical pointing and a natural, almost colloquial, manner." I cannot agree; nor, it seems to me, does Doughty, really, since he lets about a fourth of his four or five sustained pages on the work be eaten up by a long quotation from Parkman's handling of Massachusetts Governor Joseph Dudley. Further, Doughty concludes thus: "By and large . . . *A Half-Century* [*of Conflict*] is the least compelling of Parkman's histories—partly, no doubt, for reasons intrinsic to its subject matter; but also partly because, in defect of a central predominant figure, he failed to find some less loosely strung, dispersed way than is the case of organizing its diverse material" (Doughty, *Parkman*, pp. 367, 369).

Chapter Seven

1. Alvord, "Francis Parkman," pp. 394–96; George M. Wrong, "Francis Parkman," *Canadian Historical Review*, IV (1923), 289–303 *passim;* Michael Kraus, *A History of American History* (New York, 1937), pp. 253–54, 288–89, 337; DeVoto, *The Year of Decision: 1846*, pp. 62, 139–63 *passim;* Levin, *History as Romantic Art*, pp. 132–41; Harvey Wish, *The American Historian: A Social-Intellectual History of the Writing of the American Past* (New York, 1960), pp. 88, 91–93, 100; W. J. Eccles, "The History of New France According to Francis Parkman," *William and Mary Quarterly*, 3rd series, XVIII (1961), 163–75; John Higham, "Moral Factors," *American History and the Social Sciences*, ed. Edward N. Saveth (New York, 1964), p. 502; Richard Hofstadter, *The Progressive Historians: Turner, Beard, Parrington* (New York, 1968), p. 23; George H. Callcott, *History in the United States 1800–1860* (Baltimore, 1970), pp. 145, 162–64, 168, 170.

2. J. Franklin Jameson, *The History of Historical Writing in Amer-*

ica (Boston, 1891), pp. 93–95; Alvord, pp. 394–96; Joseph Schafer, "Francis Parkman, 1823–1923," *Mississippi Valley Historical Review,* X (1924), 351–64 *passim;* Joe Patterson Smith, "Francis Parkman," *The Marcus W. Jernegan Essays in American Historiography,* ed. William T. Hutchinson (Chicago, 1937), pp. 51–52; Levin, *History as Romantic Art,* pp. 219–28; David D. Van Tassel, *Recording America's Past: An Interpretation of the Development of Historical Studies in America 1607–1884* (Chicago, 1960), pp. 172, 179; Ray Allen Billington, *The Genesis of the Frontier Thesis: A Study in Historical Creativity* (San Marino, California, 1971), p. 88.

3. William Jordy, "Henry Adams and Francis Parkman," *American Quarterly,* III (1951), 52–68; J. C. Levenson, *The Mind and Art of Henry Adams* (Boston, 1957), 119–21; Ernest Samuels, *Henry Adams: The Middle Years* (Cambridge, Massachusetts, 1958), pp. 396–97, and *Henry Adams: The Major Phase* (Cambridge, 1964), p. 348; Timothy Paul Donovan, *Henry Adams and Brooks Adams: The Education of Two American Historians* (Norman, Oklahoma, 1961), pp. 161, 186–87.

4. Kraus, *History of American History,* p. 290; Smith, "Francis Parkman," p. 51; Van Tassel, *Recording America's Past,* p. 120; Callcott, *History in the United States,* p. 144.

5. John Spencer Bassett, *The Middle Group of American Historians* (New York, 1917), p. ix; Kraus, *History of American History,* p. 272; Smith, "Francis Parkman," p. 50; Donald Sheehan, *The Making of American History: Book 1: The Emergence of a Nation* (New York, 1950), pp. 31–34; Van Tassel, *Recording America's Past,* pp. 119, 125, 164; Wish, *The American Historian,* p. 94; Richard C. Vitzthum, "The Historian as Editor: Francis Parkman's Reconstruction of Sources in *Montcalm and Wolf,*" *Journal of American History,* LIII (1966), 471–86; Callcott, *History in the United States,* p. 126. On plagiarism in nineteenth-century American historians other than Parkman, see Callcott, pp. 128–29.

6. Bassett, *The Middle Group of American Historians,* p. ix; Carl L. Becker, *Every Man His Own Historian: Essays in History and Politics* (New York, 1935), p. 135; Kraus, *History of American History,* p. 272; Pease, *Parkman's History, passim;* Wilbur R. Jacobs, "Some of Parkman's Literary Devices," *New England Quarterly,* XXXI (1958), 244–52; Van Tassel, *Recording America's Past,* p. 120; Wish, *The American Historian,* p. 104.

7. Smith, "Francis Parkman," pp. 53–54; Nye, "Parkman, Red Fate, and White Civilization," in *Essays in American Literature in Honor of Jay B. Hubbell* (Durham, North Carolina, 1967), pp. 152–63; Kraus, *History of American History,* p. 294; Wish, *The American Historian,* pp. 104–08.

8. Samuel Eliot Morison and Henry Steele Commager, *The Growth of the American Republic*, 5th ed. (New York, 1962), II, 374. Elsewhere, Morison calls Parkman's treatment of Champlain "By far the best . . . in English"; he adds that because of "its matchless narrative style and hearty appreciation of Champlain, [it] should endure when all other works on him are forgotten" (Samuel Eliot Morison, *Samuel de Champlain: Father of New France* [Boston, 1972], p. 272).

9. *History of American History*, p. 272. For a comprehensive statement on the difficulty of placing Parkman among American historians, see Van Tassel, *Recording America's Past*, p. 120 n. 33.

10. *The March of Democracy: A History of the United States* (New York, 1965), II, 225.

Selected Bibliography

PRIMARY SOURCES

1. *Bibliographies*

Farnham, Charles Haight. *A Life of Francis Parkman*. Boston: Little, Brown, 1900. Has best bibliography to its date.

McCallum, John H., ed. *Francis Parkman, The Seven Years War: A Narrative Taken from Montcalm and Wolfe, The Conspiracy of Pontiac*, and *A Half-Century of Conflict*. New York: Harper and Row, 1968. Contains brief bibliographical note.

Morison, Samuel Eliot, ed. *The Parkman Reader: From the Works of Francis Parkman*. Boston: Little, Brown, 1955. Lists Parkman's historical works in book form, translations thereof, journals, letters, and other autobiographical material; valuable for discussion of revisions.

Schramm, Wilbur L., ed. *Francis Parkman: Representative Selections, with Introduction, Bibliography, and Notes*. New York: American Book Co., 1938. Includes critical bibliography, comprehensive to its date.

Spiller, Robert E., *et al.*, eds. *Literary History of the United States: Bibliography*. New York: Macmillan, 1948; Richard M. Ludwig, ed. *Bibliography Supplement*, 1959. Selective bibliography with occasional brief commentary.

Wade, Mason. *Francis Parkman: Heroic Historian*. New York: Viking Press, 1942. Lists Parkman's published writings.

Walsh, James E. "*The California and Oregon Trail*: A Bibliographical Study," *New Colophon*, III (1950), 279–85. On preparation of book for publication, all three printings of the 1849 edition, and their variants.

2. *Books (in chronological order; Roman numerals in parentheses after titles indicate their order in completed historical series)*

The California and Oregon Trail. New York: Putnam, 1849. *Prairie and Rocky Mountain Life: or, The California and Oregon Trail*. New York: Putnam, 1852. *The Oregon Trail*. Boston: Little, Brown, 1872. *The Oregon Trail*. Ed. Mason Wade. New York: Heritage Press, 1943. Contains informative Introduction. *The Oregon Trail.* Ed. E. N. Feltskog. Madison: University of Wisconsin Press, 1969. The most authoritative text, based on scholarly collation of all nine editions published in Parkman's lifetime and containing excellent critical and analytical Introduction, textual and factual notes, Frederic Remington's illustrations, and map. This splendid edition is essential to an understanding of *The Oregon Trail.*

The History of the Conspiracy of Pontiac. Boston: C. C. Little and James Brown, 1851. *The Conspiracy of Pontiac and the Indian War after the Conquest of Canada* (6th ed., rev. and enlarged), 2 vols. Boston: Little, Brown, 1870.   (VIII)

Vassall Morton: A Novel. Boston: Phillips, Sampson, 1856.

Pioneers of France in the New World. Boston: Little, Brown, 1865. *Pioneers of France in the New World* (23rd or 25th ed., enlarged and rev.). Boston: Little, Brown, 1865.   (I)

The Book of Roses. Boston: J. E. Tilton, 1866.

The Jesuits in North America in the Seventeenth Century. Boston: Little, Brown, 1867.   (II)

The Discovery of the Great West. Boston: Little, Brown, 1869. *La Salle and the Discovery of the Great West* (10th ed., rev.). Boston: Little, Brown, 1878. *La Salle and the Discovery of the Great West* (12th ed., rev.). Boston: Little, Brown, 1893.   (III)

The Old Régime in Canada. Boston: Little, Brown, 1874. *The Old Régime in Canada* (29th ed., rev.). Boston: Little, Brown, 1893.   (IV)

Count Frontenac and New France under Louis XIV. Boston: Little, Brown, 1877.   (V)

Montcalm and Wolfe, 2 vols. Boston: Little, Brown, 1884.   (VII)

A Half-Century of Conflict, 2 vols. Boston: Little, Brown, 1892.   (VI)

["Appendix"]. *Francis Parkman.* By Henry Dwight Sedgwick. Boston and New York: Houghton, Mifflin, 1904. Contains Parkman's highly revealing letter to Martin Brimmer, written October 28, 1886, as an autobiographical document to be published after Parkman's death. (Not reprinted in *Letters of Francis Parkman,* ed. Wilbur R. Jacobs.)

The Journals of Francis Parkman, 2 vols. (continuously paginated). Ed. Mason Wade. New York: Harper and Brothers, 1947. The only edition; has thorough Introduction and notes; contains raw material contributing to *The Oregon Trail* and several of the histories.

Letters of Francis Parkman, 2 vols. Ed. Wilbur R. Jacobs. Norman: University of Oklahoma Press, 1960. Definitive edition, in every way a model of scholarship; invaluable for understanding Parkman's personality and works.

3. *Collected Editions (all with same plates)*

Champlain Edition, 20 vols. Boston: Little, Brown, 1897–98. Introduction by John Fiske.
DeLuxe or La Salle Edition, 20 vols. Boston: Little, Brown, 1897–98.
New Library Edition, 13 vols. Boston: Little, Brown, 1901–02. Includes *A Life of Francis Parkman,* by Charles H. Farnham.
Frontenac Edition, 16 vols. Boston: Little, Brown, 1905–07. Adds Farnham's *Life of Parkman* as extra, unnumbered volume.
Centenary Edition, 12 vols. Boston: Little Brown, 1923.

4. *Pamphlets*

An Open Letter to a Temperance Friend, n.p., [1880].
Some of the Reasons against Woman Suffrage, n.p., [1887]. Printed at the request of an association of women.
Our Common Schools. Boston: Citizens' Public School Union, 1890.

5. *Periodical Articles (selective)*

"The Ranger's Adventure," *Knickerbocker Magazine,* XXV (1845), 198–201. Short story about ranger's meeting with Indians.
"The Scalp Hunter, a Semi-Historical Sketch," *Knickerbocker Magazine,* XXV (1845), 297–303. Parkman's best short story, about white men *vs.* Indians.
"A Fragment of Family History," *Knickerbocker Magazine,* XXV (1845), 504–18. Short story about white man's search for girl kidnaped by Indians.
"The New Hampshire Ranger, by Captain Jonathan Carver, Jr.," *Knickerbocker Magazine,* XXVI (1845), 146–48. Poem about rangers at Lake George.
"Satan and Dr. Carver, by Captain Jonathan Carver, Jr.," *Knickerbocker Magazine,* XXVI (1845), 515–25. Short story about doctor who thought he would be attacked by Indians.
"The Works of James Fenimore Cooper," *North American Review,* LXXIV (1852), 147–61. Criticizes Cooper's unrealistic treatment of Indians but praises his energetic writing and his patriotism.
"Exploring the Magalloway," *Harper's Magazine,* XXIX (1864), 735–41. Semi-fictional account of Parkman's trip during college vacation in 1842.
"The Tale of the 'Ripe Scholar,'" *Nation,* IX (December 23, 1869),

558–60. Morosely discusses inroads which materialism and democracy have made on quality of education.

Review of Pierre Margry's *Découvertes et établissements des Français dans l'Ouest et dans le Sud de l'Amérique septentrionale: mémoires et documents originaux, Nation,* XXIII (September 14, 1876), 168–69. Summarizes first volume and discusses importance of Margry's project.

"Hybridization of Lilies," *Bulletin of the Bussey Institution,* II (1877), 161–65. Distinguished little essay.

Review of M. Rameau's *Une Colonie féodale en Amérique: L'Acadie, 1604–1710, Nation,* XXV (December 27, 1877), 400. Highly critical of the book for inaccuracy and wrong conclusions.

"The Failure of Universal Suffrage," *North American Review,* CXXVII (1878), 1–20. Stresses need for sound government rather than universal suffrage.

"Mr. Parkman and His Canadian Critics," *Nation,* XXVII (August 1, 1878), 66–67. Ringing third-person rebuke of his Canadian critics.

"The Woman Question," *North American Review,* CXXIX (1879), 303–21. Argues that men should vote and perform military service and that women have higher duties.

"The Woman Question Again," *North American Review,* CXXX (1880), 16–30. Repeats position and answers critics of it.

Review of Charles Sprague Sargent's *The Forests and the Census, Atlantic Monthly,* LV (1885), 835–39. Summarizes Sargent's big book, discusses forest fires and ecology, and pleads for federal conservation program.

Review of l'Abbé H. R. Casgrain's *Un Pèlerinage au pays d'Évangeline, Nation,* XLVIII (March 14, 1889), 232–33. Challengingly criticizes Casgrain's defense of the Acadians.

"A Convent at Rome," *Harper's Magazine,* LXXXI (1890), 448–54. Discusses his brief 1844 sojourn in a Passionist convent.

"The Correspondence of Francis Parkman and Henry Stevens, 1845–1885," ed. John Buechler, *Transactions of the American Philosophical Society,* new series, LVII, Pt. 6 (August, 1967), 3–36. Includes twenty-three letters from Parkman (not in *Letters of Parkman,* ed. Jacobs) to Henry Stevens, Vermont-born London bookseller, bibliophile, and main source for British books and documents used by Parkman in *Pontiac* and *Montcalm;* with good Introduction and magnificent footnotes.

SECONDARY SOURCES

1. *Books*

Adams, James Truslow. "Francis Parkman," XIV, 247–50, in *Dictionary of American Biography*, eds. Allen Johnson and Dumas Malone, 20 vols. New York: Scribner's, 1934. Informative, balanced sketch.

Brooks, Van Wyck. *New England: Indian Summer*. New York: E. E. Dutton, 1940. Has charming portrait of Parkman as stoical Brahmin; stresses his lonely nature; omits consideration of form, style, and detailed discussion of contents of his writings.

Callcott, George H. *History in the United States 1800–1860*. Baltimore: The Johns Hopkins University Press, 1970. Splendid general survey of America's leading historians from 1800 to 1860; somewhat harsh on Parkman; contains fine "Bibliographical Note."

Casgrain, Henri R. "Francis Parkman." *Biographies Canadiennes*. Quebec: Darveau, 1875. Expanded in "Biographies Canadiennes." *Oeuvres Complètes*. Quebec: Darveau, 1885, II, 294–355. Praises Parkman in the main but criticizes his position on Canadian Catholicism.

Curti, Merle. *Human Nature in American Historical Thought*. Columbia: University of Missouri Press, 1968. Sees Parkman, unconvincingly and only in passing, as "an exponent of the limitations of human nature."

Delanglez, Jean. *Some La Salle Journeys*. Chicago: Institute of Jesuit History, 1938. Objects to Parkman's *La Salle* because of his uncritical use of documents distorted by Pierre Margry.

DeVoto, Bernard. *The Year of Decision: 1846*. Boston: Houghton Mifflin, 1943. Fits Parkman into the decisive year of westward migration; marred by inflexible opinion of Parkman as narrow, prejudiced, snobbish Puritan Brahmin.

Doughty, Howard. *Francis Parkman*. New York: Macmillan, 1962. Penetratingly considers main events in Parkman's life and with steady brilliance analyzes his major works; proves modernity of Parkman.

Farnham, Charles Haight. *A Life of Francis Parkman*. Boston: Little, Brown, 1900. First book-length biography; valuable for details which author, Parkman's secretary, could provide; wrongly depicts Parkman as solitary, silent, shadowy, and often pathetic. Reprinted by Haskell Publishing Co., Inc., in 1968.

Fiske, John. *A Century of Science and Other Essays.* Boston and New York: Houghton, Mifflin, 1900. Contains laudatory biography of Parkman and analysis of his works. Reprinted as Introduction to Champlain Edition of Parkman.

Goldman, Eric F. "The Historians." *Literary History of the United States.* Ed. Robert E. Spiller *et al.* Rev. ed. New York: Macmillan, 1953. Includes efficient, informative comparison and contrast of careers and styles of William Hickling Prescott, John Lothrop Motley, and Parkman.

Gould, George M. *Biographic Clinics* Vol. II. Philadelphia: Blakiston's, 1904. Blames most of Parkman's physical maladies on eyestrain.

Kraus, Michael. *A History of American History.* New York: Farrar & Rinehart, 1937. Includes informative, generally laudatory survey of Parkman's accomplishment.

Levin, David. "Francis Parkman: *The Oregon Trail.*" *Landmarks of American Writing,* ed. Hennig Cohen. New York: Basic Books, 1969. Stresses Parkman's pictorial skill, Brahmin condescension, and admiration of Henry Chatillon.

————. *History as Romantic Art: Bancroft, Motley, Prescott, and Parkman.* Stanford: Stanford University Press, 1959. Considers similarity of themes and Romantic literary devices in works of the four historians.

Lewis, R. W. B. *The American Adam: Innocence, Tragedy, and Tradition in the Nineteenth Century.* Chicago: University of Chicago Press, 1955. Suggests Parkman was member of American party of Memory, looking to rigorous past for spiritual and intellectual refreshment; he viewed life as unceasing struggle; and, while he paid lip service to British liberty (which triumphed over French autocracy in New World), he was sorry that any "civilization" had triumphed in America.

Morison, Samuel Eliot, ed. *The Parkman Reader: From the Works of Francis Parkman.* Boston: Little, Brown, 1955. Valuable Introduction; charmingly written.

————. *Three Centuries of Harvard.* Cambridge: Harvard University Press, 1936. Contains background information helpful for understanding Parkman's college years.

Nye, Russel B. "Parkman, Red Fate, and White Civilization." *Essays on American Literature in Honor of Jay B. Hubbell.* Ed. Clarence Gohdes. Durham, North Carolina: Duke University Press, 1967. Surveys Parkman's attitudes toward the Indians.

Pease, Otis A. *Parkman's History: The Historian as Literary Artist.* New Haven: Yale University Press, 1953. Reprinted Hamden, Connecticut: The Shoe String Press, 1968. Probing examination of literary development in Parkman's early work and then of his fusing historical facts and literary artistry; packed with insights, especially on Parkman's attitude toward heroic figures in history, handling of visual effects, and creation of sense of immediacy.

Perry, Bliss. "Francis Parkman." *Later Years of the Saturday Club.* Ed. M. A. DeWolfe Howe. Boston and New York: Houghton, Mifflin, 1927. Brief memoir.

Schramm, Wilbur L., ed. *Francis Parkman: Representative Selections, with Introduction, Bibliography, and Notes.* New York: American Book Co., 1938. Long Introduction considers Parkman's milieu, relation of his life to his writings, his theory of historical writing, his politics, philosophy, and importance.

Sedgwick, Henry Dwight. *Francis Parkman.* Boston: Houghton, Mifflin, 1904. Detailed early biography; stresses professional preparation and character.

Smith, Joe Patterson. "Francis Parkman." *The Marcus W. Jernegan Essays in American Historiography.* Ed. William T. Hutchinson. Chicago: University of Chicago Press, 1937. Pleasant biographical sketch and estimate of Parkman's achievement.

Taylor, William R. "That Way Lies Madness: Nature and Human Nature in Parkman's *La Salle.*" *In Defense of Reading.* Eds. Rueben A. Brower and Richard Poirier. New York: E. E. Dutton, 1962. Discusses social and intellectual problems influencing Parkman's portrayal of La Salle.

Tebbel, John, ed. *The Battle for North America: Edited by John Tebbel from the Works of Francis Parkman.* Garden City, New York: Doubleday, 1948. Abridgment of Parkman's histories; excludes first volume of *Pioneers, Old Régime,* and *Pontiac;* has brief Introduction.

Van Tassel, David D. *Recording America's Past: An Interpretation of the Development of Historical Studies in America 1607–1884.* Chicago: University of Chicago Press, 1960. Explains Parkman's Romanticism, places Parkman among literary historians, compares him to local historians, and accords him his place in American historiography.

Wade, Mason. *Francis Parkman: Heroic Historian.* New York: Viking Press, 1942. Painstaking, highly readable biography; makes copious use of Parkman's journals and letters.

Wish, Harvey. *The American Historian: A Social-Intellectual History of the Writing of the American Past.* New York: Oxford University Press, 1960. Contains workmanlike survey of Parkman's life and achievement.

2. Articles

Alvord, Clarence Walworth. "Francis Parkman," *Nation*, CXVII (October 10, 1923), 394–96. Places Parkman in "Middle Group" of American historians, downgrades him for being Romantic, insufficiently sociological, and provincial; praises only *La Salle* and *Pontiac;* calls Parkman grand, supremely artistic, and expressive of youth.

Bassett, John Spencer. "Francis Parkman, the Man," *Sewanee Review*, X (1902), 285–301. Considers Parkman's career as product of New England Puritanism and as protest against it; reviews his productions and nature.

Casamajor, Louis. "The Illness of Francis Parkman," *American Journal of Psychiatry*, CVII (1951), 749–52. Summarizes Parkman's physical and mental maladies; discusses mixed neurotic pattern beneath them; opposes George M. Gould.

DeVoto, Bernard. "The Easy Chair," *Harper's Magazine*, CXCVIII (1949), 52–55. Warmly but didactically praises Parkman for literary effectiveness; defends him against charge of being unaware of economic history.

Eccles, W. J. "The History of New France According to Francis Parkman," *William and Mary Quarterly*, 3rd series, XVIII (1961), 163–75. Criticizes Parkman's devotion to material progress, his "Olympian style," and his anti-clericalism; provocative but unfair at times.

Fauteux, Aegidus. "Francis Parkman," *Bulletin des Recherches Historiques*, XXXI (1925), 177–83. Combines praise and censure.

Frothingham, O. B. "Memoir of Francis Parkman," *Proceedings of the Massachusetts Historical Society*, 2nd series, VIII (1894), 520–62. Contains informative biographical material based on personal memories.

Griffin, David E. " 'The Man for the Hour': a Defense of Francis Parkman's *Frontenac*," *New England Quarterly*, XLIII (December, 1970), 605–20. Shows that Parkman's would-be detractors have adduced no real evidence to support their position.

Hart, James D. "Patrician among Savages: Francis Parkman's *The Oregon Trail*," *Georgia Review*, X (1956), 69–73. Summarizes Parkman's Western trip; criticizes title of his book; adversely discusses its Romantic style and Parkman's "patrician" attitude toward Indians and mountain men.

Howe, M. A. DeWolfe. "Two Historians," *Atlantic Monthly*, XCIV

(1904), 709–10. Compares Parkman and William Hickling Prescott.

Howells, William Dean. "Mr. Parkman's Histories," *Atlantic Monthly*, XXXIV (1874), 602–10. Laudatory survey of Parkman's work.

Jacobs, Wilbur R. "Highlights of Parkman's Formative Period," *Pacific Historical Review*, XXVII (1958), 149–58. Discusses Parkman's early education, Harvard years, youthful political opinions, reading, and facility in languages.

——. "Some of Parkman's Literary Devices," *New England Quarterly*, XXXI (1958), 244–52. Discusses Parkman's use of dramatic suspense, counterpoint of thematic and chronological presentation, plot turns at chapter endings, foreshadowing, explanatory flashbacks, reader participation, dialogue and quotation, and extensive vocabulary.

——. "Some Social Ideas of Francis Parkman," *American Quarterly*, IX (1957), 387–97. Considers Parkman's anti-democratic attitudes, his demands that one be cultured, his dislike of lower social orders, his opposition to universal and woman suffrage, his distress at quality of public education, his opposition to Roman Catholicism, his praise of self-reliance and heroic action, and his love of wilderness life; extensively documented.

Jordy, William. "Henry Adams and Francis Parkman," *American Quarterly*, III (1951), 52–68. Contrasts Parkman as narrative historian and Adams as scientific historian; highly informative.

Lodge, Henry Cabot. "Francis Parkman," *Proceedings of the Massachusetts Historical Society*, 2nd series, LVI (1923), 319–35. Laudatory personal reminiscence.

McCloin, John B. "Francis Parkman on the Jesuits," *Historical Bulletin*, XXV (1947), 57–59. Brief review of the topic.

Melville, Herman. Review of *The California and Oregon Trail*. *Literary World*, IV (March 31, 1849), 291–93. Criticizes Parkman's depiction of Indians.

Moor, Dean. "The Paxton Boys: Parkman's Use of the Frontier Hypothesis," *Mid-America*, XXXVI (1954), 211–19. Relates F. J. Turner's frontier hypothesis to Parkman's handling of the Paxton boys' raid in *Pontiac*.

Peckham, Howard H. "The Sources and Revisions of Parkman's 'Pontiac,'" *Papers of the Bibliographical Society of America*, XXXVII (1943), 293–307. Lists sources available to Parkman, explains his evaluation and use of many of them, and analyzes revisions in the editions of 1855, 1867, and 1870.

Perry, Bliss. "Some Personal Qualities of Francis Parkman," *Yale*

Review, XIII (1924), 443–48. Vigorous, brief comments on influence of Byron and Scott on Parkman, Parkman's literary skill, and his heroic accomplishment.

Rexroth, Kenneth. Review of *The Parkman Reader*, ed. Samuel Eliot Morison, *Nation*, CLXXXI (July 2, 1955), 14–15. Rancorous, often wrong-headed, thought-provoking review of Parkman as poor stylist and "bourgeois valetudinarian" whose heroes are archetypes of "robber barons" and who, like Milton, made his villains heroic because he unconsciously admired the uncivilized.

Russell, J. A. "Francis Parkman and the Real Indian," *Journal of American History*, XXI (1928), 121–29. Praises Parkman as usually accurate.

Schafer, Joseph. "Francis Parkman, 1823–1923,'" *Mississippi Valley Historical Review*, X (1924), 351–64. Slowly surveys Parkman's work; praises it usually but criticizes it slightly for occasionally leaning toward Romanticism.

Schramm, Wilbur L. "Parkman's Novel," *American Literature*, IX (1937), 218–27. Considers sources of Parkman's only novel—Scott, Cooper, Parkman's own diary, and Parkman's own personality and philosophy.

Taylor, William R. "A Journey into the Human Mind: Motivation into Francis Parkman's *La Salle*," *William and Mary Quarterly*, 3rd series, XIX (1962), 220–37. Psychoanalytically sees Parkman as self-revealingly probing recesses of human behavior in writing about La Salle, "half-crazed French explorer" of a nightmare-huge continent; provocative but curious.

Thompson, Richard A. "Francis Parkman on the Nature of Man," *Mid-America*, XLII (1960), 3–17. Discusses Parkman on savagery in all men, importance of environment, anti-commercialism, heredity, education, war (especially the Civil War), women, resolution and will, basic drives, human inequality, distinctions in social classes, ethnic distinctions, and survival of fittest.

Vitzthum, Richard C. "The Historian as Editor: Francis Parkman's Reconstruction of Sources in *Montcalm and Wolfe*," *Journal of American History*, LIII (1966), 471–86. Considers Parkman's use of various sources; discusses his effacing of voices of authors of those sources by these techniques: invention of detail, economizing of verbiage, clarification of sequences, and participation of narrator; generally favorable.

Wheelwright, Edward. "Memoir of Francis Parkman," *Publications of the Colonial Society of Massachusetts*, I (1894), 304–50. Biographically valuable because based on personal memories.

Winsor, Justin. "Francis Parkman," *Atlantic Monthly,* LXXIII (1894), 660–64. Romantically praises Parkman's Indians for being real and favorably compares his histories with those of William Hickling Prescott; effusively praises Parkman's integrity and artistry.

Wrong, George M. "Francis Parkman," *Canadian Historical Review,* IV (1923), 289–303. Thoughtful eulogy; surveys Parkman's accomplishment as historian and stylist; contains adverse criticism of his handling of Canadian religion, politics, and colonizing.

Index

Index [203]